Several Selections from the Same Anthology (Cross-Referencing)

Baker, Susan W. "Biological Influences on Human Sex and Gender." Stimson and Person 175-91.

Leifer, Myra. "Pregnancy." Stimson and Person 212-23.

Stimpson, Catherine R., and Ethel Spector Person, eds. Women: Sex and Sexuality. Chicago: U of Chicago P, 1980.

An Article in an Encyclopedia or Other Reference

A well-known reference work:

Harmon, Mamie. "Folk Arts." The New Encyclopaedia Britannica: Macropaedia. 15th ed. 2002.

"Morrison, Toni." Who's Who in America. 57th ed. 2003.

"Yodel." The Shorter Oxford English Dictionary. 1973.

A lesser-known reference work:

Hames, Raymond. "Yanomamö." South America. Vol. 7 of Encyclopedia of World Cultures. Boston: Hall, 1994.

A Preface, Introduction, Foreword, or Afterword

Bradford, Barbara Taylor. Foreword. Forever Amber. By Kathleen Winsor. 1944. Chicago: Chicago Review, 2000.

PERIODICALS AND NEWSPAPERS

An Article in a Magazine

Block, Toddi Gutner. "Riding the Waves." Forbes 11 Sept. 1995: 182+.

Jellinek, George. "Record Collecting: Hobby or Obsession?" Opera News Feb. 2003: 85.

Van Zile, Susan. "Grammar That'll Move You!" Instructor Jan./Feb. 2003: 32-34.

An Article in a Journal

Pages numbered continuously throughout the volume:

Larter, Raima. "Understanding Complexity in Biophysical Chemistry." Journal of Physical Chemistry 107 (2003): 415-29.

Each issue begins on page 1:

Mitchell, W. J. T. "The Surplus Value of Images." Mosaic 35.3 (2002): 1-23.

An Article in a Newspaper

Argetsinger, Amy. "Lobbying Gets Old College Try." Washington Post 13 Jan. 2003: B2.

Leonhardt, David. "Defining the Rich in the World's Wealthiest Nation." New York Times 12 Jan. 2003, natl. ed.: sec. 4: 1+.

Ranii, David. "New AIDS Drug Is Step Closer to Approval." News and Observer [Raleigh] 7 Nov. 1995: 1D+.

An Editorial

"Six Sigma Schools." Editorial. Wall Street Journal 15 Jan. 2003: A10.

A Letter to the Editor

Rothschild, Michelle. Letter. Kiplinger's Jan. 2003: 14.

A Review

Flanagan, Caitlin. "Get a Job." Rev. of What Should I Do with My Life?, by Po Bronson. New York Times Book Review 12 Jan. 2003: 4.

Glenn, Kenny. Rev. of Man on the Moon [film]. Premiere Jan. 2000: 20.

Rev. of Going to the Territory, by Ralph Ellison. Atlantic Aug. 1986: 91.

Stearns, David Patrick. Rev. of The Well-Tempered Clavier, by J. S. Bach [CD]. Angela Hewitt, piano. Stereophile Dec. 1999: 173+.

OTHER SOURCES

An Audio Recording

Dickinson, Dee. Creating the Future: Perspectives on Educational Change. Audiocassette. Minneapolis: Accelerated Learning Systems, 1991.

Mahler, Gustav. Symphony No. 7. Michael Tilson Thomas, cond. London Symphony Orch. CD. RCA Victor, 1999.

Shuster, George N. Jacket notes. The Poetry of Gerard Manley Hopkins. LP. Caedmon, n.d.

A Film, DVD, or Video Recording

A theatrical video:

25th Hour. Dir. Spike Lee. Screenplay by David Benioff. Touchstone, 2003.

All About Eve. Dir. Joseph L. Mankiewicz. Perf. Bette Davis, Anne Baxter, and George Sanders. Fox, 1950. DVD. Studio Classics, 2003.

A nontheatrical video:

The Classical Hollywood Style. Program 1 of The American Cinema. Prod. New York Center for Visual History. Videocassette. Annenberg/CPB, 1995.

A Lecture

Granetta, Stephanie. Class lecture. English 315. Richardson College. 7 Apr. 2003.

Kamenish, Eleanor. "A Tale of Two Countries: Mores in France and Scotland." Public lecture. Friends of the Public Library. Louisville, 16 Apr. 2003.

A Pamphlet

Golden Retriever Club of America. Prevention of Heartworm. N.p.: GRCA, 2004.

Who Are the Amish? Aylmer, Ont.: Pathway, n.d.

An Interview

Barefoot, Blake. Personal interview. 18 Sept. 2002.

(continued on next page)

Spacey, Kevin. Interview with Terry Gross. Fresh Air. Natl. Public Radio. WHQR, Wilmington, NC. 21 Jan. 2003.

Trump, Donald. "Trump Speaks." Interview with Aravind Adiga. Money Feb. 2003: 28.

A Television or Radio Program

The Crossing. Dir. Robert Harmon. Screenplay by Sherry Jones and Peter Jennings. History Channel. 1 Jan. 2000.

Stone, Susan. Report on Japanese comic books. All Things Considered. Natl. Public Radio. 9 Jan. 2003.

An Unpublished Essay

Gould, Emily. "Fast Food Comes at a High Price for Workers." Essay written for Prof. Katherine Humel's English 12 class. Fall semester 2002.

An Unpublished Letter

Cilano, Cara. Letter to author. 5 Mar. 2003.

An Unpublished Questionnaire

Questionnaire conducted by Prof. Barbara Waxman's English 103 class. Feb. 2003.

INTERNET AND ELECTRONIC SOURCES

An Online Book

Irving, David. Hitler's War. New York: Viking, 1977. 19 Jan. 2003 <http://www.fpp.co.uk/books/Hitler/>.

Richards, Hank. The Sacrifice. 1996. 3 Mar. 2003 <http://www.geocities.com/Area51/Vault/8101/>.

Wollstonecraft, Mary. Vindication of the Rights of Women. 1792. Bartleby.com, 1999. 13 Feb. 2003 <http://www.bartleby.com/144/>.

A Part of an Online Book

Coyle, Edward R. Spies and Their Work. Ambulancing on the French Front. 1918. 30 Apr. 2003. <http://www.ku.edu/carrie/specoll/medical/Coyle/Coyle04.htm#18>.

A Print Periodical (Newspaper, Magazine, or Journal) Accessed on the Publication's Web Site

Falsani, Cathleen. "Did Respect for Religion Cloud 'Clone' Coverage?" Chicago Sun-Times 10 Jan. 2003. 19 Jan. 2003 <http://www.suntimes.com/output/falsani/cst-nws-fals10.html>.

Fineman, Howard, and Tamara Lipper. "Spinning Race." Newsweek 27 Jan. 2003. 19 Jan. 2003 <http://www.msnbc.com/news/861383.asp?>.

Young, A. J., A. S. Wilson, and C. G. Mundell. "Chandra Imaging of the X-Ray Core of the Virgo Cluster." Astrophysical Journal 579.2 (2002): 560-570. 19 Jan. 2003 <http://www.journals.uchicago.edu/ApJ/journal/issues/ApJ/v579n2/54935/54935.html>.

A Nonprint Periodical Accessed on the Publication's Web Site

Clinton, Bill. "The Path to Peace." 10 Sept. 2002. Salon.com 20 Jan. 2003 <http://www.salon.com/news/feature/2002/09/10/clinton/>.

A Work Accessed in an Online Database

Jovanovic, Rozalia. "Snowmobilers Tied to Rules of the Road." National Law Journal Aug. 5, 2002: B1. InfoTrac OneFile. 20 Jan. 2003 <http://infotrac.galegroup.com/>.

Parks, Noreen. "Dolphins in Danger." Science Now, 17 Dec. 2002: 2-3. Academic Search Elite. EBSCOhost. 20 Jan. 2003 <http://web3.epnet.com/>.

"Political Inclination of the States." Associated Press. 9 Jan. 2003. LexisNexis Academic Universe. 20 Jan 2003 <http://web.lexis-nexis.com/universe>.

An Online Encyclopedia Article

"Humpback Whale." Encyclopaedia Britannica 2003. Encyclopaedia Britannica Online. 28 Jan, 2003 <http://0-search.eb.com.uncclc.coast.uncwil.edu/eb/>.

An Online Review

Ebert, Roger. Rev. of Identity, dir. James Mangold. Chicago Sun-Times Online 25 Apr. 2003. 29 May 2003. <http://www.suntimes.com/output/ebert1/wkp-news-identity25f.html>.

An Organization's Web Site

The Coral Reef Alliance. "Coral Friendly Guidelines." 21 Jan. 2003 <http://www.coralreefalliance.org/parks/guidelines.html>.

A Course Web Page

Reilly, Colleen. English 204: Introduction to Technical Writing. Course home page. U of North Carolina at Wilmington. Spring 2003. 29 Apr. 2003 <http://people.uncw.edu/reillyc/204/>.

An Academic Department Page

Dept. of English home page. U of North Carolina at Wilmington. 10 Mar. 2003 <http://www.uncwil.edu/english/>.

A Personal Web Page

Hemming, Sally. Home page. 4 Feb. 2003 <http://www.sallyhemming.com>.

Computer Software

Atoms, Symbols and Equations. Vers.3.0. Software. 2002 <http://ourworld.compuserve.com/homepages/RayLec/atoms.htm>.

Twain's World. CD-ROM. Parsippany, NJ: Bureau Development, 1993.

E-Mail

Wilkes, Paul. E-mail to author. 29 Dec. 2002.

RESEARCH

RESEARCH
The Student's Guide to Writing Research Papers
FOURTH EDITION

Richard Veit

University of North Carolina at Wilmington

New York   Boston   San Francisco
London   Toronto   Sydney   Tokyo   Singapore   Madrid
Mexico City   Munich   Paris   Cape Town   Hong Kong   Montreal

Senior Vice President and Publisher: Joseph Opiela
Vice President and Publisher: Eben W. Ludlow
Executive Marketing Manager: Ann Stypuloski
Senior Supplements Editor: Donna Campion/Teresa Ward
Production Manager: Ellen MacElree
Project Coordination, Text Design, and Electronic Page Makeup: Nesbitt Graphics, Inc.
Cover Designer/Manager: Wendy Ann Fredericks
Cover Art: Copyright © 2003 by Celia Johnson/c/o theispot.com
Manufacturing Buyer: Lucy Hebard
Printer and Binder: Hamilton Printing Company.
Cover Printer: Coral Graphic Services

For permission to use copyrighted material, grateful acknowledgment is made to the copyright holders on page 277, which is hereby made part of this copyright page.

Library of Congress Cataloging-in-Publication Data

Veit, Richard.
    Research : the student's guide to writing research papers / Richard
Veit.-- 4th ed.
      p. cm.
    Includes bibliographical references and index.
    ISBN 0-321-19834-4
       1. Report writing. 2. Research. I. Title.
    LB2369.V43 2003
    808'.02--dc22

                                                            2003016410

Please visit our Web site at http://www.ablongman.com

ISBN 0-321-19834-4

1 2 3 4 5 6 7 8 9 10—HT—06 05 04 03

Contents

To the Instructor

Perhaps the most important feature of the fourth edition of *Research: The Student's Guide to Writing Research Papers* is its attitude toward research and the student researcher. This book teaches all the important conventions of college research but, more importantly, it presents those conventions not as ends in themselves but as means to achieving the real goals of research and research writing: the discovery and communication of ideas. Students new to college research need a text that speaks to them honestly and clearly and that builds confidence in their ability to do research and write effective papers. *Research* addresses those needs, and, by showing the *purpose* behind conventions, prepares students to think on their feet and to adapt to unforeseen research situations.

Research, Fourth Edition, is meant to be practical, both as a classroom textbook and as a guidebook for student researchers. Its organization provides instructors with a workable (and flexible) teaching sequence, and it provides students with a sequenced introduction to the stages of the research process. Features like the handy guides on the inside covers make the book a useful reference tool for current and future research projects.

Two sample student research papers documented in the MLA style are featured, and the experiences of the student authors are used throughout the book to exemplify the process of typical college researchers. These papers represent contrasting uses for research. One, an informative paper (with a point of view) about workers at fast-food restaurants, is a successful academic research paper in the traditional sense. The other, a student's inquiry about whether a certain career choice is right for him, represents a more personal style of research writing. The range of these papers demonstrates to students that research is more than an academic exercise and that it can take many forms, each of which can be important, rewarding, and interesting.

An organizational innovation of *Research* is its presentation of the polished final drafts of the student papers near the beginning, rather than at the end, of the book. Although in all other respects the stages of the research process are examined chronologically from the earliest invention exercises to final copyediting, students will learn more about each stage if they can see it in relation to a goal, the end product. Readers of this book are first shown two papers produced by actual first-year college students. They are then shown how these writers, like most students, began with uncertainties and anxieties, and worked to discover their topics, research them, and write successfully about them.

The text features the MLA style of parenthetical citation, as updated in the sixth edition of the *MLA Handbook for Writers of Research Papers*. Other styles are explained in appendixes: APA style, numbered-references style, and the alternative MLA footnote/endnote style.

Research, Fourth Edition, provides clear, up-to-date information about research sources, both within and outside the library. In the first edition of this book, published in 1990, the chapter on the library predicted, "In the near future, most searches for library information will be conducted with the aid of a computer." That time has certainly arrived, bringing not just a profusion of electronic indexes but also unanticipated marvels such as the World Wide Web. The "library" chapter of this book has long since been renamed "Tools for Finding Sources," and this fourth edition of *Research*, like its predecessors, has been revised to keep current with the latest developments in search tools and citation of electronic sources. The two student papers also exemplify the use of a variety of electronic, as well as print, sources.

Supplements

The instructor's manual provides answers to the exercises and offers instructions for using *Research* in the classroom.

Acknowledgments

I owe the greatest debt to our students, from whom I have learned most of what I know about teaching composition. In particular, I would like to thank Emily Gould and Justin Stafford, the two student writers who shared their notes and drafts with me and allowed me to use their papers and experiences in this book.

I owe very special thanks to Christopher Gould, my friend and collaborator on *Writing, Reading, and Research*, Sixth Edition, a full-length composition textbook and reader. Almost everything in *Research*, Fourth Edition, appears in that book as well (and I will take this opportunity to recommend the sixth edition of *Writing, Reading, and Research* to instructors seeking a text that fully integrates research into a college composition course). Because we collaborated so closely, Chris contributed many ideas—and, in some cases, actual language—to this book as well, and Chris's daughter Emily authored one of the student papers featured in this book.

I would also like to thank the following reviewers whose wise and thoughtful suggestions made an immeasurable contribution to this fourth edition: Tom Amorose, Seattle Pacific University; Shirley Hart Berry, Cape Fear Community College; Deborah K. Chappel, Arkansas State University; Lu Ellen Huntley, University of North Carolina, Wilmington; Bryan Moore, Arkansas State University; Gregory J. Pulliam, Illinois Institute of Technology; and George T. Vaughn, Maysville Community College. Finally, my thanks to Eben Ludlow, vice president and publisher, and to my friends and colleagues at the University of North Carolina at Wilmington.

Richard Veit

RESEARCH

1 *Introduction: What Is Research?*

▪ DOING RESEARCH

It would not be surprising if you find yourself tempted to give a sarcastic answer to the question in the chapter title. Many students expect research to be an excruciating ordeal, and the idea of THE RESEARCH PAPER looms in student mythology as the academic equivalent of a root-canal session at the dentist's office.

Fortunately, the myth is wrong. Research needn't be a tedious ordeal, though it can be for those who begin without knowing what they are doing or why. *Research* is nothing more than finding out what you need to know. If you are good at it—if you have learned a few elementary skills—it can be useful and satisfying; it can even be fun.

You are already skilled in certain kinds of research. Right now, for example, if you wanted to find your dentist's telephone number, you could easily do so, even though your phone book contains thousands of names. Your research skills enable you to find out what movies are showing on television tonight and the current price of Raleigh mountain bikes. Research in college involves additional skills that are equally useful and not any more difficult to acquire. These skills not only help you become a competent college researcher, but also prove useful after you graduate.

Research takes many forms, from looking up the definition of a word to conducting an opinion poll. Depending on what you want to find out, you may ask the opinions of experts, undertake fieldwork or laboratory experiments, interview eyewitnesses, analyze photographs, or observe the behavior of people who don't know they're being watched. Other research methods—those explained and illustrated in this book—involve written sources. You can discover general information in reference works such as encyclopedias and almanacs. More specific information and ideas can be found in magazines, newspapers, journals, pamphlets, books, and Web sites. Your college library and computer databases are two valuable resources for conducting this type of research.

The skills you develop as a researcher provide personal benefits outside of college. For example, knowing how to use the library can help a pharmacy major locate a summer job. Or it can help consumers find out which videorecorders are most reliable. Unlike these more private kinds of inquiry, the research you perform as a college student has a more public purpose. It may be part of a larger project in which you share your findings with other scholars, communicating what you have learned through *research writing.*

In short, any organized investigation can be called research, and any writing you do as a result—from poetry to scientific reports—may be called research writing. Research is an important academic skill because college students rarely begin a major assignment with all the information they need. When you write about personal feelings, research is unnecessary; no one is likely to challenge expressions of feeling. However, if you write about dating customs of the early twentieth century, you must rely on more than feelings or casual conversation. Since readers expect your writing to be dependable and accurate, research is indispensable.

■ THE RESEARCH PAPER

Suppose you are a smoker who has finally decided to kick the habit. Knowing that your addiction will be hard to overcome, you wonder if you should try to cut down in successive stages, or if you should take the more drastic step of quitting cold turkey. Determined to succeed, you visit the library and find that people who quit all at once have the best results. You also learn that you can expect withdrawal symptoms, but that after seventy-two hours, the worst of these are over. You grit your teeth, toss your remaining cigarettes in the garbage, and resolve that you, not tobacco, will prevail.

In the case at hand, reading about nicotine addiction carries a clear personal benefit. However, research often helps others as well A college *research project* is an undertaking that should not only satisfy your own curiosity but also inform anyone else who reads the *research paper* in which you present your findings. However, the paper itself is only the final step in a project that seeks out and discovers information about a particular topic. After making your discoveries, evaluating and selecting among them, and then organizing the material you wish to report, you finally present what you have learned in a documented paper. Of course, not all research papers are alike; in years to come you probably will make frequent use of research in your writing, though not always in what you may think of as "research papers."

Although papers that draw on research can take many different forms, most fall into one of two categories. The more common of the two is the *research-based paper.* Papers of this type consist largely of information found through research; the writers of such papers present relatively few of their own opinions or discoveries. For example, a student seeking to learn whether the fearsome reputation of great white sharks is justified could write a paper based almost entirely on what she found from reading and from interviewing experts. Her own observations on the subject might play only a small part in her paper. In contrast, the *research-supported paper* presents the writer's own ideas, with research findings used to support or supplement them. Argumentative essays are frequently research-supported. For example, a student arguing for increased funding for intramural athletics could use research in part of his paper; he could demonstrate feasibility by citing published budgetary figures, and he could support his own arguments with expert testimony on the need for greater fitness. Still, his original ideas would constitute the heart of his paper.

In practice, the distinction between research-based and research-supported writing is far from absolute. It is not possible to present information in a completely impersonal or neutral way. Assume, for example, that the student writing about great white sharks tried to make her paper objective and impersonal, presenting only the facts and ideas she had learned from her reading and offering no personal opinions or speculations. Even so, the paper she wrote would be very much hers, since it was she who interpreted her sources, selected which facts and ideas to include, and shaped the material so that it represented her understanding of what great white sharks are like. Whatever type of research writing you engage in, you are expected to *think;* even research-based papers are written by human beings, not by computers.

■ PRIMARY AND SECONDARY RESEARCH

We can also distinguish between types or methods of research. Most library research undertaken for college papers is **secondary research,** so called because it involves the second-hand discovery of information. Through secondary research we learn what others have previously discovered or thought about a topic. In contrast, when we make our own original discoveries, we engage in **primary research.** To give an example of primary research, an agricultural scientist might plant a standard variety of corn in one field and a new hybrid variety in another to test which provides higher yields and is more resistant to drought and disease. On the other hand, a farmer who reads a report written by that scientist to find out the best seed to plant is engaging in secondary research.

As a college student, you will have opportunities to undertake both primary and secondary research. When you conduct an experiment to test the behavior of laboratory rats or survey voter reactions to a presidential speech, you engage in primary research. When you read a history or a chemistry textbook, consult an encyclopedia, or get a printout from a computer database, you engage in secondary research.

However, not every use of a print source is secondary. Written sources can be either primary or secondary. A historian researching the slave trade in colonial America would seek sources from that era. Newspaper stories about slavery, diaries written by freed slaves and slave owners, slave auction notices and bills of sale, tracts written by abolitionists, and census figures and other records from that time are all examples of **primary sources.** In addition, the historian would consult such **secondary sources** as books and articles by other historians who have also researched and written about the slave trade.

In your upcoming research project, you may have occasion to make both secondary discoveries (in library works) and primary discoveries (by interviewing or corresponding with sources). The research you do is determined by the nature of your project and the resources at your disposal.

■ BENEFITS OF DOING RESEARCH

If research papers were not a requirement in college classes, it is doubtful that many students would have the opportunity or motivation to undertake such projects on their own. By the same token, few instructors are surprised when students, after their projects are completed, say that they were glad to have had the opportunity. Often students say they have gained more from the experience than they expected. They find that research writing can have unanticipated benefits.

Learning an Essential Skill

One aim of this book is to help you become a competent college researcher with all the tools you need to produce quality research papers. A more general—and important—aim is to give you the confidence and skills to discover and use available information about any topic that arouses your curiosity.

It is likely that you will need to write many research papers during your college career and afterward. In other classes, you may be asked to gather information on a topic and report what you discover. After college, in your professional career, you may be faced with questions that you will have to answer through research. In these cases, you will need to consult what others have written, to evaluate and select what is pertinent from this information, and to write reports on your findings.

One reason you are being asked to do one or more research projects in your current course is to give you the experience you will need to conduct future projects with confidence. Practice now will make things easier later. When you are assigned to write a research paper in an art history, marketing, or anthropology class, for example, your instructor will not have time to tutor you in the basics of research. And after you graduate, you will have no instructor at all. College students and college graduates are simply expected to have mastered these skills. Now is the time for you to become an experienced researcher.

While students in a college composition course have the opportunity to learn research skills, they are also at a disadvantage compared with other researchers. Others do research not to practice a skill but to learn about specific topics. What they are discovering is important to them, and the research process is merely a means to that end. In the composition class, however, learning about the research paper can be an end in itself, and the topic you are writing about may seem of only peripheral importance. In that regard, your research project may seem artificial to you, an exercise that is useful in teaching skills for later use but one that has no real importance of its own. This *can* happen, but it is up to you to make sure it does not. For that reason, it is essential for you to choose with care the topic that you will research and write about. Because you will be spending much time and effort on this project, you should become as involved as you can with your topic. If you pursue a topic you genuinely care about, you will gain many rewards: Not only will you spend your time profitably, but you will also write a far better paper and, in the process, learn what you need to know about research methods. If you take an interest in your topic and pursue it avidly, the skills you are seeking to acquire will take care of themselves.

Contributing to Scholarship

Although competence in research and research writing are practical skills, there is yet another reason to engage in research besides its personal usefulness to you. By doing research and then making your discoveries public in a paper, you are benefiting your readers as well.

Research is at the very heart of education—it represents the cooperation that is essential to learning. Most knowledge that you have gained is a result of such cooperation. None of us would have been able to figure out the principles of algebra, to mention just one example, if we had been left entirely on our own. Fortunately, throughout the centuries, mathematicians have shared the results of their discoveries with each other and (through our school algebra classes and textbooks) with us as well. A major function of higher education is to share with students the most important thoughts and discoveries of other scholars.

School classes are not the only means by which scholars share their work with us. They also publish their findings so that we and other scholars can have access to them. To make this sharing even easier, the books and articles they produce have been gathered in a central, accessible place: the college library. Engaging in research is simply taking advantage of what other scholars have learned. Like all scholars, you have the right to read about and learn from the discoveries of others. But scholarship is more than just passively receiving the gift of knowledge. As a scholar, you play an active role. Even when you write a research-based paper reporting on the findings of others, you are still creating something new, a fresh synthesis of information, shaped with your own wisdom and insights, a *new source* that was not available to scholars before. Every research paper makes at least a modest contribution to the domain of knowledge. As a student researcher, you are fully entitled to think of yourself as a scholar engaged in a scholarly enterprise. It is for this reason that you are expected to share your findings in a written, public form.

Gaining Personal Knowledge

In traditional college research writing, the author's aim is to report findings, to share information with readers. Authors of these papers keep their writing focused on their topic, while directing attention away from themselves as authors. (The word *I* rarely appears in conventional research writing.) But while you write such a paper to inform others, no one benefits more from your project than you yourself. Before you can inform your readers, you must first inform yourself about your topic through research. Research writing is a sharing of the knowledge you have gained.

Even the act of writing contributes to your learning. Creating a focused, unified paper forces you to see your topic in new ways. It causes you to bring together information from various sources, to make connections, to take vague ideas and make them concrete. Writing has been properly called a *learning tool;* research writers continue to gain personal knowledge while they are writing about what they have read.

On some occasions, however, personal benefit is not just a byproduct but your principal motive for conducting research. At times, you need to seek answers to questions important to you personally. Writing about such privately motivated research can be just as beneficial and worthy as carrying out conventional research projects. For that reason, one type of paper that has become increasingly popular in composition courses is the **personal research paper.*** Unlike the standard research paper, this paper does not call for impersonal writing; as its name implies, it aims to be intensely personal. If you write a personal research paper, you should pick a topic that has real importance to you—or as one author puts it, you should let a topic pick you (Macrorie 66).† Perhaps your research will help you make a decision, such as what major or career to choose, or even which motorcycle to buy or what vacation to take. Perhaps it will just satisfy some strong curiosity. In any case, a personal research paper is a record of your quest for answers. You write your paper not only about *what* you found but also about *how* you went about finding it. The word *I* appears often in personal research writing. Even when such projects are approached with purely personal goals in mind, they provide far wider benefits. Besides being informative, they can be especially instructive because a strong motivation to find answers is the best teacher of research skills. Although personal research papers center on the writer's interest and focus on the writer's experiences, readers often find them interesting. The writer's deep involvement in the subject usually translates into lively writing.

---

*It was also given the name "I-search paper" by Ken Macrorie in his book *The I-Search Paper,* rev. ed. (Portsmouth, NH: Boynton, 1988).

†As Chapter 9 explains, "Macrorie 66" is a form of shorthand telling the reader that the authors are citing an idea by Ken Macrorie on page 66 of his book (identified in the preceding footnote).

2 Two Sample Research Papers

THE RESEARCH PROCESS

Like all other forms of writing, a research paper does not happen all at once. Many steps are involved. Although a research paper may seem complicated and difficult, you can learn to produce one quite capably if you take one step at a time. This book examines each stage in the research process. To illustrate the tasks involved, we will trace the experiences of two first-year college students as they undertake research and write papers for their composition classes. By examining the steps they follow, the problems they encounter, and the solutions they discover to overcome them, you can observe the skills that go into writing a research paper. The same procedure can be adapted for research writing in your other courses and in your future career.

A RESEARCH ASSIGNMENT

In any given semester, students in different composition classes receive a wide variety of assignments for research projects. Some are given open-ended assignments with many options, whereas others are assigned more focused tasks, such as projects related to a particular theme the class has explored in reading and discussion.

Emily Gould and Justin Stafford, first-year college students enrolled in composition courses, were given different assignments by their instructors. In Emily's class, each student was asked to write a standard college research paper. Students in Justin's class were offered the option of writing either a standard or a personal research paper. In both classes, students were asked to choose their own topics.

Following is an assignment similar to the one that students in Justin's class received. Your own research assignment may differ from it, and your instructor may provide additional criteria for the length, scope, and format of your paper. Make careful note of any ways in which your own instructor's assignment differs from the one given here.

Investigate a question or problem that intrigues you and write an informative essay, based on your findings from research. Observe the following guidelines, depending on the option you choose or are assigned.

Option A: The Standard College Research Paper

- *Subject.* Frame your research task in the form of a question that you want your investigation to answer. You may explore any subject that arouses your curiosity and interest. You might choose a topic related to your career goals or the field you plan to major in. Perhaps a certain topic in one of your other courses has aroused your curiosity. Perhaps an event or person from recent or earlier history would be worth learning more about. Perhaps in your reading, in conversation, or in viewing a film or television documentary, you have encountered a subject you would like to explore.

- *Audience.* Assume that the other members of your class are your audience. Write a paper that is appropriate for this audience—one that they will find informative and interesting.

- *Voice.* You are the author of this paper, and it should be an honest presentation of what you have learned. But remember that your readers' interests, not yours, should come first. Although sometimes research writers use the word *I* in their papers (e.g., when they present their personal experience as a source), the focus of the paper should be on the subject matter, not on you as a person.

- *Information and opinion.* Be certain that your paper is principally based on the findings of your research rather than on personal speculation. This does not mean, however, that your paper must avoid any ideas and opinions of your own. Your paper may adopt a point of view, but if it does, you should make it clear to your readers from the beginning.

- *Length.* A typical paper is six to twelve pages long, but the length of your paper should be determined by the nature of your subject.

- *Sources.* Your paper should be based on a variety of research, including (where appropriate) such secondary sources as books, periodicals, and newspapers. If you find that additional sources are appropriate for your topic, you should also interview or correspond with experts or participants. Most papers will cite between eight and sixteen sources. In upcoming classes, you will learn how to locate appropriate sources, how to make use of what you learn from them, and how to acknowledge them in notes and in a works-cited page—that is, how to give your sources credit for their contributions to your paper.

Option B: The Personal Research Paper

Most of the guidelines for the standard research paper apply here as well, but there are some differences.

- *Subject.* You should pick a topic that is already a personal concern in your life. That is, you should seek a question you have a good reason to answer, one that can benefit you directly. Any topic that can help you make a decision or that can provide you with information that will enhance your life in some way is likely to be a good choice.

- *Voice and audience.* You should write honestly and unpretentiously about your research experience. Since your topic is of personal interest to you, the word *I* may occur often in your paper. However, you should also write so as to inform readers who may share your interest.

- *Form.* Unlike the standard paper, which is limited to the subject of the writer's research, the personal paper tells about the writer's process of discovery as well. Although no pattern for what to include and how to arrange it is right for all papers, here is a typical pattern suggested by Ken Macrorie. If you choose, your paper can follow this general outline, found in Macrorie's book *The I-Search Paper:*

  1. What I Knew (and didn't know about my topic when I started out).
  2. Why I'm Writing This Paper. (Here's where a real need should show up: The writer demonstrates that the search may make a difference in his life.)
  3. The Search (an account of the hunt, usually in chronological order; what I did first, what I did next, and so on).
  4. What I Learned (or didn't learn. A search that failed can be as exciting and valuable as one that succeeded). (Macrorie 64)

Parts 3 and 4 can be merged if it makes sense to combine your accounts of what you found and how you found it.

- *Sources.* Interview experts, people who are likely to have the answers you want or who know where you can find answers. Consult these primary sources as well as library materials and other secondary sources.

You are also asked to keep a research notebook (explained on pages 44–45) throughout your research project. Save all your notes, outlines, and rough drafts (more about these later), and submit them in a folder with your completed paper. Your current priority is to choose one of these options and to begin focusing on a specific topic. Use the time between now and the next class to think more about potential topics for your paper.

When their instructors announced the assignment, Emily and Justin had a reaction typical of most first-year college students in this situation: a sinking feeling in the stomach, followed by varying degrees of anxiety. It seemed more intimidating than the papers they had written before. Although both are competent writers, they weren't sure they could do it. At least momentarily, they were afraid their deficiencies would be exposed, that they would be revealed as imposters impersonating college students.

As grim as this sounds, there is nothing unusual about what Emily and Justin felt. All writers are apprehensive at the beginning of an assignment, especially one as unfamiliar and as complex as this research paper seemed. But despite their early fears, Emily and Justin not only wrote their papers but also received high grades for them. Afterward they admitted that the project was not the ordeal they had expected. In fact, it was not only rewarding but also interesting, informative, and, despite much hard work, even enjoyable.

What Emily and Justin did you can do. The trick is to divide the long project into a sequence of smaller, manageable tasks. As we examine these tasks, we will consider these two students' experiences as examples—following the progress of research from chaos to clarity, from panic to finished product. Since you will be making a similar trek, the journeys of Emily and Justin are worth your attention.

THE FINISHED PRODUCT

Before you examine all the steps Emily and Justin took to produce their papers, first look at where they ended up. Their polished, final drafts—the completed papers that were the results of all their work—appear on the following pages.

A Sample Standard Research Paper

First is Emily's response to option A, her research paper on teenage workers in fast-food restaurants. Note that despite her impersonal voice, Emily's paper expresses her point of view about a controversial topic.

Gould 1

Emily Gould

English 12

Professor Katherine Humel

4 October 2002

Fast Food Comes at a High Price for Workers

McDonald's, Burger King, KFC, Wendy's, and other popular chains have brought countless innovations to the restaurant industry, delivering food fast and at low cost year after year. Convenience and value have come at a price, however, and many believe that benefits to the public are outweighed by the costs that this giant industry imposes on its workers.

In his best-selling book Fast-Food Nation, Eric Schlosser shows just how much such popular chains revolutionized America's eating habits. In 1970, Americans spent $6 billion on fast food. By 2000, that figure had soared to $110 billion. Schlosser says Americans "spend more on fast food than on movies, books, magazines, newspapers, videos, and recorded music--combined" (3). Every day about a quarter of the U.S. adult population eats fast food in some form. Few, however, give much thought to the workers who prepare and deliver their meals.

Hiring teenagers to serve us food in a fast-food setting has become "so natural, so normal, and so

Gould 2

inevitable that people often think little about it," says
Stuart Tannock, a lecturer in social and cultural studies
at the University of California at Berkeley (qtd. in Ayoub
A20). Nevertheless, while fast-food workers have become an
essential component in the service industry, a fast-food
job is usually viewed as undesirable, dead-end work.

One-third of all workers under the age of 35 have
gotten their first jobs working for restaurants (Yum!
Brands), and about one-eighth of all workers in the United
States have, at some point, worked for McDonald's
(Schlosser 4). Yvonne Zipp of the Christian Science
Monitor observes that such jobs have become "a teen rite
of passage as universal as driver's ed" (1). They are
ideal for teens because they require no special skills,
and many believe that such jobs provide the educational
benefit of teaching responsibility and good time and money
management. These benefits may be more than offset by
costs, however. Zipp cites a study by the National
Research Council and the Institute of Medicine in
Washington that teens who work more than 20 hours a week
are "less likely to get enough sleep and exercise, less
likely to go on to higher education, and more likely to
use alcohol or drugs." These findings are disturbing,
since four-fifths of American teens work at least part-

Gould 3

time during the school year, and of these, half work more than 20 hours weekly (Zipp 1).

Child labor laws offer some protection, governing the number of hours teens can work and the kinds of work they can do. Those who are 14 or 15 years of age may work up to three hours on a school day and up to eight hours on other days, for a maximum of 18 hours during a school week and 40 hours during a non-school week. They may work only between the hours of 7 a.m. and 7 p.m., except in the summer, when the hours extend to 9 p.m. Once they reach 16, however, teens may work an unlimited number of hours ("General").

These boundaries were set by the Fair Labor Standards Act of 1938, and many believe they are no longer suitable to current realities. At the beginning of the twentieth century, most teens left school at 16, and restrictive laws for children up to 15 years of age were designed to introduce them to the workforce before becoming full-time workers at 16. Today, however, 90% of teens graduate from high school at 18, and most work primarily for extra spending money or luxuries such as new cars. Relatively few now work to help support their families (Zipp 1).

Since 2000, Congress has been debating the Young American Workers' Bill of Rights, a bill that would update the 1938 labor law. If it is enacted as law, 14- and 15-

year-olds could work no more than 15 hours weekly, and
teens 16 and 17 would be limited to a 20-hour work week
(Kiger). While this bill would only affect work hours,
some critics of teen employment, such as Janine Bempechat,
assistant professor in Harvard's Graduate School of
Education, want to keep teens away from fast-food counters
altogether, claiming that they can get a similar sense of
responsibility and self-esteem from jobs such as peer
tutoring or volunteer work. Others, however, noting that
some teens use their paychecks to save for college, worry
that limiting hours could keep them from earning enough to
pay for tuition (Zipp 1).

Teens are also restricted in the kinds of work they
can do. Workers at 14 or 15 are not allowed to cook and
are limited to jobs such as cashier, bagger, or member of
the cleanup crew. More options are available to 16- and
17-year-olds, who can cook but cannot use hazardous
machinery such as automatic slicers, grinders, choppers,
or machines that form hamburger patties ("Prohibited").
Even though such regulations are intended to ensure safety
in the workplace, many employers are either not obeying
the laws or not doing enough to protect young workers. A
teen gets injured on the job every 40 seconds, and one
dies from a work-related injury every five days. Responding
to these alarming statistics, the U.S. Department of Labor

Gould 5

has tried to crack down on violations of child labor laws
with heavy fines (Kiger). Funding for these efforts has
increased, with money going toward inspection of workplaces,
investigations, and occasional sweeps of industries
suspected of serious violations. The Department can impose
fines of up to $10,000 on employers who willfully break
labor laws and can sentence individuals to six-month jail
terms for each employee working in violation of the law.
One of the largest fines was incurred by a fast-food
company in Ohio, when a 15-year-old cut her finger while
using a meat slicer, a piece of equipment that should have
been off-limits to her according to federal law. The
company was ordered to pay $333,450 after it was found to
have 32 other unauthorized employees using similar
equipment, including one under the age of 14 (Pass and
Spector).

In recent years, reported cases of employer
misconduct have declined, but the injury rate among teens
at work has not seen a similar drop. Although fines for
violators are steep, critics worry that the Labor Department
is not doing enough to reduce violations. Only a thousand
inspectors are responsible for the safety of all 100
million workers in the nation. As a result, most employers
are not fined until someone is injured. Under the proposed
Young American Workers' Bill of Rights, an employer who

willfully ignores child labor laws could be sentenced to
as long as five years in prison for each teen who is
seriously injured on the job and up to ten if a teen dies
as a result of the employer's neglect. Regardless,
however, of whether stricter child labor legislation is
passed, companies and young workers alike have a strong
economic incentive to break whatever laws are on the
books. U.S. businesses save an estimated $155 million each
year by employing teens, and the economic gains that
result from hiring them to do jobs meant for older, more
experienced workers often outweigh the consequences of
getting caught (Kiger). Furthermore, teens are unlikely to
refuse an illegal assignment and risk losing the only job
they are qualified to hold.

Because most fast-food jobs require little skill,
they are among the worst paying in the United States. The
fast-food industry pays minimum wage to a higher proportion
of its workers than any other sector of employment. While
a minimum-wage job may be a good source of spending money
for a teenager living at home, it is nearly impossible
for an adult to live off such wages, much less support a
family. Between 1968 and 1990, the boom years for
fast-food restaurants, the purchasing power of the minimum
wage dropped 40 percent, and even now, despite increases
mandated by federal law, it still purchases about 27

Gould 7

percent less than it did in 1968. At the same time, the earnings of restaurant executives have risen dramatically. Nevertheless, the National Restaurant Association opposes any further increase in the minimum wage, and some large fast-food chains, such as Wendy's and Jack in the Box, have backed legislation that would allow states to exempt certain employers from federal minimum-wage regulations (Schlosser 73).

Critics of a higher minimum wage fear the effects of increased labor costs on the restaurant industry. Scott Vincent, director of government affairs for the National Council of Chain Restaurants, says, "A lot of chains are franchised, which means they're small businesses with thin profit margins that can't handle more labor costs" (qtd. in Van Houten). Higher wages, he maintains, would result in reduced hiring, layoffs, or even closings. The only way to compensate would be price increases, which would lessen the appeal of fast food to customers with limited means and therefore reduce business.

A spokesperson for the Coalition on Human Needs expresses a contrary view, asserting that the effects of previous increases in the minimum wage suggest that no serious consequences to the restaurant business would result, while low-income neighborhoods would derive the greatest benefits from a minimum-wage increase

Gould 8

(Van Houten). Author Eric Schlosser calculates that an
increase of one dollar in wages would cause the price of a
hamburger to increase only two cents (73). Furthermore,
Jill Cashen, a representative of the United Food and
Commercial Workers Union, argues that better wages and
working conditions for workers would actually benefit the
consumer:

> The service that customers get when going to
> shop is one of the main reasons why they'll come
> back and be repeat customers. . . . When workers
> are happier--when they have better wages and
> feel like they have a voice at work--their
> service is going to be better, and customers are
> going to come back, and that's what helps build
> a good company.

Without a minimum-wage increase, however, the pay
that fast-food workers receive is unlikely to rise because
they have so little bargaining power. The industry
recruits part-time, unskilled workers, especially young
people, because they are more willing to accept lower pay.
Today, fast-food restaurants also hire disabled persons,
elderly persons, and recent immigrants, for similar
reasons (Schlosser 68, 70). When such employees grow
dissatisfied, they are replaced quickly and easily, with
little disruption of the restaurant's operations.

Gould 9

Fast-food restaurants see an annual turnover rate in
employees of over 75% (White). To accommodate easy
replacement of workers, companies are steadily reaching a
goal of "zero training" for employees by developing more
efficient methods and adopting the most advanced kitchen
technology. The fast-food kitchen is like an assembly
line. Food arrives at the restaurant frozen, and
preparation, which involves little actual cooking, is
regimented by a manual, which includes such details as how
hamburger patties are to be arranged on the grill and the
thickness of the fries (Schlosser 68-72). One college
student who worked at Wendy's said, "You don't even think
when doing work, and you never make any decisions. You're
always told what to do. When you make hamburgers there are
even diagrams about where the ketchup goes" (Williams).
All these factors have contributed to the "de-skilled"
nature of fast-food jobs, which corporations believe to be
in their best interest because it increases output and
reduces the cost of training and wages.

Others, however, claim that the high turnover in
fast-food jobs costs employers more than they save through
low wages. Fast-food restaurants lose at least $500 for
each employee who has to be replaced. Managers are forced
to spend time in recruiting, hiring, and training new
employees, and additional staff is often needed to help

process applications. Current employees are also burdened
with extra responsibilities when they pick up the tasks of
replaced workers (White).

Other controversies involving wages have plagued the
fast-food industry. In 1998, a Washington state jury found
Taco Bell guilty of cheating as many as 13,000 workers out
of overtime pay (Broydo 20), which, according to federal
law, must be paid whenever an employee works more than 40
hours in a week and must be at least one and a half times
the normal hourly wage ("General"). In the Taco Bell case,
the jury found that managers had forced workers to wait
until the restaurant got busy to punch in, had them work
after punching out, and failed to record hours correctly.
One worker claimed that she regularly worked 70 to 80
hours a week but was paid for only 40. While these are
among the worst violations, there is evidence that many
other companies deprive workers of earned overtime pay.
The Employment Policy Foundation estimates that employees
lose $19 billion in unpaid overtime wages every year
(Broydo 20).

Fast-food restaurants adopt several other tactics as
well to lower costs. Workers are employed "at will,"
meaning that they are employed only as needed, so if a
restaurant is not busy, a manager can send them home early.
Managers also avoid the cost of benefits for full-time

Gould 11

employees by hiring large crews and keeping all workers
employed for less than 30 hours per week. Fast-food chains
often reward managers who keep labor costs down, leading
to such abuses as compensating workers with food instead
of money and requiring them to clean the restaurant on
their own time. When such abuses do occur, corporations
try to distance themselves from responsibility. For
example, the McDonald's corporation has no formal wage
policies, so it accepts no blame for the abuses of its
franchisees (Schlosser 74-75).

In various industries, dissatisfied workers have
turned to labor unions to gain a voice in the workplace
and to secure better wages and working conditions. At
fast-food restaurants, however, union representation is
rare. Organizers attribute their failed attempts to
unionize McDonald's restaurants during the 1960s and 70s
to the high turnover of workers and the corporation's
opposition to unions. John Cook, U.S. labor-relations
chief for McDonald's during the 1970s, said, "Unions are
inimical to what we stand for and how we operate" (qtd. in
Royle 40).

While the company no longer publicizes its anti-union
stance, its efforts to forestall unions have continued. In
1998, two McDonald's employees in Ohio claimed that they
were fired for trying to organize a union (Hamstra). In

1973, during a union drive at a McDonald's in San Francisco, a group of employees claimed that they had been threatened with dismissal if they did not agree to take polygraph tests and answer questions about their involvement in union activities. The company was found in violation of state law and was ordered to stop; nevertheless, the attempt to unionize was unsuccessful (Schlosser 76).

Ads for fast-food companies always show smiling, well-scrubbed, contented workers, and the corporations boast of their employee-friendly policies. Restaurants recruit workers with slogans such as "Everybody's Somebody at Wendy's" (Wendy's) and "A Subway restaurant is a really neat place to work" (Subway). On its website, McDonald's proclaims, "We're not just a hamburger company serving people; we're a people company serving hamburgers," and it claims that its goal is "to be the best employer in each community around the world" (McDonald's). While many thousands of teenagers who annually accept work serving fast food find the experience rewarding, many others regard the job as anything but friendly. As author Eric Schlosser concludes, "The real price [of fast food] never appears on the menu" (9).

Gould 13

Works Cited

Ayoub, Nina C. "Nota Bene." Rev. of Youth at Work: The
    Unionized Fast-Food and Grocery Workplace, by Stuart
    Tannock. Chronicle of Higher Education 25 May 2001:
    A20.

Broydo, Leora. "Worked Over." Utne Reader Jan./Feb. 1999:
    20-21.

Cashen, Jill. Personal Interview. 10 Sept. 2002.

"General Information on the Fair Labor Standards Act
    (FLSA)." U.S. Dept. of Labor Employment Standards
    Administration Wage and Hour Division. 29 Sept. 2002
    <http://www.dol.gov/esa/regs/compliance/whd/
    mwposter.htm>.

Hamstra, Mark. "Unions Seek Momentum from Canadian McD's
    Certification." Nation's Restaurant News 7 Sept.
    1998: 3. MasterFILE Premier. EBSCOhost. 15 Sept. 2002
    <http://web3.epnet.com/>.

Kiger, Patrick. "Risky Business." Good Housekeeping Apr.
    2002: 114. MasterFILE Premier. EBSCOhost. 15 Sept.
    2002 <http://web3.epnet.com/>.

McDonald's USA. "Why McDonald's Has a People Promise and a
    People Vision." 22 Sept. 2002. <http://
    www.mcdonalds.com/corporate/promise/>.

Pass, Caryn G., and Jeffrey A. Spector. "Protecting
    Teens." HR Magazine Feb. 2000: 139. MasterFILE

Premier. EBSCOhost. 15 Sept. 2002 <http://
    web3.epnet.com/>.

"Prohibited Occupations for Non-Agricultural Employees."
    U.S. Dept. of Labor. Elaws--Fair Labor Standards Act
    Advisor. 29 Sept. 2002 <http://www.dol.gov/elaws/esa/
    flsa/docs/haznonag.asp>.

Royle, Tony. "Underneath the Arches." People Management 28
    Sept. 2000: 40.

Schlosser, Eric. Fast Food Nation: The Dark Side of the
    All-American Meal. Boston: Houghton, 2001.

Subway Restaurants. "Subway Job Opportunities." 22 Sept.
    2002 <http://www.subway.com/>.

Van Houten, Ben. "Moving on Up?" Restaurant Business 1
    July 2001: 15. MasterFILE Premier. EBSCOhost. 15
    Sept. 2002 <http://web3.epnet.com/>.

Wendy's International. "Welcome to Wendy's Career Center."
    22 Sept. 2002. <http://www.wendys.com/w-5-0.shtml>.

White, Gerald L. "Employee Turnover: The Hidden Drain on
    Profits." HR Focus Jan. 1995: 15. InfoTrac OneFile.
    21 Sept. 2002 <http://infotrac.galegroup.com/>.

Williams, Tamicah. Personal interview. 24 Sept. 2002.

Yum! Brands. "Great Jobs." 22 Sept. 2002. <http://
    www.yumjobs.com/>.

Zipp, Yvonne. "Virtues of Work vs. Finishing Homework."
    Christian Science Monitor 15 Dec. 1998: 1. MasterFILE

Gould 15

Premier. EBSCOhost. 15 Sept. 2002 <http://
web3.epnet.com/>.

A Sample Personal Research Paper

True to the nature of personal research papers, Justin's paper on whether he should pursue a career in pharmacy is more personal and informal than Emily's paper on fast-food restaurants. Justin's style, however, is fully appropriate for the kind of paper he is writing.

Stafford 1

Justin Stafford

ENG 102

Prof. Richard Veit

8 Oct. 2002

Becoming a Pharmacist: Prescription for Success?

I. Why I Am Writing This Paper

Next to finding the person I will marry, selecting the profession that will occupy me for the rest of my life is the most important decision I am likely to make. At various times as a boy and a teenager, I dreamt about exciting jobs, such as being an astronaut, a soldier, a senator, and a rock star. Lately, however, my plans have become more practical, and for the last year I have given serious thought to a career with considerably less sex appeal. Rather than piloting the space shuttle or winning a Grammy, I have begun to think that I can be successful and happy by becoming a pharmacist.

Because the consequences are so great, I do not want to make a hasty decision, and this assignment has given me an opportunity to learn if pharmacy is the right choice and, if so, what I will need to do to pursue this career path.

II. What I Knew

Science has always been one of my interests and strengths, so I have focused on science-related fields, including pharmacy as well as medicine, dentistry, electrical engineering, and marine biology. All have their attractions as well as drawbacks. Doctors, for example, have high incomes and great prestige, but their hours can be irregular, and their stress level is high. Marine biology fascinates me, but the number of interested students far exceeds the number of available jobs.

Although I was much less informed about pharmacy before writing this paper than I am now, I did know that a pharmacist spends fewer years in school than either a doctor or a dentist. I had heard about a nationwide shortage of pharmacists, so jobs are easy to get and the pay is excellent. Unlike engineers, pharmacists work on a daily basis with the general public, something I enjoy. My guidance counselor in high school raised the possibility of a career in pharmacy, and the idea appealed to me from the first. In my hometown, our neighbor, Mr. Eric Marshburn, was a pharmacist who drove a restored classic Thunderbird and had a good life. He was an excellent role model, one of the people I admired growing up, and he is one reason I am leaning toward this profession.

Stafford 3

About the required education, I knew that I would need to transfer to a pharmacy school, but the details were hazy. Learning the practical aspects of getting from where I am now as a first-year college student to the end point as a professional pharmacist was a major goal of my search. But first, and even more important, I needed to find out for certain if this profession was the right one for me.

III. The Search

My first step was a visit to the university's Career Services Center, where the receptionist directed me to books and brochures about health professions. At his suggestion, I also went online to the Center's career-planning page and took several tests intended to match me with professions suited to my skills and interests. Based on my answers, the "Career Key" test told me I scored highest in "investigative" jobs, followed by "social" and "enterprising." I scored lowest in the "artistic" category. The 70 "investigative" jobs listed on the program include biological scientist, speech pathologist, historian, and--I was pleased to see--pharmacist (Jones). The "Career Interests Game" from the University of Missouri combined several traits and narrowed the list of professions to a dozen choices, one of which, again, was

Stafford 4

pharmacy. The "Career Key" program also linked me to the Department of Labor's <u>Occupational Outlook Handbook</u>, which contained a wealth of information about the pharmacy profession and which provided still more links to Web sites of professional organizations such as the American Association of Colleges of Pharmacy.

I then went online to the university's library databases. I did not find any useful books on my topic, but I had much better luck with periodicals. I searched the EBSCOhost, InfoTrac, and Lexis-Nexis databases using various keywords, including "pharmacy career," "pharmacy education," "pharmacy degree," and "pharmacist shortage," and I was led to many useful articles. I also did an Internet search with the Google search engine using similar phrases. The phrase "pharmacy degree" led me to several sites of universities that offer pharmacy degrees, and I learned about their requirements and the application process. I visited the public library and found one helpful reference book on pharmacy careers.

I next read about the pre-pharmacy major in our university catalog, and I talked with the pre-pharmacy advisor, Ms. Claudia Stack. She gave me information about what courses I would need to take in the next three semesters to be eligible to transfer to a pharmacy program after sophomore year. Finally, when I had read widely

Stafford 5

enough to ask intelligent questions, I undertook what
turned out to be the most valuable step in my search, an
interview with a working pharmacist. I called the Target
discount store and spoke to Mr. Blake Barefoot, the head
pharmacist, who readily agreed to speak with me. We made
an appointment to talk during the slowest part of his day,
and during the twenty-minute interview, he answered all my
questions and discussed the pros and cons of his
profession.

At this point I had an abundance of information. I
was not only informed but enthusiastic and ready to put it
all together. Later, as I made note cards and began
writing, I found some gaps and had further questions,
which caused me to conduct additional searches in the
library's databases.

IV. What I Found

As everyone knows, pharmacists dispense drugs
prescribed by doctors. In the past they mixed ingredients
to form powders, tablets, and ointments, but today most
drugs are packaged by pharmaceutical companies in pills
and capsules in a standard dosage ("Pharmacists," Bureau).
Nevertheless, pharmacists must still be experts in
medications so they can advise patients and doctors about
the effects and dosages of drugs. They must be able to

protect patients by identifying errors in prescriptions, and they must keep careful records of all the drugs prescribed to each customer by different physicians to be able to identify duplicate drugs or combinations of drugs that can lead to harmful side effects or interactions ("Pharmacists," Encyclopedia 103).

Skills in dealing with people are just as important for pharmacists as scientific skills. Pharmacists advise patients about the proper use and effects of drugs, answer questions about symptoms, and advise about non-prescription medications such as vitamins and cough syrups. Being a drug counselor is an increasingly important role for pharmacists as many doctors have less time to spend with patients than in the past ("Pharmacists," Encyclopedia 103).

Winning the trust of patients and being able to give clear, careful advise are vital since one third of all Americans have "low health literacy" (Kaufman). Todd Dankmyer of the National Association of Retail Druggists says, "If patients don't feel comfortable talking with their pharmacist, they may discontinue prescribed medication on their own, make wrong treatment decisions, or avoid seeking medical help until the side-effects become life-threatening" (qtd. in "Your Local"). Blake Barefoot, the chief pharmacist at the Wilmington Target store, says, "Good people skills are essential, and

Stafford 7

pharmacists who lack them usually hate their work."
Others, like Barefoot, consider working with the public
"the most valuable and rewarding part of my job."

In addition to skill in both science and communication,
pharmacists must be orderly and meticulous. Qualifications
listed in the Encyclopedia of Careers and Vocational
Guidance include the following:

> You must be diligent in maintaining a clean and
> ordered work area. You must be exceedingly
> accurate and precise in your calculations, and
> possess a high degree of concentration, in order
> to reduce the risk of error as you compound and
> assemble prescriptions. You must be proficient
> with a variety of technical devices and computer
> systems. ("Pharmacists," Encyclopedia 104)

Clearly, not every personality is suited to this
profession.

When most people think of pharmacists, they picture
the druggists they encounter when getting their
prescriptions filled, but a pharmacy degree can lead to
many different career options. In addition to drug stores
and retail chains, pharmacists can work in primary-care
clinics and nursing homes. They can be employed by
government agencies such as the U.S. Public Health Service
and the Indian Health Service, or they can assess the

safety and effectiveness of drugs as agents of the Food and Drug Administration (American, "Career"). They can also work to discover new drugs as university research pharmacists, or they can work for a drug manufacturer, where they can test the chemicals that go into the company's products, supervise their preparation, or make sure the company's literature and advertising about drugs are truthful ("Pharmacists," Encyclopedia 105).

Even being a pharmacist in the local community presents several career choices, including working in a hospital, owning an independent pharmacy, and being a salaried employee in a retail store. Like the others, hospital pharmacists dispense drugs, but an advantage of a hospital setting is they can work more closely with doctors and nurses on patient care as members of a healthcare team--often right on a patient floor (Levenson). They can also specialize in areas that may interest them such as nuclear pharmacy, drug and poison information, and intravenous therapy (American, "Hospital"). On the other hand, hospitals are open around the clock, so working hours are less regular and predictable. As an incentive, some hospitals offer pharmacists the option of working seven days on, seven days off, which gives them frequent mini-vacations and can cut child-care costs in half. Because hospitals pay pharmacists about six percent less

Stafford 9

than stores, some hospitals offer scholarships for pharmacy school as an incentive, paying for one year of schooling for each year the student agrees to work at the hospital after graduation (Costello 2).

Owning a retail drug store is potentially the most lucrative option, and it allows pharmacists to be their own boss and to set store policies. Retail pharmacists usually begin as salaried employees before gaining the funds and experience to be store owners or co-owners ("Pharmacists," Bureau). A drawback is that the initial capital investment is high and so are the risks. Competition is great, and independent pharmacies now account for only 17% of the prescription market, compared to chain stores at 30%. Mail-order companies (13%) and even supermarket pharmacies (9%) are also growing rapidly and capturing market share (Frederick 45). Profits are further threatened as health insurance companies and Medicare have cut the fees they pay for each prescription. Drug stores are now filling more prescriptions than ever but making less money doing so. One owner lamented, "All I can do is try to survive by controlling expenses and focusing on the part of my business that is profitable-- cards and gift items" (qtd. in Martinez).

Perhaps to avoid the problems of ownership, most pharmacists, by far, choose to work as salaried employees in retail stores, but they face problems there as well. In addition to filling prescriptions and advising patients, pharmacists spend on average almost 20% of their time on insurance claims and other paperwork related to payments (Mistretta 37). Hours can be long, but the biggest cause of stress comes from customers. Rafael Saenz, a pharmacy student who worked part-time for a chain drug store, gave an example:

> The clients could be incredibly rude. One Saturday, when we were filling out something like 500 prescriptions, a man demanded to know what was taking so long, and why we couldn't just count the pills and slap a label on the bottle. He didn't realize we were looking for drug interactions and fighting with his insurance company to pay for the medication. (Qtd. in Mangan A43)

To Blake Barefoot, the greatest cause of stress in his job is in "trying to be fast--everyone wants their prescription in five minutes." He says delays come when drugs cannot be refilled or people give the wrong insurance information.

On the positive side, pharmacists are in demand, and employers go to great lengths to make the job attractive. Dramatic growth in the number of pharmacies has led to

over 5,600 unfilled openings for full-time pharmacists in
chain stores alone, and the shortage is expected to
continue for the foreseeable future ("Pharmacist
Shortage"). As a result, employers are offering high wages
and hiring assistants to take on more of the paperwork.
The average starting salary of full-time pharmacists in
2000 was $67,824 ("Pharmacists," Bureau). Entering
salaries of $80,000 are now common in mid-size cities and
can reach $120,000 in parts of New York and California
(Mangan). Chain stores also offer opportunity for
advancement, and a pharmacist who is willing to relocate
can become a chief pharmacist when a store is opened in a
new location (Barefoot).

Until recently, a five-year college degree was the
standard for becoming a licensed pharmacist, but today
most states require a six-year Doctor of Pharmacy degree.
At colleges that do not offer this degree, students enter
a pre-pharmacy program in the first two years, where they
take a range of courses, with a focus on the sciences.
They then apply to transfer in their third year to a
pharmacy program to begin a demanding four-year course of
study leading to the D. Pharm. degree. Pre-pharmacy
students are advised that, since admission to a pharmacy
program isn't guaranteed, they should also be working
toward another major. In addition, they should get a job
in a pharmacy part-time or during the summer to gain

Stafford 12

experience and be certain they are choosing the right profession (Pre-Health 13-14).

Despite some negative aspects to the job, pharmacist Blake Barefoot enthusiastically recommends pharmacy, which he has found to be "a wonderful career" that provides "endless potential for personal growth and learning." It is also a job with good pay and security, since "people will always need medicine" (Barefoot).

V. Conclusion

My research has taught me much I did not previously know about pharmacy and has given me a solid basis for making the crucial career decision that faces me, although questions still remain in my mind. From aptitude tests I have learned that my personality and interests are suited to the demands of this career. Income and benefits for pharmacists are even better than I expected, and, at a time when the economy is questionable, it would be comforting to be in a high-paying profession where employment is all but guaranteed.

Still, I must be careful not to take too rosy a view of what may be in store. I must consider, for example, whether I am prepared to spend long hours filing Medicare claims or haggling with insurance companies over a patient's coverage. I must consider the stress and

Stafford 13

frustrations that pharmacists endure. Fortunately, I have always thrived under pressure and enjoyed challenges. I love talking and working with people, and I don't get flustered or angry when confronted by rude or angry people. I am also famous among friends and family for being a "neat freak," so the detail and orderliness of the job also appeal to me.

Writing this paper has solidified my intention to become a pharmacist. I intend to take the pre-pharmacy curriculum and apply to several pharmacy schools next year. I will also be ready for a major in chemistry or biology in case I am not accepted. During the school year I am too busy to take a part-time job, but this summer I will certainly work in a pharmacy to gain first-hand experience before making a final commitment to the field.

The one question I am least close to answering is which branch of pharmacy I will enter, because several look attractive. I can picture myself, for example, as a uniformed officer of the Public Health Service, traveling to different assignments and assisting in disasters and health emergencies. I can also imagine myself in a laboratory doing drug research, although I would miss the interaction with people that other options provide. Most likely--and realistically--I will choose to become a retail pharmacist, dispensing drugs and drug-related advice to neighbors in my community. Fortunately, I will not have to lock into any of these options until pharmacy school. During my study for the Doctor of Pharmacy degree, I will be able to take internships in several areas to learn which is right for me. Pharmacist Blake Barefoot told me, "I learned more doing my internship and in my first six months on the job than in my first four years of college."

My research into pharmacy has made me enthusiastic about my future. Although several momentous decisions lie before me, I am now increasingly hopeful and confident that this profession offers me the best prescription for my happiness and success.

Works Cited

American Association of Colleges of Pharmacy. "Career
Options." 16 Sept. 2002 <http://www.aacp.org/>.

---. "Hospital and Institutional Practice." 16 Sept. 2002
<http://www.aacp.org/>.

Barefoot, Blake. Personal interview. 18 Sept. 2002.

"The Career Interests Game." U of Missouri Career Center.
14 Sept. 2002 <http://success.missour.edu/career/>.

Costello, Mary Ann. "More than a Job." AHA News 5 Feb.
2001: 2. Health Source. EBSCOhost. 15 Sept. 2002
<http://web3.epnet.com/>.

Jones, Lawrence K. "The Career Key." 14 Sept. 2002.
<http://www.careerkey.org/english/>.

Kaufman, Jeffrey. Report on health literacy. ABC World
News Tonight. 16 Sept. 2002.

Levenson, Deborah. "Hospitals Struggle to Fill Pharmacy,
Radiological Technology Staff Positions." AHA News 3
Apr. 2000: 1-2. Health Source. EBSCOhost. 15 Sept.
2002 <http://web3.epnet.com/>.

Mangan, Katherine S. "Pharmacy Schools Struggle to Fill
Their Classes." The Chronicle of Higher Education 2
Mar. 2001: A43.

Martinez, "Independent Druggists Feel the Pinch." Wenatchee
Business Journal Mar. 1997: 1+. MasterFILE Premier.
EBSCOhost. 15 Sept. 2002 <http://web3.epnet.com/>.

Stafford 16

Mistretta, A. J. "Pharmacists' Ranks Thinning as Demand
    for Recruits Grows." New Orleans CityBusiness 20 Aug.
    2001: 36-37.

"Pharmacist Shortage Is Long Term." Chain Drug Review. 5
    Aug. 2002. InfoTrac OneFile. 8 Sept. 2002.
    <http://infotrac.galegroup.com/>

"Pharmacists." Bureau of Labor Statistics. U.S. Dept. of
    Labor. Occupational Outlook Handbook, 2002-03
    Edition. Bulletin 2570. Washington: GPO, 2002.
    257-59. 14 Sept. 2002 <http://stats.bls.gov/oco/
    ocos079.htm>.

"Pharmacists." Encyclopedia of Careers and Vocational
    Guidance. Ed. Holli R. Cosgrove. Vol. 4. Chicago:
    Ferguson, 2000. 103-07.

"Pre-Health Professions Student Manual." UNCW. Handout.

"Your Local Pharmacist Could Be Your Lifesaver." Executive
    Health's Good Health Report Mar. 1995: 1-3. Health
    Source. EBSCOhost. 15 Sept. 2002 <http://
    web3.epnet.com/>.

Justin's paper is about a decision that may have important consequences for him. Personal research projects also work well with less momentous topics; any question that arouses your curiosity is a worthy candidate for such a paper. Emily's paper on fast-food jobs, for example, would also have worked well as a personal paper, particularly if she had her own experience with fast-food work. Likewise, Justin could have written his pharmacy paper as a standard research paper. In fact, he chose to keep himself out of one part of his paper, the "What I Found" section. You might try to imagine what each of these papers would have been like if its author had chosen a different format for it.

Analysis and Discussion   **EXERCISE**

Before reading on to learn how Emily and Justin went about researching and writing their papers, answer these questions about their final drafts:

  a. What is your impression of the strengths and weaknesses of each paper? Does each have a clear focus; that is, can you give a brief summary of its topic or central idea? Do you find it interesting? informative? clearly written? well organized? Did the author seem to do an adequate job of researching his or her topic?

  b. If you were the author's instructor, how would you respond to each paper? If you were the author, would you change it in any way to improve it?

Both Emily's paper about fast food and Justin's about his career decision impressed their instructors and classmates, but they did not get that way all at once. Many stages involving much labor, some frustrations, and many changes preceded the final versions. The history of their creation is as informative as the papers themselves.

3 *Selecting a Research Topic*

YOUR RESEARCH SCHEDULE: PLANNING IN ADVANCE

Writing a research paper is a labor-intensive project. Between now and the time you submit your final draft, you will be busy. You will be choosing a topic, exploring it, refining it, chasing down leads, riffling through sources, taking notes, thinking, jotting down ideas, narrowing your project's focus, doing more research and more thinking, writing a tentative draft, revising and revising again.

Obviously, a research project cannot be completed in a day or two. You need to plan now so that you have enough time to undertake each step in the process and so that you can make efficient use of your time. Like Emily Gould, you may be assigned separate deadlines for the various steps in your project. Or you may be given only the final deadline for submitting the completed paper, in which case you should establish your own intermediate deadlines for completing each stage. Emily's instructor gave the class a form much like the one shown in Figure 3.1, with a date for each deadline. You can use the form for recording your own schedule.

Some instructors may supply an even more detailed schedule, which may include dates for such additional activities as library orientation, additional editing sessions, and student–instructor conferences. Whatever your schedule, your instructor will certainly concur in this advice: Budget your time wisely, and get started on your project without delay.

A RESEARCH NOTEBOOK

At the beginning of your project you may already have a clear vision—or only the vaguest notion—of what your final draft will eventually look like. Nevertheless, it is probably safe to say that your final paper will be very different from anything you currently imagine. A research project involves many discoveries, and the act of writing usually inspires us to rethink our ideas. Rather than being *assembled,* research papers typically *evolve* through a process of development and change. Prepare for an adventure in which you discover what eventually emerges on paper.

Your finished paper is the end product of that adventure, the last of several stages in the research process. What you learn during that process is probably

```
┌─────────────────────────────────────────────────────────────────────┐
│                       RESEARCH PROJECT                                │
│                                                                       │
│      Principal Deadlines:                          Due Dates:         │
│                                                                       │
│      1.  Research prospectus due, including a                         │
│          statement of your research topic and a                       │
│          working bibliography (see page 89):        _____        │
│                                                                       │
│      2.  Note cards and preliminary outline due                       │
│          (see page 117):                            _____        │
│                                                                       │
│      3.  In-class editing of completed draft                          │
│          (see pages 195–96):                        _____        │
│                                                                       │
│      4.  Typed good draft due (see page 228):       _____        │
│                                                                       │
│      5.  Final draft due (see page 245):            _____        │
│                                                                       │
└─────────────────────────────────────────────────────────────────────┘
```

Figure 3.1 A schedule for a research project.

more important in the long run than the paper itself. It was for this reason that Emily's and Justin's instructors asked each student in their classes to keep a *research notebook.* At every stage of the project, researchers were expected to keep a personal record of their progress. The research notebook is like a diary. In it Emily and Justin recorded what they were doing and what they were expected to do. They wrote about what they had found, the problems they were facing, and their plans for their next steps. Justin used his notebook as the raw material for the "search" section of his personal research paper.

The writing you do in a research notebook should be informal, not polished. Unlike the research paper itself, the notebook is written to yourself, not to outside readers. When you are finished, you have a record of your research process. But there is also another benefit to keeping a notebook. Both Emily and Justin found that it helped them make decisions and focus their thoughts. In addition, many of the passages both writers used in their papers came from ideas they had scribbled in their notebooks.

You should use a spiral notepad that you can carry with you when you do research, though you may also want to use your word processor (if you have one) to record some entries. You will start using your notebook from the very beginning—now—as you select and focus your research topic.

▮ YOUR RESEARCH TOPIC

Only on rare occasions do researchers have to *choose* a topic. Such an occasion might come about for a freelance writer of magazine articles who wants to select not only a fresh subject that will interest readers and an editor but also one about which she can find enough information through interviews, legwork, and library research.

In most cases, however, researchers already have their topics before them. A situation arises that demands exploration. For example, in order for a detective novelist to write convincingly about a counterfeiting ring, he must do research to learn how counterfeiters actually operate. A historian with a theory about the causes of the Russian Revolution would have to discover the available facts about the period as well as learn what theories other historians have proposed. A lawyer writing a brief for a criminal case must research legal precedents to know how similar cases have been decided in the past and to provide herself with convincing arguments. Most researchers begin with a strong curiosity about a topic and a need to know.

As you begin your own research project, you may already have decided on a topic. Perhaps your class has been reading and talking about an interesting issue such as nuclear policy, teenage suicide, the future of the family farm, or dating practices in foreign countries. Your discussion may have raised questions in your mind, questions that you can answer only through research. Besides satisfying your own curiosity, you can perform a service for your instructor and classmates by informing them about what you have learned. For you, a research paper is a natural.

On the other hand, you may not yet have chosen a specific topic. Perhaps your instructor, like Emily's and Justin's, has left the selection of a topic up to you. Perhaps you have been given a choice within a limited area, such as a current event, the life and views of a public figure, or your career goals. In any case, it is important for you to select a topic you can work with. Because many hundreds of topics may appeal to you, deciding on any one can be hard.

You begin with your curiosity. Your research is aimed at answering a question in your mind, at satisfying your urge to know. For that reason, it is usually helpful at the outset of a project to state your topic in the form of a *research question.* Rather than just naming a general area for your paper, such as "racial policy in the armed forces," it is often more useful to frame your project as a question to be answered, such as "How has the military dealt with discrimination?" or "How has the struggle against discrimination in the American armed forces compared with the struggle in the civilian world?" Perhaps you have formed a *hypothesis,* a theory that you would like to test. In this case your question would begin, "Is it true that . . . ?" For example, in reading about the plagues that devastated Europe during the thirteenth century, you might have speculated that in spite of modern scientific advances, the reactions of people to epidemics have not changed much in seven hundred years. If you decided to test this hypothesis through research, your question might be, "Are effects of the AIDS epidemic on our society similar to the effects of the Black Death on medieval Europe?"

Three factors are critical in framing a good research question. Your topic should have the following qualities. It should be

1. **Appealing.** This is the most crucial factor. Your research should be aimed at answering a question that genuinely arouses your curiosity or that helps you solve a problem. If you are not involved with your topic, it is unlikely that you will write an essay that will interest readers. The interest you have in your topic will also determine whether the many hours you spend on it will be rewarding or agonizing.

2.   **Researchable.** You may be curious about the attitudes of college students in Japan toward religion, for example, but if you can locate only one or two sources on the subject in your local libraries, you will not be able to write a research paper about it.

3.   **Narrowed.** If your question is "What is astronomy?" you will find no shortage of materials. On the contrary, you will certainly discover that your topic is too broad. You can find hundreds of books and entire journals devoted to astronomy. However, you cannot do justice to so vast a topic in a paper of a few thousand words. You will need to narrow your topic to one you can research and cover adequately. You may decide to concentrate on black holes, for example, as a more focused topic. Later on, as you continue your research and begin writing, you may narrow the topic still more, perhaps to a recent theory or discovery about black holes.

GENERATING IDEAS

Unless you already have a question in mind that you are eager to answer, or unless you are facing a pressing decision for which you need information, you will have to do some exploring and thinking about a general subject before you arrive at a properly appealing, researchable, and narrowed research question. Several techniques for stimulating ideas can help you in your selection, including brainstorming and clustering.

Brainstorming

If you were asked right now to declare some possible research topics, you might find it difficult to do so. After a few minutes of wrestling with the problem, you might finally come up with a few topics, but you might find them to be neither original nor exciting. Yet there are literally hundreds of topics that you not only would enjoy researching but also could write about well. The trick is to stimulate your mind to think of them. *Brainstorming* is one helpful technique. It is simply a way of forcing your mind to bring forth many possible topics, under the theory that one idea can lead to another and that, if enough ideas are brought forth, at least one will click.

On the day they announced the assignment, Emily's and Justin's instructors led their classes through several activities to stimulate their thinking. Following are some examples of brainstorming exercises.

Brainstorming: Random Listing	EXERCISES

1.   Let's start with a light and unintimidating exercise. The following is a random list of concepts in no particular order and of no particular significance. Read the list rapidly and then, in your research notebook, begin your own list, adding as many items to it as you can. Give free play to your imagination. List whatever comes to mind without regard to whether it is serious or would make a

reasonable research topic. Save those concerns for later. For now, write rapidly, and have some fun with your list.

surnames	water fountains	swimsuits
clowns	sea horses	salesmanship
cans	con artists	pro wrestling
lip sync	cremation	campaign buttons
lipstick	hiccups	prep schools
war paint	blueprints	sponges
juggling	Russian roulette	snuff
teddy bears	triplets	fads
cave dwellers	women's weightlifting	cavities
haircuts	chocolate	advertising jingles
ways to fasten shoes	frisbees	plastic surgery
high heels	coffins	bartending
hit men	chain letters	mirrors
cheerleaders	tanning	juke boxes
revenge	baldness	icebergs
bicycles	wigs	mermaids
televangelists	facial hair	tribal societies
silicon chips	earrings	fast food
college colors	longevity	cyclones
company logos	boomerangs	Beetle Bailey
roller skates	fuel injection	toilets
tractors	fertility	laughing
warts and birthmarks	nomads	cable cars
freckles	film editing	Mardi Gras
tattoos	spelunking	free gift with purchase

2. Because one idea leads to another in brainstorming, the ideas of other people can stimulate your own thinking. You can cross-fertilize your imagination by looking at other students' lists. After you have listed items for a few minutes, you can (a) exchange lists with one or more classmates or (b) join members of your class in calling out items (perhaps in orderly turns, perhaps randomly) as one or more people write them on the blackboard.

3. Stimulated by these new ideas, resume listing for another few minutes.

4. When you have finished, reread your list and circle the items that seem most interesting to you. What about these items stimulates your curiosity? See if you can now pose five or six questions about them for which you would like answers.

You may be concerned that some of the topics you listed or some of the questions you posed are not particularly serious or do not seem scholarly or deep. You need not worry, since any subject that provokes your genuine interest and curiosity is worth exploring and can be given serious treatment in a research paper. The item "lipstick" in the preceding list, for example, may seem frivolous at first, but it can lead to many serious questions: What is lipstick made of (now and in the past)? How long have people been using lipstick? How has society regarded its use in earlier times? Does it symbolize anything? Is its use widespread throughout the world? Is it ever prohibited by governments or by religions? Why do American women use it but not (for the most part) American men? Such questions point to an interesting and rewarding research project. A student who pursued them would find much information. In the course of research, the student could certainly narrow the topic—perhaps to "What has society thought about lipstick?"—and write an informative, worthwhile paper.

Brainstorming: Focused Listing

EXERCISE

This brainstorming exercise is more focused than the preceding one. In your notebook, list as many ideas as you can in response to the following questions. Write rapidly, listing whatever comes to mind. List phrases, rather than complete sentences. If one topic strikes you as having possibilities as a research topic, keep listing ideas about it until you have explored it to your satisfaction. You do not need to answer every question, but do not stop listing ideas until your instructor tells you that time is up.

- What have been your favorite courses in high school and college? What topics in those courses did you find interesting? For each topic, write as many phrases associated with it as you can.

- What major are you considering? List some particular subjects you hope to explore in your major.

- What career are you considering? What specific branches of that field interest you? What jobs can you imagine yourself holding in the future? List several possibilities.

- What recent or historical events or discoveries are associated with your career interests or major field? What notable persons are associated with these areas? List some things you know about them.

- List magazine articles, books, movies, and memorable television programs that you have encountered lately. List some specific ideas or topics that they bring to mind.

- List some events or controversies that concern you. What news stories have aroused your interest or concern? What historical events have you wanted to learn more about? What do you consider the major changes that have taken place during your lifetime in world affairs? In science and technology? In the way we lead our lives? What problems face us in the future?

- What topics have you read about because you needed or wanted to learn more about them? What problems do you now need to resolve?

- What decisions will you have to make soon? Decisions about school? career? lifestyles? morality? romance? friends? family? purchases? leisure time?
- What areas are you an expert in? What are your chief interests and hobbies?
- What are some of the major gaps in your background? What should you know more about than you do?
- What notable people do you most admire? What people have had achievements that mean something to you? Think of men, women, historical figures, living people, scientists, artists, athletes, politicians. What famous people do you pity or consider villains?

Emily's class spent about fifteen minutes listing ideas for the preceding exercise. Afterward, students shared lists with classmates and discussed their ideas. They also jotted down any new ideas that came to them. Emily's list filled two pages in her notebook. Here are excerpts:

> Favorite subjects
>   History
>   —American history
>   —20th century
>   Government and politics—current events, law school?
> Possible careers
>   Journalism
>   —TV news
>   —print media—Time, Newsweek
>   —politics based
> . . . Controversies—healthy and unhealthy food
>   —vegetarian vs. meat-eating
>   —health risks
>   obesity—heart disease, diabetes
>   causes—fatty diets, fast food, large portions, overeating
>   —risky diets, eating disorders
>   —body image

Emily's list was not an orderly, logical outline, nor was it meant to be. However, this short excerpt shows her mind actively at work, listing and shaping ideas. Clearly she hadn't yet found her research topic at this point, but even at this early stage the germ of her topic was apparent in her list. Among the controversies she noted was unhealthy eating, and, almost as a tangential thought, she mentions fast food, which, several permutations later, would become the eventual topic of her paper. The complete list included many other ideas as well, most of which turned out to be dead ends. But several ideas captured Emily's interest and provided options as she journeyed toward her topic.

Here are some excepts from Justin's list:

...3. Careers
   a. Pharmacy—most promising
       benefits: income, job in demand
       skills: science, sales/personal
   b. Marine biologist
   c. Research chemist
   d. Physician's associate
   e. Other science-related
   f. Military—short-term
4. Recent events
   a. Anthrax scare
   b. Ban on whale meat
   c. Medicare prescription benefits
   d. Required doctoral degree for pharmacists
...8. Major decisions
   a. Career
   b. Major
   c. Marriage
   d. Part-time job ...

In contrast to Emily, Justin hit on his topic—his interest in pursuing a career as a pharmacist—almost immediately. The brainstorming question "What career are you considering?" coincided so exactly with a decision he was wrestling with that he knew instantly what he would research and write about. Justin's certainty about his topic at this point is a rarity. In many cases, brainstorming activities do not lead directly and immediately to a topic the writer recognizes as ideal. Instead, they open up many pathways for the writer to explore. When pursued, some of those paths will lead to still other paths for the writer to take, until eventually the right destination is reached.

Developing an Idea: Clustering

A more concentrated form of brainstorming can be called *clustering* or *mapping.* It is a technique designed to stimulate the development of many ideas related to one given idea. Emily's instructor gave her class the following exercise.

Clustering Ideas   EXERCISE

Review the lists you have made thus far and circle all the items that look promising as research topics. If you have time, ask one or two classmates to do the same thing, each using a different color ink. Finally, select one possible topic (this is not a final commitment) and write it in the center of a blank page in your notebook. Using it as a starting point, radiate from it whatever ideas come to mind. The clusterings of Emily and Justin are shown in Figures 3.2 and 3.3.

Figure 3.2 Emily's clustering.

Finally, Emily's instructor asked class members to call out questions that arose from the idea they had listed (or new ones that occurred to them), while she wrote them on the board. Here are some typical questions offered by the students:

- Does having a baby increase a mother's IQ?
- What effects does El Niño have on weather?
- Are big-time college athletics corrupt?
- Do high CD prices represent price fixing?
- Was Susan B. Anthony an American hero?
- How is wireless technology changing American society?
- Are violent video games harmful to children?
- What strategies work in quitting smoking?

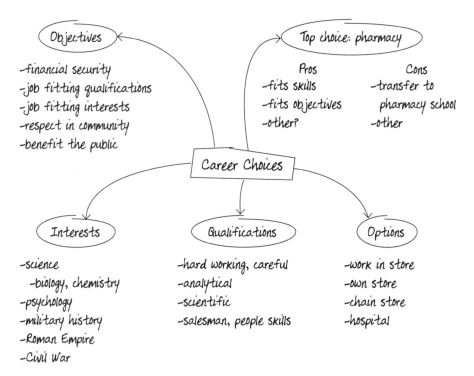

Figure 3.3 Justin's clustering.

- What are causes of body dysmorphic disorder?
- Why do wealthy people shoplift?
- Is phonics a useful strategy for teaching reading?
- What are benefits and drawbacks of state lotteries?
- What role did music play in the Civil Rights movement?

Also on the list was a question from Emily, "What effects does fast food have on our health?"

Prewriting exercises are not magic formulas that instantly produce perfect research topics. Instead, if all goes well, they begin a chain reaction that leads you, however circuitously, to your eventual topic. The idea-generating exercises that Emily and Justin engaged in pointed them in helpful directions. Justin was that rare student who knew almost immediately exactly what would be the focus of his research. His mind was already occupied by a decision with an upcoming deadline: If he was going to enter a career in pharmacy, he would need to declare a pre-pharmacy major almost immediately. Emily, in contrast, arrived at her research topic by a far more indirect route. Most of her brainstorming centered around food-related health issues, a topic she had been reading about. As her clustering shows, she thought about vegetarianism, diets, and obesity. The latter led her to causes of obesity, including the eventual topic of her paper, fast food.

At this early stage, she was focusing on the health effects of fast food, and it would still be some time before she settled on the ultimate topic of her paper, workers in fast-food restaurants.

A research project is like a puzzle. When you begin, you never know how it will turn out. After all, the purpose of research is to answer questions for which you do not currently have answers. When you start, you cannot know what answers you will find. You cannot even be sure your questions are good ones. These discoveries are made only as you undertake the actual research and as you begin to write about your findings. You are almost certain to find that the research paper you end up writing will be quite different from your current expectations. What you learn along the way will cause you to change plans and go in new and often unexpected directions. You are sure to meet surprises. A good researcher must be flexible, able to adapt to whatever new ideas and information present themselves. For this reason you need not be concerned if you now have only a tentative idea of the topic of your paper. Your topic will take firmer shape (and perhaps a very different shape) as you undertake your research. The following chapters show you how to conduct that research.

4 Tools for Finding Sources

■ BEGINNING YOUR RESEARCH

Having generated ideas about likely topics for papers, Emily and Justin needed to do preliminary research to learn more about these topics and to bring their research questions into sharper focus. A visit to the library and some exploration of the resources available to them via computer were the logical next steps. From their instructors they received assignments similar to the one that follows.

Preliminary Research   ASSIGNMENT

Do some preliminary research to explore the topic you are considering.

- Learn more about your topic by reading about it in encyclopedias and other general reference sources. If the topic seems appropriate, take notes and see if you can narrow your focus to a specific question.

- See if your topic is researchable by assembling a working bibliography of about a dozen sources that you intend to consult. (Working bibliographies are further explained in Chapter 6.) Use a variety of search tools (explained in this chapter), and include books, periodicals, newspapers, and electronic media, as appropriate for your topic. If, for example, you are writing about a recent event, newspaper articles will be a significant source of information. On the other hand, if you are writing about an event from ancient history, you may not discover any newspaper sources.

- If adequate sources are not available, see if you can broaden your topic or switch to another one. If you find too many sources, read more about the subject and narrow your paper's focus within more manageable limits.

- Make sure your sources are available. Find out if the library has the periodicals and newspapers you are seeking. Check books out. If necessary, order books from other libraries through InterLibrary Loan. Ask the circulation desk to recall desired books that have been checked out by others. If most of the books are gone, however, someone else is probably writing on your topic, and the sources you need may not become available in time. If so, avoid needless frustration by switching now to another topic.

- Do some quick reading in your sources to learn more about your topic. It might be wise to ask a professor or some other authority on your subject for suggestions about the topic and for further research sources.

- Decide what additional sources can provide valuable information for your project. Write letters to request information, if necessary. Arrange interviews in advance by setting up appointments. (Letters and interviews are discussed in Chapter 5.)

- Be sure to record your discoveries, questions, and other experiences with locating sources in your research notebook.

As they begin their first research project in college, few students are experts in using the library. Many are confused and intimidated by electronic resources such as online databases and the World Wide Web. By the time students have finished the project, however, they have learned how to find information in their library as well as to access other sources throughout the world via electronic communication.

■ YOUR CAMPUS LIBRARY

Your purpose in conducting a research project is not only to inform yourself about your topic by discovering information but to inform others as well by making your discoveries available in a paper. Learning is, after all, a cooperative venture, and scholars have an obligation to pass on to others what they have learned. For that reason, a wealth of important information and ideas produced by scholars has been collected and located in a convenient place for your use—your college library.

As any quick browse through the library will make abundantly clear, there are a great many potential sources out there—written about an almost unlimited number of topics. Finding information about any particular topic might seem an impossible task. Fortunately, however, the means are available for locating almost anything you are looking for. Your library offers not only *research sources* themselves, such as books and periodicals, but also *search tools,* which allow you to discover what research sources are available for your topic and to locate them. These tools include the library's book catalog, online and printed guides to periodical and newspaper sources, and reference librarians. Search tools can give you a great deal of power, allowing you to discover information on almost any topic. Of immediate interest to you, of course, is that they allow you to find sources for your research paper. This chapter, with its accompanying exercises, is intended to make you proficient in the use of various search tools.

ELECTRONIC RESOURCES

A generation ago, college students searched for books about their research topics by flipping through index cards alphabetized in drawers in a library's card catalog. To find periodical and newspaper sources, they paged laboriously through dozens of bound indexes. The computer revolution changed all that, and today most library searches are conducted at a keyboard in front of a computer screen. Not only have searches become simpler and more convenient, but today's students have easy access to vastly more sources than did scholars just a few years ago.

Electronic searches have themselves undergone rapid change. A few years ago, the student researcher had to visit many different library terminals, each dedicated to a particular index or database. Today it is typical for a college library to have a *central information system,* a single online site from which a student can locate all the library's holdings, find sources in any of dozens of electronic databases, and even read many sources directly on the viewing screen. Because most library information systems are accessible on the Internet, students may avail themselves of many library resources from their home computers or at computer workstations around campus.

Being able to link up with your college library from home is only a small part of the research power now available to you through computers. For example, if you wanted, you could also search the holdings of a university library in Australia, copy a file stored on a computer in Scotland, or ask a question of a scholar in Nigeria. Before we explore the various tools for locating sources, both within and outside the library, we need some general background about electronic resources. To understand electronic resources and acquire skill in using them, there is no substitute for hands-on practice, but the following can provide a useful introduction.

A collection of material that is available electronically (by computer) is generally referred to as a *database.* Databases can be classified as either portable or online. A *portable database* is one that can reside within a particular computer, such as a program on a diskette or a CD-ROM file. In contrast, an *online database* is located at a distant site, such as a host computer or another computer on a network. For you to access it, your computer must communicate with that site. A vast and ever-growing number of databases is available online. These include valuable search tools such as indexes that enable you to locate sources, electronic encyclopedias, and whole libraries of data.

Networks

To gain access to an online database, your computer terminal needs to be connected to another computer containing the database. Such an arrangement by which a number of computers can contact each other is called a *network.* Your college is likely to have its own *local network* in which most computers on campus are connected through a central computer, known as a *server.* This connectivity allows students and faculty to share files and use e-mail to communicate. Most *college library networks* are tied in with the larger campus network, providing patrons with access to library information from classroom, office, and dormitory computers. Since colleges put restrictions on who may use their network, you may need to apply for an *account* and receive an *address* and a *password.*

Smaller networks are often joined in a larger network. For example, your college library network may be joined with networks from other regional libraries, so that you can search for works in several different libraries simultaneously. The linking of libraries in such a consortium also enables students at one campus to find and borrow works owned by another campus.

Finally, networks throughout the world, most likely including your campus network, are joined together in the largest and grandest network of them all, the *Internet.* Originally begun by the U.S. government, this network has grown to allow computer users almost anywhere on the planet to communicate and share information. Any Internet user can send and receive messages with any other user via e-mail. For example, you could direct an inquiry about your research question to a scholar in Finland, provided you knew that person's e-mail address. You could also join one of countless *discussion lists* devoted to particular topics. A message sent to a list is automatically forwarded to all its subscribers. For instance, if you were researching voting patterns of women, you might post an inquiry on the PoSciM list, which is devoted to a discussion of political science issues (and maybe also to WmSt-L, a women's studies list). Other subscribers interested in your topic would be likely to reply. An index to thousands of discussion lists can be found online at http://paml.alastra.com.

Another way to follow an ongoing e-mail discussion about a particular topic is by consulting a *newsgroup* or a *bulletin board.* These are very much like actual bulletin boards, where anyone can read and post messages. Unlike discussion lists, where all items are e-mailed directly to subscribers, newsgroups and bulletin boards are "places" on the network that you can "visit" whenever you choose, but no messages are sent to your e-mail in-box.

By far the most popular component of the Internet is the *World Wide Web,* which allows users to read (and create) attractive presentations of text, graphics, and sound known as *Web pages.* Because virtually anyone can post material on the Web, there is no limit to the variety of available presentations. For example, you can explore your college's *home page,* which is linked to many other Web pages containing information about its programs, faculty, and resources. You can also read electronic "magazines" (often called *zines*) on the Web or consult the Web for instant news, weather, and sports updates. The variety is so great that "surfing the Net" has become a recreational obsession for many. However, because almost anyone can post whatever they choose on the Web without oversight or restriction, much information found on Web pages is of dubious merit. Students need to take special care in evaluating material from Web sources.

USING YOUR LIBRARY'S RESEARCH TOOLS

It is worth repeating that while search tools can give you access to a vast quantity of information, the *quality* of that information varies widely. More than ever, student researchers need to use careful judgment about the reliability of their sources and the usefulness of information they encounter. Since the number of channels by which you can access research sources is so great, the following sections of this chapter will focus on those most likely to be helpful. Still, many such tools—old and new—are described, and they can seem intimidating at first. Don't allow yourself to be overwhelmed. It is not necessary for you to absorb all the information in a single sitting. Nor do you need to memorize the names of all the available reference sources and the procedures for using them. Instead, regard this chapter as a guide that you can consult whenever you need it, now and in years to come. By examining the resources that are described here one at a time and by gaining experience with their use through the practice exercises, you will soon develop a solid and confident command of the tools needed for doing college research.

Most college libraries allow you access to a great variety of resources, and you can begin your search from one convenient online screen, the home page of the library's central information system. Once you log on to this page, you are presented with a menu of choices. Different libraries set up their home pages in different ways, but most have similar features, and we will explore some typical and important research tools likely to be available through your college library's online system.

The following two menu options are a staple of most college library systems:

- **Search the library catalog.** This option allows you to find books and other items in your library's holdings.
- **Search electronic indexes and databases.** This option allows you to find articles in journals, newspapers, and other periodicals.

In addition, the menu may allow you to learn library hours, view your own library record and renew items you have borrowed, see what materials your instructor has placed on reserve, and even search catalogs at other libraries.

Finding Books and Other Library Holdings

Let us begin by examining the first of the two options just mentioned, a search of your library's catalog. The library's holdings include books, periodicals, videocassettes, sound recordings, and many other materials—and all are indexed in its online catalog. The catalog menu will present you with a number of search options, including the following:

- Author search
- Title search
- Subject search
- Keyword search
- Call number search

If you know what author or book title you are seeking, you can do an ***author search*** or a ***title search.*** Merely enter the name of the author or title, and information is displayed.

When you are engaged in a research project, you will be looking to find what books are available on a particular topic, and you will want to conduct a ***subject search*** or a ***keyword search.*** In a subject search, you enter the subject you are searching. Only particular subjects are indexed, namely the subject headings designated by the Library of Congress. Since you may not know the exact subject heading, a keyword search may be the handiest way to begin your search for books on your topic.

Doing a Keyword Search

In a keyword search, you enter one or more words that are likely to appear in a work's title, in its subject, or in catalog notes about its contents. Imagine, for example, that you are interested in researching the widely believed myths known as "urban legends." These are popular but unfounded stories, such as the rumor that a certain brand of bubble gum contained spider eggs or the myth that alligators live in the sewers of New York City. If you entered "legend," you would find that hundreds of works in your library are referenced by this keyword, most of which would have nothing to do with urban legends. (In my library, the entries I found included a book about basketball legend Michael Jordan and a CD of Irish fairy tales.) To eliminate the clutter, you can narrow your search by typing in two or more words, such as "urban legend." Most library catalogues treat two words as a phrase and will search for instances of those words appearing side by side.

Library Catalog Searches

- Type in one or more words that may appear in the title, subject, author name, or notes.
- Multiple words are searched as a phrase: The entries "college English" and "English college" will produce different results.
- Use *AND* to search for entries containing *both* words (not necessarily together):

    alcohol AND law
- Use *OR* to search for entries containing *either* word:

    college OR university
- Use a wildcard symbol (asterisk) to represent missing letters: The entry "educat* polic*" will produce results for "educational policy" and "education policies," but also "educating police."

One limitation to keyword searches is that a computer is very literal-minded. If you include the word "legend," it will ignore instances of "legends." Most catalogs allow you to use a ***wildcard symbol,*** usually an asterisk, to represent optional characters. For example, in a keyword search of the college catalog, I found only

Num	Mark	KEYWORDS (1–6 of 13)	Medium	Year
		KEYWORD ⬍ urban legend* UNC Coastal Library Consortiur ⬍ [Search]		
		Sorted by Date		
1	☐	Net crimes & misdemeanors : outmaneuvering the spammers, swi	Book	2002
2	☐	Encyclopedia of urban legends / Jan Harold Brunvand ; artwor	Book	2001
3	☐	The truth never stands in the way of a good story / Jan Haro	Book	2000
4	☐	Urban legends : the as–complete–as–one–could–be guide to mod	Book	2000
5	☐	Urban legends final cut [videorecording] / Columbia ; Phoeni	Videorecording	2000
6	☐	Spiders in the hairdo : modern urban legends / collected and	Book	1999
		[Save Marked Records] [JUMP TO AN ENTRY] [13]		

Figure 4.1 Results of a keyword search for "urban legend*" in a library catalog.

one entry by entering just "urban legend." However, I found thirteen entries when I entered the term "urban legend*." Researchers must be judicious in their use of wildcards, however, because they can sometimes make a search too broad. For example, a search for "urban*" would return entries about urban legends, but also many unwanted entries containing the words "urbane," "urbanization," "Pope Urban VIII," and "Urbana, Illinois." Partial results of a search using the keywords "urban legend*" are shown in Figure 4.1, in which the first six of thirteen titles are shown on the screen.

You could make a list of all the works that interest you by checking the boxes to the left of their titles. Later, when you have finished all your searches, you could ask for a display of all the works you marked. Alternatively, you could examine entries immediately. For example, if you clicked on the sixth title in Figure 4.1, *Spiders in the Hairdo: Modern Urban Legends*, you would be shown a record, part of which is reproduced in Figure 4.2. This screen gives much information about the book, including its authors, title, publisher, and length (111 pages). The fact that the book was published in 1999 tells you how current it is. The fact that the book contains "bibliographic references" tells you that you might go to pages 110 and 111 to find a list of other works on the topic. The information in the boxes tells you where to go to find the book (its location and call number) and

Author	Holt, David
Title	**Spiders in the hairdo : modern urban legends / collected and retold by David Holt & Bill Mooney**
Publisher	Little Rock, Ark. : August House, 1999

LOCATION	CALL #	STATUS
UNCW General Collection	GR105 .H63 1999	AVAILABLE

Description	111 p. : ill. ; 22 cm
Bibliography	Includes bibliographical references (p. 110–111)
Subject	Urban folklore -- United States
	Legends -- United States
	United States -- Social life and customs
Alt author	Mooney, William
Add title	Modern urban legends
ISBN	0874835259 (tpb. : alk. paper)

Figure 4.2 Excerpt from a book record.

that it is available (not checked out by another patron). When a book's status is "unavailable," you can ask the circulation desk to send a *recall notice* to the borrower, but you would receive no guarantee that it will be returned in time to meet your project's deadline.

Notice that in Figure 4.2, seven different items are underlined, which means that each is a computer *link* to further data, and each provides a useful way to find additional sources on your topic. If you were to use your mouse to click on the first author's name, "Holt, David," you would be shown a list of all the holdings in the library written by that author. If you clicked on the books's call number, you would be shown a list of works with similar call numbers. Since books are numbered according to their topic, this is a handy way to see what other related items (in this case, about folktales) are in your library. Finally, three different subject headings are listed. You could click on any one of them to do a subject search for this heading.

It should also be noted that your search need not be limited to the holdings in your own library. One useful tool for searching the holdings of over 40,000 libraries worldwide is the OCLC *WorldCom* database, which is available among the online tools on most college library Web sites. A search on WorldCom for books using the keywords "urban legends" found forty-nine entries. For each entry, WorldCom noted if the work was available in our library. For a work not available locally, WorldCom provides a list of libraries in nearby states that hold the book. A work found in another library can be borrowed by your library through an *InterLibrary Loan*. You may find it useful to check the collections of libraries specializing in your subject. If you were researching automotive engineering, you would be wise to check libraries of major universities in Michigan, a state with a large automobile industry. Likewise, if you were researching manatees, you would expect to find more works on the subject at the University of Florida than, say, at the University of North Dakota. Ask your librarian for help in searching the collections of other libraries.

EXERCISES | **Using Your Library's Central Information System**

Use your college library's online catalog to answer the following questions. Although these exercises may remind you of a scavenger hunt, they are intended to familiarize you with the resources in your library and to practice important research skills that you will use many times in the future.

1. These questions can be answered by doing an author search on your college library's catalog:

   a. How many authors with the surname Churchill have works in your library?

   b. How many author listings are there for Sir Winston Churchill (1874–1965)?

   c. View the record for one book by Sir Winston Churchill (and print it, if your computer terminal is connected to a printer). What is the book's full title? its call number? Is the book currently available in your library, or has it been checked out? In what city was the book published? by what publisher? in what year? How many pages long is the book? What subject headings could you use in a subject search to find similar works on the same topic?

2. Do a subject search, using one of the subject headings found in 1c, above. How many works does your library have on that subject? What are the title, author, and call number of one of those works (other than the Churchill book)?

3. Find an author whose last name is the same as or close to your own. Record the title and call number of one book by this author.

4. How would you use your library catalog to locate works *about,* rather than by, Sir Winston Churchill? How many works does your library have about him? Record the author, title, and call number of one such book.

5. How many books does your library have with the title (or partial title) *Descent of Man?* Who are the authors of these books?

6. Do a call number search to answer these questions: How many works are there in your library whose call numbers begin with TL789? What subject(s) are books with this number about? Record the author, title, and call number of one such book.

7. To answer this question, you may need guidance from your instructor or librarian: How can you limit your call number search to only those works (with call number TL789) that were published after 1990? How many such works are there in your library's collection? Can you limit your search to TL789 works with the word "flying" in the title? How many such works are in your library?

8. Do a keyword search to find works on your research project topic (or another topic that interests you). What subject headings do you find for these works? Use the most appropriate of these headings to do a subject search. Now use the WorldCom database to see what additional works on your topic are available at other libraries in your state. Record information about works likely to help you in your research project.

Encyclopedias and Other General Reference Works

General reference works, books, periodicals, newspapers, and microforms are some of the resources in college libraries. Because so many sources are available, it is helpful to approach a search for information with a strategy in mind and to turn first to resources that are most likely to be of help. Before you search in particular directions, you need a broad overview of your topic. General reference works are often a good place to begin.

General reference works, such as encyclopedias and almanacs, offer information about many subjects. They are located in the reference section of your library, where they can be consulted but not checked out. Many encyclopedias, dictionaries, and almanacs are also available online or in CD-ROM format. In addition to text and pictures, some online works allow you to view film clips and hear audio as well. Another advantage of online encyclopedias is that they are frequently updated, and the latest edition is always available to you.

General encyclopedias have alphabetically arranged articles on a wide variety of subjects. *Encyclopedia Americana* and *Collier's Encyclopaedia* both contain accessible articles that can provide you with helpful introductions to unfamiliar subjects. The print version of the *New Encyclopaedia Britannica* is somewhat more complicated to use in that it is divided into various sections, including the "Micropaedia," which consists of short articles and cross-references to other articles in the set, and the "Macropaedia," which consists of longer, more detailed articles. Encyclopedias published on CD-ROM disks or available online include *Encarta* and *Britannica Online.* One-volume *desk encyclopedias,* such as the *New Columbia Encyclopedia,* can be quick and handy guides to basic information about a subject. *Almanacs,* such as *Information Please Almanac, Atlas and Yearbook,* and *The World Almanac & Book of Facts,* contain tables of information and are handy sources of much statistical information.

Specialized encyclopedias, restricted to specific areas of knowledge, can provide you with more in-depth information. Many such works are available—the online catalog at the university where we teach lists over a thousand works under the subject heading "Encyclopedia." By way of example, here are just a few from the beginning of the alphabet: *Encyclopedia of Adolescence, Encyclopedia of African-American Civil Rights, Encyclopedia of Aging and the Elderly, Encyclopedia of Alcoholism, Encyclopedia of Allergy and Environmental Illness, Encyclopedia of Amazons, Encyclopedia of American Social History, Encyclopedia of Animated Cartoons, Encyclopedia of Arms Control and Disarmament,* and *Encyclopedia of Assassinations.* You can use your college catalog to locate a specialized encyclopedia dealing with your research topic. You can also browse the reference section in the appropriate stacks for your topic; sections are marked by Library of Congress call numbers (e.g., BF for psychology, HV for crime, N for art, etc.).

EXERCISES | Using General Reference Works

1. Locate a specialized encyclopedia dealing with your research topic or another topic that appeals to you.
2. Look up that same topic in the print version of the *New Encyclopaedia Britannica* (look first in the index, which will direct you to either the "Micropaedia" or the "Macropaedia") and then in an online or CD-ROM encyclopedia. Compare the treatment and coverage of the topic in these different works.
3. Determine if information about the same topic can also be found in a desk encyclopedia or in an almanac.

4. Finally, write a one-page account of what you discovered. In particular, what kinds of information are found in the different reference works? How do the treatments of the topic differ?

■ FINDING ARTICLES: MAGAZINES, JOURNALS, AND NEWSPAPERS

Articles in magazines, journals, and newspapers are among the sources used most frequently by student researchers in composition classes, for several reasons: Articles are written on a variety of subjects; they make timely information available right up to the most recent issues; and, being relatively brief, they tend to focus on a single topic. Your college library is likely to have recent issues of hundreds of magazines and journals and of many local, national, and international newspapers. In addition, back issues of these publications are available either in bound volumes or on *microforms* (miniaturized photographic copies of the material). Many electronic indexes that you may use to find articles on your research topic allow you to view the articles directly on your screen, saving you the step of finding the article in print or on microform.

Locating Periodicals

If you are in doubt about whether your library has a magazine or journal you are looking for, you can consult a list of all the periodicals your library owns. Such a list is usually found in the library's online catalog. In most libraries, current issues of magazines and journals are shelved on open stacks; back issues are collected and bound by volume or copied onto microforms. Recent back issues, not yet bound, are sometimes available at a periodicals or service desk. If you have difficulty finding an article, ask at the periodicals or reference desk for assistance.

Microforms

As a space-saving device, many libraries store some printed materials on microforms, miniaturized photographic copies of the materials. The two principal types of microforms are *microfilm,* which comes in spools that resemble small movie reels, and *microfiche* (pronounced *MY-crow-feesh*), which comes in individual sheets of photographic film. The images they contain are so small that they can store large quantities of material. A projector is required to enlarge these images so they can be read. Most college libraries have projectors for both microfilm and microfiche. Some projectors also allow for photocopying of what appears on the projector's screen. Follow the directions on these machines or ask a librarian for assistance. Although sturdy, microforms are not indestructible, so it is important to handle them with care and to return them in the same condition as you received them.

Library Vandalism—A Crime Against Scholarship

Since scholarship is a cooperative enterprise, it is essential that all scholars have access to sources. Students who steal, deface, or mutilate library materials commit a crime against the ethics of scholarship. An unforgivable sin is to tear articles from magazines, permanently depriving others of their right to read them. Many a frustrated scholar, looking for a needed source only to find it stolen, has uttered a terrible curse on the heads of all library vandals—one that it might be wise not to incur. On the more tangible side, most states have made library vandalism a criminal offense, punishable by stiff fines and in some cases jail sentences.

Actually, there is no excuse for such vandalism. Short passages can be hand-copied. Longer excerpts, to be used for legitimate academic purposes, can be photocopied inexpensively. Most libraries have coin-operated or debit-card photocopy machines in convenient locations. (Some photoduplication violates copyright laws; consult your instructor or librarian if you are in doubt.)

▮ USING ELECTRONIC DATABASES

Most college libraries provide links to electronic databases, which have replaced printed indexes as the most popular means for students to locate articles, electronic files, and other materials related to their research topics. These databases are either online (through an electronic connection to the database host site) or portable (stored on a CD-ROM disk). *Databases* are usually accessed through the library's central information system.

College libraries allow you access to dozens of databases, and the number is increasing at a rapid rate. In this chapter we will introduce a few of the more popular and useful databases, but you should explore your library to learn what databases are available. Most databases work in a similar way, and you need to master only a few simple principles to conduct a successful search. Once you have practiced searching one database, you should have little trouble negotiating most other databases as well. It is usually advisable to search several different databases when you are looking for articles and other information about your research topic.

A Sample Search for Periodical Sources

Your library may subscribe to several *online reference services*, such as EBSCO-host, FirstSearch, InfoTrac, LexisNexis Academic Universe, ProQuest, and WilsonWeb. Each service allows you to search a number of databases either singly or simultaneously. As an example of how you could use an online reference service, we will demonstrate a search using the EBSCOhost service. Let us imagine you are doing a research project on college students who are binge drinkers.

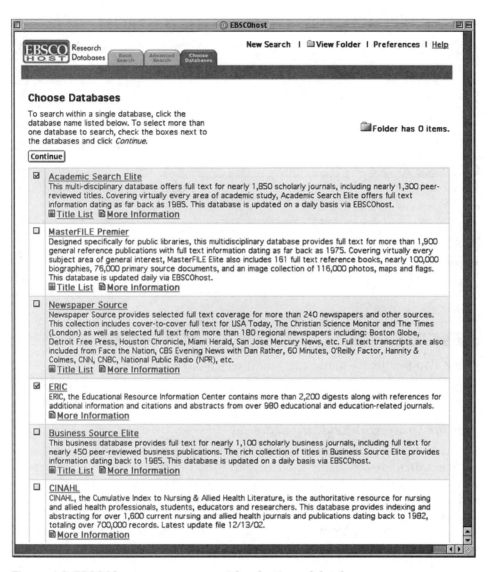

Figure 4.3 EBSCOhost menu screen with selection of databases.

Figure 4.3 shows part of the EBSCOhost menu of databases. Scrolling down the screen would reveal many other databases as well. To the left of each database is a box. As a first step in your search, you would click on the boxes of all the databases that might be pertinent. Let us assume you decided to search the Academic Search Elite database (a database of articles in scholarly journals) and ERIC (a database of education-related journals and documents). By clicking first in those two boxes and then on the *Enter* button, you bring up the search page shown in Figure 4.4.

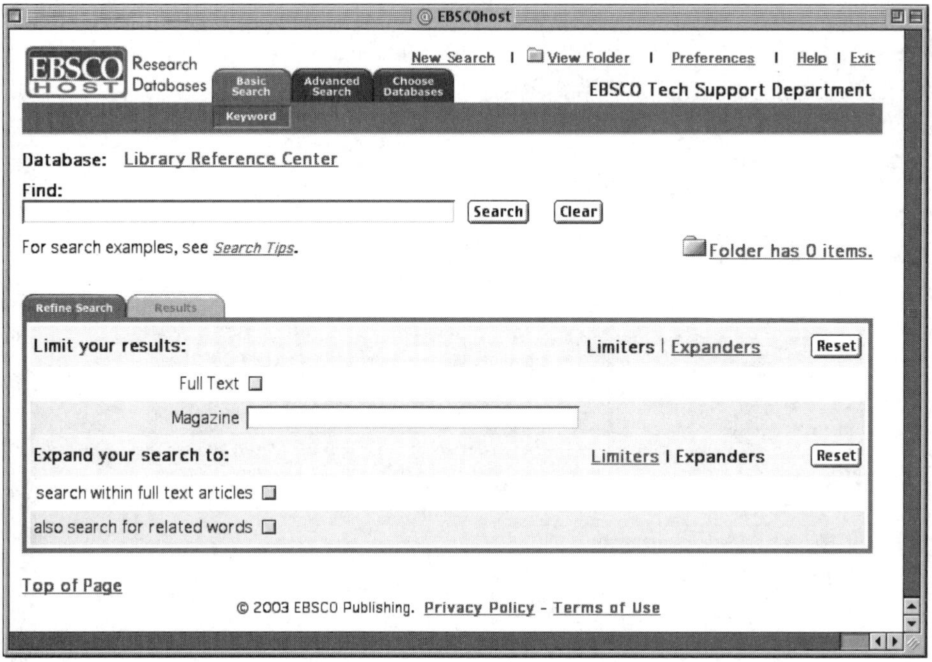

Figure 4.4 Search page in the EBSCOhost search engine.

Tips for Successful Keyword Searches

The next step in your search is to enter **keywords** on the screen in Figure 4.4 to tell the **search engine** (that's another term used to describe an online program that searches a database) what words or phrases to look for as it searches the titles and abstracts of articles. If you enter "binge drinker" in the *Find* box and then click on the *Search* button, a results list will soon appear with fifty-seven documents, the first several of which are shown in Figure 4.5. Although this may seem a respectable return, unfortunately it does not come close to capturing all the articles available on the subject.

But wait! Computers are very literal. You have asked the search engine to restrict its search just to that one phrase, greatly limiting the results. A useful tip is to use an asterisk as a **wildcard character** to find any of several related words. Entering "binge drink*" instead of "binge drinker" will broaden your search to any phrase that begins with those characters, including *binge drinker*, *binge drinkers*, and *binge drinking*. Click on the *Search* button, and instead of fifty-seven results, the search engine now reports it has found 393 items—a more satisfactory outcome.

But perhaps a search of these keywords is still too limiting. The EBSCOhost search engine assumes that two or more words side by side constitute a phrase, and it will look only for the words *binge* and *drink** when they occur next to each other, not when they are separated by other words. A solution is to conduct what is known as a **Boolean search**, using the signals *AND, OR,* or *NOT.* For example, if

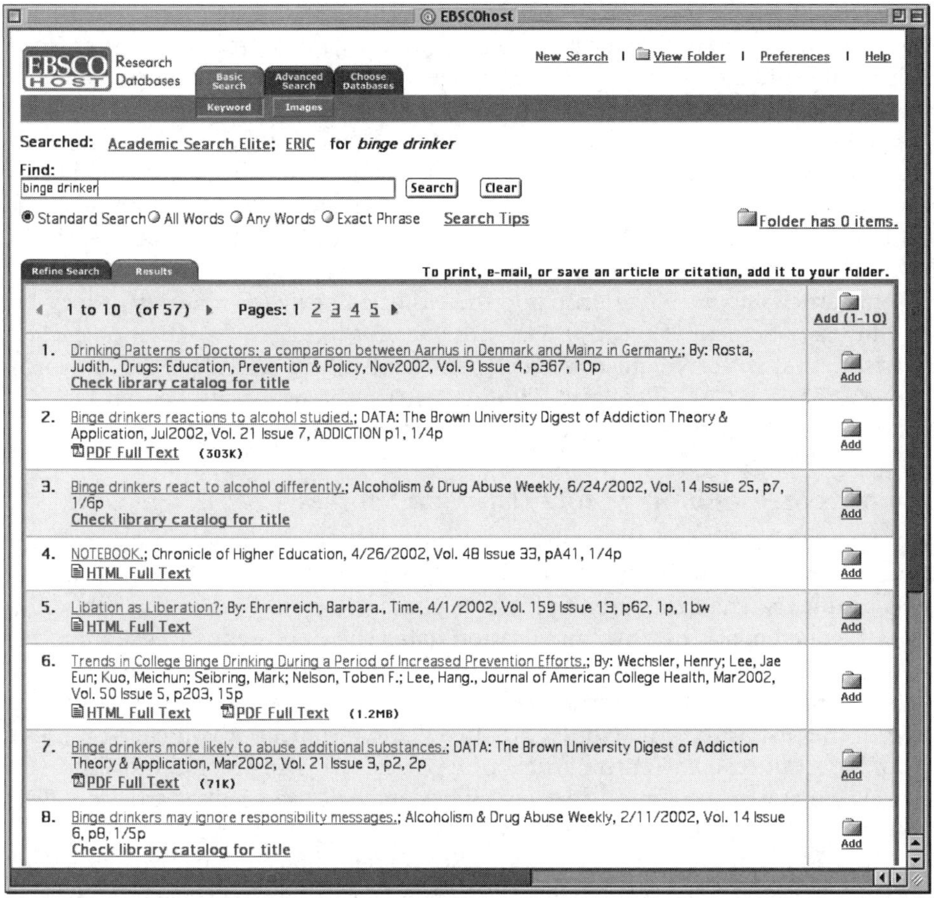

Figure 4.5 A "results list" in the EBSCOhost search engine.

Using Boolean Operators to Refine Your Search

- The *AND* operator combines search terms to find documents that contain *both* terms:

    alcohol AND college

- The *OR* operator combines terms to find documents that contain *at least one* of the terms:

    alcohol OR drugs

- The *NOT* operator *excludes* terms:

    alcohol NOT drugs

    This will find documents on alcohol but will ignore those in which the word "drugs" appears.

you asked EBSCOhost to search for "binge AND drink*," it will look for articles that contain both of those words, even if they are separated from each other. That is, it would find articles that contain "binge drinkers" as well as those that contain "drinkers who go on a binge" and so on.

More is not always better, however, and now your search may be too broad. You aren't interested in binge drinking among business executives, just among college students, so a useful strategy is to refine your search further to eliminate unwanted articles. Make the search topic "binge AND drink* AND college*" to eliminate any documents in which the words *college* or *colleges* do not appear. However, in some articles about binge drinking, the word *university* (or *universities*) may be used instead of *college*. You can use the OR operator to search for either *college** or *universit**. That is, you might have your best results if you search for the keywords "binge AND drink* AND (college* OR universit*)." The search results that EBSCOhost returned when different keywords were entered are shown in Figure 4.6.

The Next Step—Finding More Detail on Sources

In a sample search for articles about collegiate binge drinking, I used the keywords "binge AND drink* AND (college* OR universit*)," and EBSCOhost found 265 documents. The first screen of these results is shown in Figure 4.7. Each result gives the document's title and publication data. The next step is to examine the most promising articles to find useful sources. You can click your mouse on the title of an article to read an ***abstract*** (a brief summary) of its contents. Beneath the titles of the first article, the words "HTML Full Text" appear. If you click on these words, you can read the entire article on your screen. The second and third entries also give you the option to view photocopies of the original articles ("PDF Full Text"). For the fourth entry, an abstract is available online, but you would have to read the article in your library. To see if your library has back issues of the journal *International Journal of Eating Disorders*, you can click on the words "Check library catalog for title."

Keywords entered	Number of documents found
binge drinker	57
binge drinkers	66
binge drinking	356
binge drink*	393
binge AND drink*	427
binge AND drink* AND college*	250
binge AND drink* AND (college* OR universit*)	265

Figure 4.6 Number of documents found in an EBSCOhost search using different keywords.

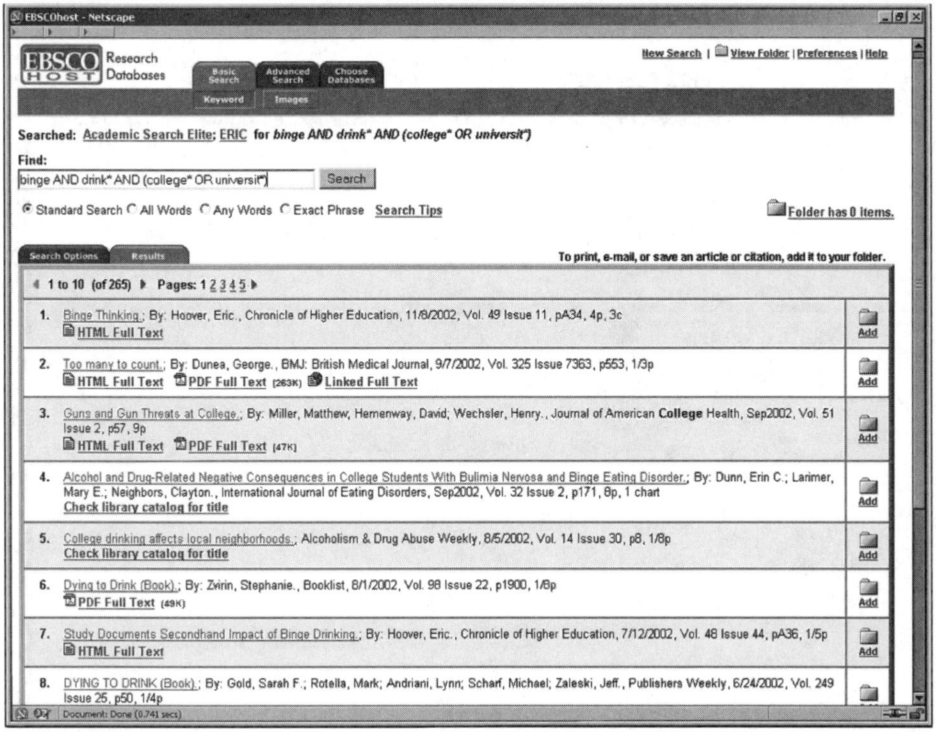

Figure 4.7 Search results for "binge AND drink AND (college* OR universit*)."

If you were to click on the title of the first item in Figure 4.7, "Binge Thinking," you would see the detailed information shown in Figure 4.8. In addition to the title, author, and source of the article, this screen contains several other useful items. The abstract summarizes the article and is your best guide to whether the article is likely to be a useful source for your research project. If so, you can read the full text by scrolling down the page or by clicking on "HTML Full Text" above the title. If you believe the article is a useful research source, you can take notes on the article immediately if you like. You also are given several other options at the top of the page. You can *Print* it for later use; *E-mail* the article to yourself (this is especially useful if you are working in a library); *Save* it on a diskette; or *Add to folder*. The last option allows you to select all the articles that you have found to be likely sources for your project.

Another useful feature of Figure 4.8 is the "Subject(s)" heading. This article is indexed under four different subjects. If you were to click on the third subject, "DRINKING of alcoholic beverages—United States," you would find additional articles related to that subject.

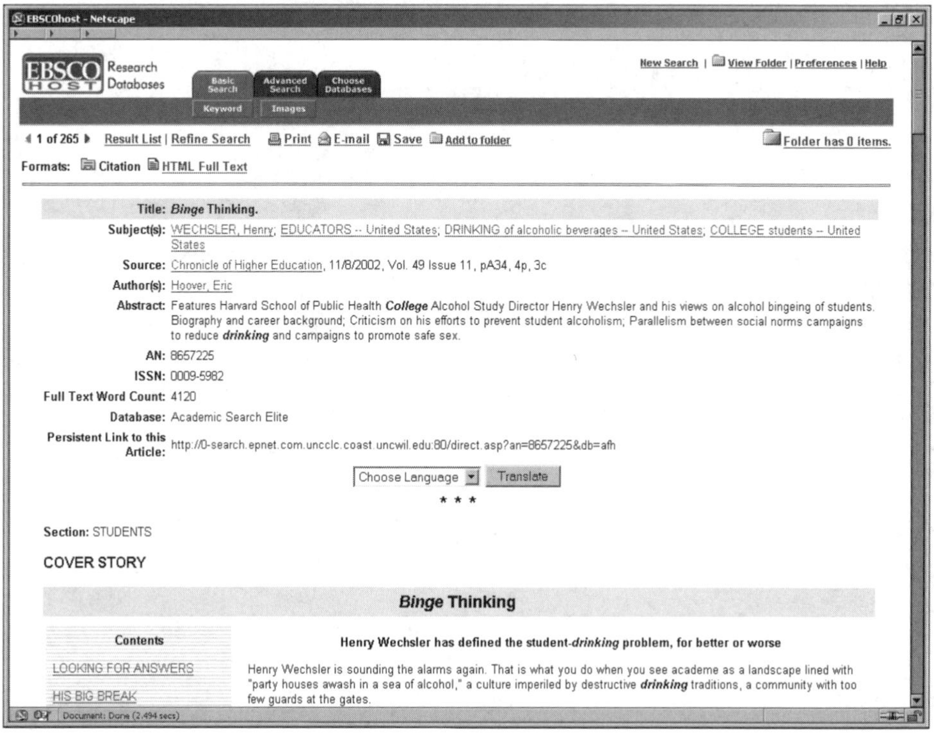

Figure 4.8 An EBSCOhost citation screen.

EXERCISES | ## Using an Online Reference Service

1. In Figure 4.3, which of the databases shown would be your best source to find articles in academic journals? Which database(s) would you search if you were writing a paper on the issue of social promotion in the schools? Which database(s) would be most useful to locate sources for a research project on student entrepreneurs who start Internet businesses? What is the difference between the MasterFILE Premier database and the Newspaper Source database?

2. Figure 4.4 shows an EBSCOhost search page. If you were looking to find articles about psychological warfare, what keywords would you enter in the "Find" box, and which of the four buttons immediately below the "Find" box would you click? What would you do if you were looking for articles about penguins in Chile? What if you were looking for articles about either anorexia or bulimia? If you were searching for articles about the town of Paris in Texas, how could you use Boolean operators to eliminate articles about the movie named *Paris, Texas*? What if you were looking for articles about the censorship of music or television in China or Vietnam?

3. In Figure 4.4, how could you limit your search to articles that can be read online? Which box would you check if you wanted to limit your search just to articles that

appeared in scholarly journals? What if you wanted to conduct the search for your keywords not just in the titles or abstracts of articles, but in the articles themselves?

4. In Figure 4.7, who were the authors of the article "Guns and Gun Threats at College"? In what publication did it appear? What is the length in pages of the article? Of the eight articles listed on screen, which ones can be read online? Which ones would you have to look for in your library? If you wanted to email articles numbered 1, 4, and 5 to your home, what would your first steps in the process be?

5. The page shown partially in Figure 4.7 gives the first ten of 265 documents. Where would you click with your mouse pointer to view the next ten results?

6. Figure 4.8 shows a citation page for an article. What is the title of the article? Where would you find a brief summary of the article? How many words long is the article? In what publication did it appear? Would clicking on any of the four listed subject headings be helpful in finding additional articles about binge drinking among college students? How could you read the full article?

7. Figure 4.9 shows a search screen using the InfoTrac search engine in which a student has filled in some of the boxes. What subject(s) is the student researching? In addition to entering keywords, what other limitations did the student put on the search?

InfoTrac OneFile

INFOTRAC

- Help - Search
- Title List

- Subject guide
- Relevance search
- Keyword search
- Advanced search
- Start over

Back to ...

- Gale Group Databases

Keyword search

Click in the entry box and enter search term(s)

bond funds AND target maturity funds NOT Asia   [Search]

Search for words ○ in title, citation, abstract ● in entire article content
Type words to search for. You can use AND, OR, NOT. Results are sorted by date.

Limit the current search (optional)
☐ to articles with text
☐ to refereed publications
by date [mm/dd/yyyy or mm/yyyy or yyyy] 06/01/2000 - 01/01/2003
to the following journal(s) _____   [Browse]

———————————— **History** ————————————

No Search Results

InfoTrac OneFile has 28,777,876 articles and was last updated on Jan 12, 2003.

THOMSON
GALE   Copyright and Terms of Use

Document: Done (0.421 secs)

Figure 4.9 A keyword search using the InfoTrac OneFile search engine.

Figure 4.10 A LexisNexis™ search.

8. Figure 4.10 shows a search using the LexisNexis™ search engine. Describe what the student who filled in this page was seeking?

9. Log on to your college library's central information system. Does it allow you to search for articles online? If so, which online reference services (e.g., EBSCO-host, FirstSearch, LexisNexis, WilsonWeb) does it allow you to search? Are there other databases you can use to search for articles?

10. Use your college library's resources to find a newspaper article about Medicare fraud published within the past year.

11. Use a different database to find an article in an academic journal about the sleeping disorder known as sleep apnea. If you can, print out the citation screen for the article; if not, copy the name of the author, title, publication, date, and page numbers.

FINDING GOVERNMENT DOCUMENTS

The vast array of documents published by the U.S. government constitutes another useful resource for research in almost any field of study. Many government

documents are available online. In addition, each state has at least one designated depository library that receives all documents distributed by the Government Printing Office (GPO), as well as several other partial depository libraries
that receive selected government publications. Items not in your college library
can usually be borrowed through the InterLibrary Loan service. Government documents are usually shelved in a special library section and identified by a call
number (called a *GovDoc* or *SuDoc* number). Many library catalogs do not index
all their government documents along with their book holdings. To find documents and their call numbers, you need to consult one of several indexes that can
search GPO databases. The **Catalog of U.S. Government Publications** is a gov-
ernment-sponsored online search engine, located at http://www.access.gpo.gov/
su_docs/locators/cgp/.

Another index is the **GPO Monthly Catalog** available in many university libraries through the FirstSearch online reference service. Imagine, for example,
that you were writing a research paper on the prevalence and causes of teenage
smoking. A search of the GPO Monthly Catalog using the keywords "teen*" and
"smoking" would yield many documents, including one called "Changing Ado-
lescent Smoking Prevalence: Where It Is and Why." Clicking on the title would
call up on your screen the record of that publication shown in Figure 4.11.

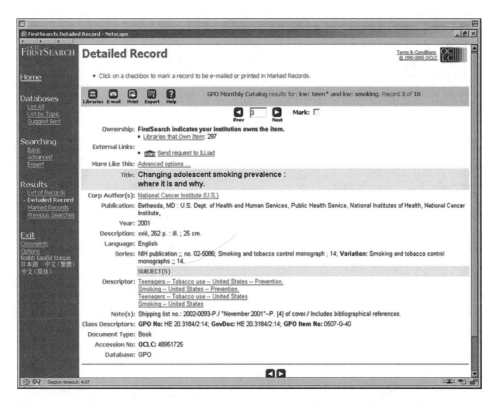

Figure 4.11 A government document record in the GPO Monthly Catalog.

Finding Government Documents

1. This exercise can be undertaken by one or two students who can report their findings to the class. Find out if your college library is your state's regional depository for U.S. government documents or a partial depository. If the latter, what percentage of available government items does it receive? Where are government documents shelved in the library? How can students gain access to government documents not in your library?

2. Figure 4.11 is the record of one of the government documents found from a search about teenage smoking. Which government agency authored the report? In what year was it published? On what subject heading(s) might you click to find more documents about teen smoking?

3. Use a GPO index to search for a government document related to your research topic. Report briefly on what you find.

■ INTERNET RESOURCES

Library sources can be accessed in systematic ways; by contrast, finding sources on the Internet is much more a hit-or-miss affair. Whereas the library's staff controls its collection and creates an index of all the library's holdings (its on-line catalog), no one runs the Internet, much less controls access to it or creates a comprehensive index. The Internet is really a vast interconnected network of smaller networks, which virtually anyone can access and where virtually anyone can publish anything. Navigating the Internet and finding resources that can aid your research project require much practice, some skill, and considerable luck.

The best Internet tutorial comes from hands-on exploration, aided by your curiosity and an adventurous spirit. Here I can give only some brief information and hints to get you started.

Web Search Engines

When you seek Web sources for a research project, you will probably not know the addresses for specific sites. Although no comprehensive index to the millions of Web pages exists, several commercial indexes (known as *search engines*) provide access to a large number of sites. Search engines are of two general types: Web crawlers and human-powered directories, which work in radically different ways. *Web crawlers* automatically pore through the Web and index what they have found. When you search for a specific term, the search engine examines its index and returns a list of relevant sites. A *human-powered directory* relies on people to examine sites and to classify them according to category. Most search engines are actually hybrids, combining both crawler and human-powered results.

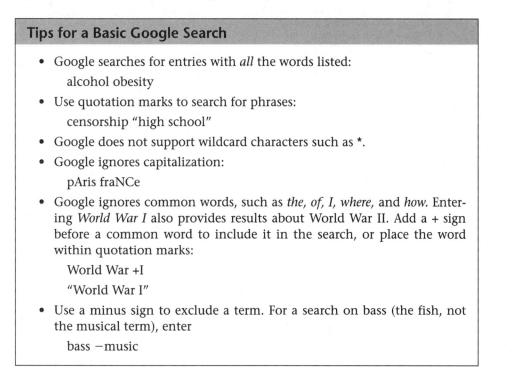

Figure 4.12 Screen for a basic Google search.

Tips for a Basic Google Search

- Google searches for entries with *all* the words listed:

  alcohol obesity

- Use quotation marks to search for phrases:

  censorship "high school"

- Google does not support wildcard characters such as *.

- Google ignores capitalization:

  pAris fraNCe

- Google ignores common words, such as *the, of, I, where,* and *how.* Entering *World War I* also provides results about World War II. Add a + sign before a common word to include it in the search, or place the word within quotation marks:

  World War +I

  "World War I"

- Use a minus sign to exclude a term. For a search on bass (the fish, not the musical term), enter

  bass −music

Because different search engines provide different results, it is often best to use more than one in researching your topic. Here are the addresses of some of the more prominent search engines:

Google	http://www.google.com
AllTheWeb.com (FAST)	http://www.alltheweb.com
Yahoo (crawler)	http://www.yahoo.com
Yahoo (directory)	http://dir.yahoo.com/
MSN Search	http://search.msn.com
Lycos	http://www.lycos.com
Ask Jeeves	http://www.askjeeves.com

One of the most popular and highly regarded search engines is Google. The Google address *www.google.com* produces the basic search screen shown in Figure 4.12 on the previous page. Unlike most library catalogs and periodical search engines such as EBSCOhost, Google does not treat keywords as phrases; that is, it

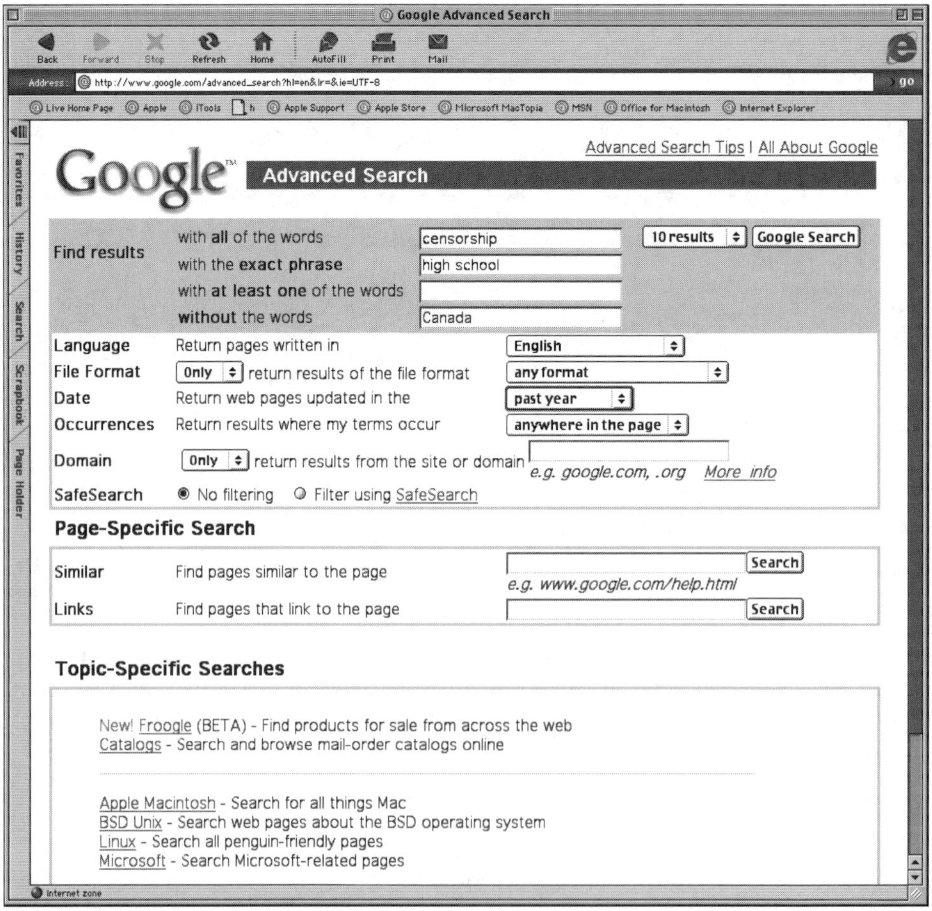

Figure 4.13 Screen for an advanced Google search.

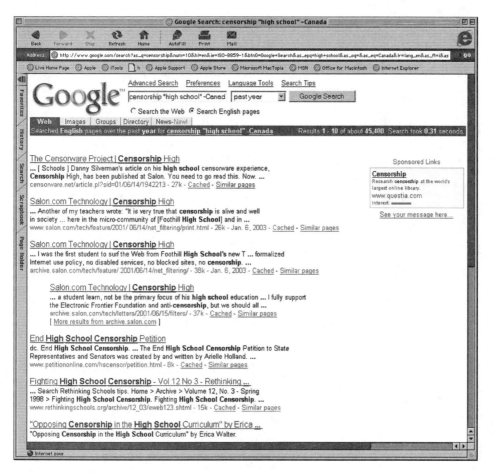

Figure 4.14 The results page of a Google search.

will search for sites containing all the words listed, regardless of whether they occur side by side. If you were searching for sites about the relationship between
alcohol and obesity, you could enter *alcohol obesity*. You don't need the *AND* operator between the words (in fact, Google ignores *AND* or *and*). See the box on
page 77 for other tips about a basic Google search.

For greater control in an Internet search, click on the "Advanced Search" link.
An advanced search can allow you to return the most pertinent results while ex-
cluding unwanted sites. For example, Figure 4.13 shows how you might search for
pages in English produced within the last year about censorship in high schools,
but not those in Canada. Figure 4.14 shows the results of this search. Because
all search engines provide different results, it is often worthwhile to conduct
searches on more than one search engine.

A second option for Web searching is to use the search engine's human-
powered directory. Figure 4.15 shows the Yahoo directory at *dir.yahoo.com*. You
can either browse the directory by following links through relevant categories

Figure 4.15 The Yahoo directory page. *(Reproduced with permission of Yahoo! Inc. Copyright © 2003 by Yahoo! Inc. Yahoo! and the Yahoo! logo are trademarks of Yahoo! Inc.)*

(e.g., *Science*, then *Biology*, then *Evolution*, etc.) or you can do a keyword search of the directory. Because items in the directory have been selected by humans, a search will provide fewer, but more selective results.

Some words of caution about Web searches are in order. Students should evaluate Web pages with a careful, critical eye. Remember that anyone can post Web pages, and so not everything on the Web is valuable or accurate. Find out who has created the document and how reliable or comprehensive it is. For example, if you are researching a scandal in the widget industry, you will likely find many widget pages. Knowing if the page is created by a widget trade organization (which would be expected to have a pro-widget bias) or by an anti-widget consumer group (with the opposite bias) is essential if you are to assess the sources and determine whether and how to use them.

Because Web searches often return hundreds, if not thousands, of results, visit only those that look promising. When you find worthwhile sites, you can take notes on them, print the pages, or bookmark them for later use.

Using the World Wide Web

Do the following exercises using the World Wide Web:

1. See what you can find on the Web on the following three topics: identical twins, Peru, and archery. Use one or more of the above search engines to explore these topics. Follow links from page to page as your curiosity leads you. Write a narrative describing your search and discoveries.
2. The Yahoo directory at *dir.yahoo.com* is organized around a number of topics (business & economy, computers & Internet, etc.). Select one that interests you, and continue to choose from among options until you arrive at an interesting page. Print the page (if equipment allows) or summarize its contents.
3. Use other search engines to find Web sources on your research topic.

THE REFERENCE LIBRARIAN—THE MOST RESOURCEFUL RESOURCE

By far the most valuable resource in any library is the librarian, a professional who knows the library well and is an expert in locating information. Use the other resources in this chapter first, but if you become stuck or do not know where to look or cannot find the sources you need, do not hesitate to ask a librarian for help. College libraries have *reference librarians* on duty, usually at a station marked as the *reference desk.* Their job is to assist when you need help in finding sources. Reference librarians are almost always helpful, and they have aided many students with the same kinds of research problems and questions that you are likely to have.

There are some limits, however, to the services reference librarians can provide. One librarian requested that we mention some problems they are sometimes asked to solve but cannot. They cannot pick a topic for you, interpret your assignment, or answer questions about the format of your bibliographic citations. Those questions should be addressed to your instructor. The librarian's job is to assist when you need help locating library sources.

Although printed and electronic materials are of great value to researchers, they are not the only sources available. Chapter 5 discusses ways to use other sources in your research project.

5 Finding Sources outside the Library: Conducting Interviews and Writing Letters

▮ INTERVIEWING SOURCES

In addition to print sources, interviews with experts can provide valuable material for your paper. Because the people you interview are primary rather than secondary sources, the firsthand information they provide is exclusively yours to present—information that readers will find nowhere else. Therefore, interviewed sources can make a favorable impression, giving readers the sense that they are getting expert testimony directly and reliably. Your own reliability and credibility may also be enhanced, since you demonstrate the initiative to have extended your search beyond the usual kinds of sources.

On a college campus, professors are an accessible source of expert information. Being familiar with research in their individual fields, they also can suggest published and unpublished resources you might not have found in your library research. You may also find experts living in your local community. In his research on a pharmacy career, Justin Stafford interviewed Blake Barefoot, a working pharmacist in a chain store in his city. Justin found it invaluable to talk with someone who had direct experience in the profession and could answer his many questions and give him expert advice. Similarly, Emily Gould gained valuable firsthand information about labor issues in fast-food restaurants when she interviewed Jill Cashen, an official for a union active in the food industry.

Participants and eyewitnesses are also valuable sources. Emily also interviewed Tamicah Williams, a fellow student with a part-time job in a fast-food restaurant. If you were researching, say, biological terrorism, you could interview persons responsible for emergency preparedness in your community, such as police and hospital staff. Be resourceful in considering interviewees who can contribute to your knowledge and understanding.

Conducting interviews may not be the first order of business in your research project, but because interviews require advance planning, it is important to set up appointments as early as possible—even before you are ready to conduct them. Soon after Justin had decided on his topic, he knew he would want to talk to a pharmacist. He wanted to do some reading first in order to be sufficiently informed to ask intelligent questions, but he also knew that pharmacists are busy during their work hours and that it would be wise to arrange an interview well in advance.

Arranging the Interview

Like every other stage in a research project, arranging interviews can lead to inevitable frustrations. For example, if you were researching a career in psychiatry, you might find it difficult to arrange an interview with a psychiatrist. After all, psychiatrists spend their days talking with patients; they may have little interest in giving up their precious free time to talk with someone else (without compensation).

When you telephone someone you don't know, be courteous and explain your purpose simply and clearly. For example, if you were calling an executive at a computer company to ask for an interview, you might say something like this:

> Hello, Ms. Smith, I'm [your name], a student at [your school]. I'm conducting a research project concerning the future of computers in the workplace. I'm particularly interested in talking to a person in the industry with your expertise, and I would like to learn your views on the topic. I wonder if I could meet with you briefly to ask you a few questions.

You can expect the person to ask you further questions about the nature of your project and about the amount of time the interview will take. If you are courteous and open and if your purposes seem serious, people are likely to cooperate with you to the extent that they are able. Be prepared to meet at a time and place convenient to the interviewee. Many interviews can be conducted in fifteen to thirty minutes. If you wish to tape-record the interview, ask for permission at the time you arrange the meeting.

Professors are usually available to students during office hours, but business people and other professionals are usually not so easy to reach. Before talking to the executive, you might have to explain your need to a receptionist or secretary, who might be reluctant to connect you. Often a letter written in advance of your telephone call can be effective in securing an interview. For example, a student who wishes to arrange an interview with a computer executive might send a letter like this one:

```
                                        202 Willow Street
                                        Wilmington, NC 28401
                                        2 March 2003

Ms. Denise Smith
Vice-President for Research and Development
CompuCosmos Corporation
Wilmington, NC 28401

Dear Ms. Smith:
        I am a student at the University of North Carolina at
Wilmington engaged in a research project concerning the future
of computer use in business offices. I have learned much about
```

```
the topic from written sources, but I still have some
unanswered questions. Your observations and expert opinions
would be invaluable for my report. I know your time is
valuable, and I would be grateful if I could meet with you for
a brief interview. I will telephone Wednesday morning to see if
I can arrange a meeting. If you wish, you can reach me by phone
at 555-1893.
```

Sincerely,

Blair Halliday

Blair Halliday

Conducting the Interview

Some interviews may consist of a simple question or two, designed to fill specific gaps in your knowledge about your topic. Others may be extended question-and-answer sessions about a variety of topics. The success of your interviewing depends on your preparation, professionalism, and interpersonal skills. The following guidelines should be followed when you conduct an interview:

1. *Before the interview:*

   • **Be well prepared.** The most important part of the interview takes place before the questions are posed. Become as informed about your subject as you can so that you can ask the right questions. Use your reading notes to prepare questions in advance.

   • **Dress appropriately for the interview.** How you dress can influence how the interviewee behaves toward you; people are most comfortable talking with someone who dresses as they do. Business and professional people, for example, are more likely to take you seriously if you are wearing standard business attire. On the other hand, formal attire would be inappropriate when interviewing striking factory workers, who might be reluctant to speak freely with someone who looks like management.

   • **Arrive on time for your appointment.** Not only is arriving on time a matter of courtesy, but it is essential in assuring the interviewee's cooperation.

2. *During the interview:*

   • **Take careful and accurate notes.** If you intend to quote your source, you must be certain that you have copied the person's words exactly. A tape recorder can give you an accurate transcript of your interviews.

   • **Behave politely and ethically.** Be certain you have the interviewee's permission if you tape-record the conversation. If you take notes, offer to let the interviewee check the transcript later to ensure accuracy (doing so may elicit further elaborations and additional statements that you can use).

• **Be relaxed and friendly.** People who are not accustomed to being interviewed are often nervous at first about having their comments recorded. By being friendly and relaxed, you can win their confidence and put them at ease. The most fruitful parts of interviews occur when interviewees become absorbed in what they are saying and forget they are being recorded. Begin with general questions that can be answered with ease and confidence. Later introduce more specific and pointed questions. (For experienced interviewees, these precautions may not be necessary.)

• **Make your recording as unobtrusive as possible.** Many people will not speak freely and naturally when constantly reminded that their comments are being recorded. Place the tape recorder out of the interviewee's direct line of sight. Do not write constantly during the interview; write down key phrases and facts that will allow you to reconstruct the conversation immediately after the interview.

• **Be interested in what the interviewee says.** People will speak much more freely with you if they sense that you are responsive to their comments. It is a mistake for an interviewer to read one prepared question after another, while barely listening to the interviewee's responses. Such wooden interviewing produces an uncomfortable atmosphere and strained responses.

• **Stay flexible.** Do not be a slave to your prepared questions. Listen with real curiosity to what the person says and ask further questions based on what you learn. Request explanations of what is not clear to you. Ask probing questions when a topic is raised that you would like to learn more about.

• **Let the interviewee do the talking.** Remember that it is the interviewee's ideas that you are interested in, not your own. Avoid the temptation to state your own opinions and experiences or to argue points with the interviewee.

3. *After the interview:*

• **End the interview professionally.** Check your notes and questions to determine if any gaps still need to be filled. Thank the interviewee. Ask if the person would like to check your use of statements and information for accuracy, and whether you can call again if you have further questions. Offer to send the interviewee a copy of your paper when it is completed.

• **Be fair to the source.** When you write the paper, be certain that any ideas or statements you attribute to the source are true reflections of the sound and spirit of the person's answers and comments. Be accurate in quoting the person, but eliminate slips of the tongue and distracting phrases like *uh* and *you know.*

• **Send a thank-you note.** Whether or not you send a copy of your paper to the interviewee, you should send a note expressing your appreciation for the help that the person provided.

Justin prepared the following list of questions before he interviewed Blake Barefoot, a pharmacist at a chain store in his community:

Possible Interview Questions for Mr. Barefoot

- Why did you decide to be a pharmacist?
- Is your job what you expected?
- What do you do on a typical day?
- Are you "following doctor's orders" or do you make decisions affecting people?
- What are your working conditions?
- Is the job enjoyable and rewarding? What are the major satisfactions?
- Is it stressful? What are your major frustrations?
- Is there opportunity for advancement?
- What training did you have?
- What was pharmacy school like?
- Would you recommend this career to others?

Although he used his prepared questions as a point of reference, Justin found himself departing from them as he responded to Mr. Barefoot's comments. During his interview, Justin took notes in his research notebook. Here are some excerpts. (In some cases we have recast them to make them clearer to other readers.)

Notes from Interview with Mr. Barefoot

—Grew up in a small town. I wanted to be a lawyer, but my brother decided to go to pharmacy school and steered me in that direction.

—Most valuable work is interacting with people. Answer questions about side effects, alleviate their fears or steer them to other therapies. Check drug interactions.

—Long hours, not bad--no qualms. Target is a good company to work for.

—Stressful? High level of stress, trying to be fast. Everyone wants prescription in 5 minutes. Delays: no refills, people give us the wrong insurance company. Juggling 10 people's work schedules.

—Many argue they fill too many prescriptions in one day. What is safe? Stress factors involved.

—Advancement: extensive. Pharmacy business has done well, especially in last 5 years. Dramatic growth. If willing to relocate, if opening a new store, can be supervisor.

—5 years of school, now 6. 1 year of internship, "preceptor program." You can choose: retail, hospital, ER. I learned more doing my internships and in the first 6 months on job than in first 4 years of college.

—Retail: money is better. My personality lends itself to retail.

—Owning a store is very difficult nowadays. Insurance billing & low payments from insurance companies. Hard to be independent without specialization in something in addition to pharmacy. Hard to compete.

—Good people skills needed. Pharmacists who lack them usually hate pharmacy.

—Would definitely recommend. A wonderful career. Endless potential for personal growth and learning, plus good income. People will always need medicine.

WRITING FOR INFORMATION

It frequently happens that information helpful to your project is unavailable in the library. For example, if you were doing a project on nutrition in children's breakfast foods, you might visit a supermarket to record nutritional information and ingredients of various brands from the sides of cereal boxes. You could also write letters of inquiry to cereal manufacturers, such as the one that follows.

November 3, 2003

```
Public Relations Officer
Breakfast Foods Division
General Foods Corporation
250 North Street
White Plains, NY 10625

Dear Public Relations Officer:
     As a student at [your university], I am undertaking a
research study of nutrition in breakfast cereals. I am
particularly interested in learning if there is a market for
low-sugar cereals targeted specifically for the children's
market. Could you please tell me the sales figures for your
low-sugar Post Crispy Critters cereal? I would also appreciate
any additional information you could send me related to this
subject.
     I would be grateful if you could respond before [date],
the deadline for my research paper.

                              Sincerely,
                              [your signature]
                              [your name]
```

Business directories in the reference section of your library, such as the *Directory of Corporate Affiliations*, can help you find company addresses. Your library may also subscribe to online databases that provide corporate information, such as *Dow Jones Interactive*. You can also consult a "yellow pages" search engine, such as www.switchboard.com. If you need further assistance, consult with the reference librarian.

It is wise to tell correspondents how you plan to use the information you are requesting. They are more likely to respond if convinced that your project will not be harmful to their interests. (Some businesses, such as tobacco or liquor companies, are understandably leery about supplying information for studies that may attack them.) You can increase your chances of getting a response by including a self-addressed stamped envelope with your letter. If time is short, a telephone call, e-mail message, or a fax may get a speedier response than a letter.

STILL OTHER SOURCES

Researchers can avail themselves of many other sources besides library materials, interviews, and letters. *Lectures, films, television programs,* and *audio recordings* are among the sources often cited in student research projects. In your paper, for example, you might quote a person who appeared in a television documentary, or you might describe an event portrayed in a news program. A song lyric or a line from movie dialogue might effectively illustrate a particular theme.

On many campuses there is a *media center* in which videotapes (including television documentaries), films, and various audio recordings are available. It may be housed in the library or in a separate building. Some campuses belong to a regional network of media centers that share their materials, usually with little or no charge to the borrower. If your campus has a media center, ask how you can find what sources are available on your topic and whether it is possible for you to gain access to materials from other campuses.

6 *Assembling a Prospectus and a Working Bibliography*

A RESEARCH PROSPECTUS

A *prospectus* is a statement of your plans for a project. During the early stages of their projects, Emily Gould and Justin Stafford were asked by their instructors to submit a research prospectus. Emily's class received the following assignment.

Research Prospectus   **ASSIGNMENT**

Bring to our next class a prospectus of your research project. It should consist of the following elements:

1. **A statement of your research question.** Your topic may be tentative at this point, so you needn't feel locked into it. In upcoming days, you may decide to alter your question or shift its focus as you conduct further research and learn more about the subject.

2. **A paragraph or two about your progress so far.** You can summarize why you chose your topic, what you already know about it, and what you hope to discover. You can also discuss any problems or successes you have had with focusing your topic and finding sources.

3. **A working bibliography** (a list of the sources you have located so far). Use the MLA format (explained in this chapter) for your bibliography. This is a list of raw sources—sources you have not yet had much chance to examine and evaluate—so it is likely to contain some items that you will not use in your paper and therefore will not appear in the works cited page of the final draft.

Emily and Justin by now had a general idea of their topics. They had done some browsing in encyclopedias and other reference works, and each was beginning to assemble a list of potential sources. Following are some excerpts from Emily's research notebook, written as she was beginning her search. Emily's notes are informal, in the style of journal entries. I have edited them somewhat to make them clearer for other readers.

> [After searching for books,] I went to the library's
> database/article search [using my computer]. I clicked
> on EBSCOhost's "MasterFILE Premier" and searched several
> topics concerning fast food. I started by typing in
> "fast food and nutrition" and found quite a few articles.
> I knew that it would be easy to find articles that would
> accuse fast food of being a cause of obesity, so first I
> looked for articles that gave a balanced view, since
> I wanted to provide a variety of opinions in the paper.
> I found an article titled "Can Fast Food Be Part of a
> Healthy Diet?" which stressed the idea of moderation in
> diet above all. . . . The health issue involved spokespeople
> from fast-food restaurants and the restaurant business deny-
> ing responsibility for obesity and denying the fact that fast
> food was unhealthy. I found several interesting articles
> talking about meatpacking plants, but for the most part
> they were too graphic and many of the articles seemed too
> emotional.

Here is another entry from Emily's notebook a few days later:

> . . . I looked for articles about the labor issues in
> fast food. One of the first articles I found was called
> "Worked Over." I could not find the full text online,
> so I went to the library to make a copy from the actual
> [print] periodical. It discussed the abuses of workers by
> employers in fast food who required their employees to
> work overtime but shortchange them in their paychecks.
> I decided to check what the actual laws concerning work
> hours and pay were, so I used the "Search" tool on my
> browser to find the Web site for the U.S. Department of
> Labor and followed links to "Youth Employment" where
> I found a list of all of the labor regulations
> including pay and minimum wage, and age-labor
> regulations. . . .

After more searching with their college library's central information system and online databases, Emily and Justin had settled on their topics and were ready to write their prospectuses. Emily's prospectus and working bibliography are shown in Figure 6.1. Her original interest in the health aspects of fast food had begun to broaden, and she was also exploring the effects of fast food both on society and on the employees in the restaurants.

Gould 1

Emily Gould
Research Prospectus

1. Research question: How has America's love affair with fast food changed our lives, and what have the consequences been?

2. After reading journalist Eric Schlosser's 2001 book Fast-Food Nation this summer, I became aware of many controversies surrounding fast food. I have decided to research the topic further, focusing on three aspects: The proliferation of fast-food restaurants has changed the eating patterns of Americans and other aspects of our culture. Second, these restaurants affect the lives of thousands of workers, whom they employ in low-wage, unskilled jobs. Finally, fast food itself has been blamed for causing obesity, diabetes, and heart attacks in thousands of Americans who had no knowledge that the food they were eating was unhealthy until recently.

My searches of the library catalog and of periodicals have turned up hundreds of books and articles on the topic. I have checked out a book and have printouts of the articles in my bibliography. If anything, I am finding too many sources and will probably narrow my topic as I do more research.

Figure 6.1 Emily's Research Prospectus.

Gould 2

3. Working bibliography

Broydo, Leora. "Worked Over." Utne Reader. Jan./Feb. 1999:
      20-21.

Cardial, Denise. "Multicultural Breakdown." Des Moines
      Business Record. 6 May 1996: 16. MasterFILE Premier.
      EBSCOhost. 10 Sept. 2002 <http://web3.epnet.com/>.

Cooper, Marc. "The Heartland's Raw Deal." The Nation 3
      Feb. 1997: 11-17.

"Fast-Food Explosion 'A Threat to Global Health.'" Daily
      Mail 18 Feb. 2002. Newspaper Source. EBSCOhost. 10
      Sept. 2002 <http://web3.epnet.com/>.

Greenburg, Jan C. "Fast-Food Lawsuits May Be Successful
      Legacy of Big Tobacco Penalties." Chicago Tribune 30
      Aug. 2002. Newspaper Source. EBSCOhost. 10 Sept. 2002
      <http://web3.epnet.com/>.

Matorin, James. "Obesity Awareness Campaign Needed, but
      Regulations Won't Curb Fast-Food Appetite." Nation's
      Restaurant News 27 Aug. 2001. MasterFILE Premier.
      EBSCOhost. 15 Sept. 2002 <http://web3.epnet.com/>.

Ritzer, George. The McDonaldization Thesis: Explorations
      and Extensions. London: Sage, 1998.

Schlosser, Eric. Fast-Food Nation. Boston: Houghton, 2001.

Zipp, Yvonne. "Virtues of Work vs. Finishing Homework."
      Christian Science Monitor 15 Dec. 1998: 1. MasterFILE
      Premier. EBSCOhost. 15 Sept. 2002
      <http://web3.epnet.com/>.

Figure 6.1 (*continued*)

THE WORKING BIBLIOGRAPHY

A *bibliography* is a list of research sources. One of the last tasks in your search project is to type a *list of works cited* at the end of your paper—a formal bibliography or listing of all the sources you have used in writing it. But this occurs much later in the research process. For now, your task is to continue gathering sources; that is, you need to use the library databases and other research tools described in Chapter 4 to locate books and articles for your paper. The list of possible sources you draw up as you begin your search is your *working bibliography.* You add to the working bibliography during the course of your project as you discover additional sources, and you subtract from it as some sources on the list turn out not to be helpful.

A working bibliography is tentative, informal, and practical. The only requirement for a good working bibliography is that you are able to use it conveniently. Since it is for your own use—not part of the paper itself—you can record the information you need any way you like. For example, when you find a likely book from a subject citation in the library catalog, you can jot down in your notebook the key information that will enable you to locate it—perhaps only its title and call number. On the other hand, there are advantages to including more complete information in your working bibliography, as Emily did, in that you will use this information later, at the end of the project, when you type your works-cited page. Therefore, you can save considerable time by including all the information you may need later. For that reason, it is important for you to be acquainted with the standard conventions for citing sources.

BIBLIOGRAPHIC FORMATS

A list of works cited is expected to conform to a certain *bibliographic format*—a prescribed method of listing source information. Every academic field, such as English, sociology, or mathematics, has a preferred format that dictates not only what information about sources should be in the list of works cited but also how it should be arranged and even punctuated.

Unfortunately, each format has its own quirks and peculiarities. Which one you use will depend on the academic discipline in which you are working. If you are writing a paper for a psychology course, for example, you may be required to use a different format than you would use in a chemistry paper. The research papers by Emily and Justin follow the *Modern Language Association (MLA) format,* which is widely used in humanities courses (courses in such fields as literature, history, philosophy, theology, languages, and the arts), and it is frequently accepted for use in other courses as well. Two other formats widely used in the social and applied sciences—that of the *American Psychological Association (APA)* and the *numbered references* system—are presented in Appendix A. Fortunately, you do not need to memorize the details of these various formats. However, it is important that you know they exist, that you know how to find and use them, and that you follow whatever format you use with care. These chapters can serve as a reference guide to the various bibliographic formats you may encounter throughout your college career.

■ GENERAL GUIDELINES—MLA FORMAT

The following general guidelines apply to MLA-style bibliographies. Notice how Emily Gould followed the format in her working bibliography in Figure 6.1 on pages 91–92.

1. **What to include?** Emily's working bibliography listed the sources she had discovered during the preliminary stages of her project. She had not yet examined all of them, and some she would not use in her paper. Later, in her list of works cited, she would include only the sources she used in writing the paper. You should include a source in your list of works cited if you have quoted or paraphrased from it or if you have made reference to it. Do not list a work if you consulted it but did not make use of it in writing the paper.

2. **In what order?** Sources are presented in alphabetical order, *not* in the order in which they are used in the paper. Do not number the items in your list.

3. **What word first?** Each entry begins with the author's last name. When a work is anonymous—that is, when no author's name is given—the title is listed first. If the first word is *a, an,* or *the,* put that word first, but use the next word of the entry to determine its place within alphabetical order.

4. **What format for titles?** In typed or handwritten papers, titles of longer works, such as books and magazines, are *italicized* or <u>underlined</u>. Do not underline the period that follows a title. Titles of shorter works, such as articles and book chapters (which are published as subparts of longer works), are printed within quotation marks (" "). Thus in Figure 6.2 we observe that the article "Worked Over" was published in the magazine *Utne Reader*.

5. **What format for publishers?** Publishers' names are shortened in MLA style. If a publishing firm is named after several persons, only the first is used (e.g., *Houghton* instead of *Houghton Mifflin Co.*). Omit first names (write *Knopf* instead of *Alfred A. Knopf, Inc.*), and omit words such as *Books, Press,* and *Publishers.* Use the abbreviation *UP* to represent *University Press* (e.g., *Indiana UP, U of Michigan P,* and *UP of Virginia*). When questions arise, use your judgment about identifying a publisher accurately. For example, you may write *Banner Books* to distinguish it from *Banner Press*.

6. **What margins?** The first line of each entry begins at the left margin (one inch from the left edge of the page). The second and all following lines are indented one-half inch. In other words, each entry is "*out*dented" (also called a *hanging indent*), the reverse of the way paragraphs are *in*dented. The purpose is to

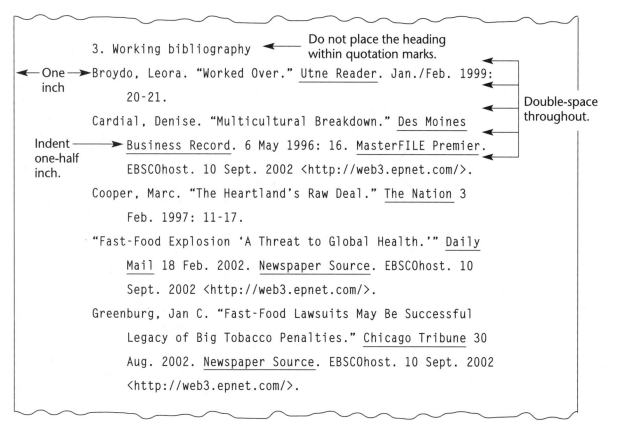

Figure 6.2 Format for a working bibliography.

make it easy for readers to find the first word of the entry so they can quickly lo-cate individual items from a long list.

7.   **What spacing?** Double-space throughout, both within and between entries. Do not skip extra lines between entries.

8.   **What punctuation?** Punctuation conventions, however inexplicable they may seem, should be observed with care. Follow the models in this book when-ever you create a list of works cited, paying close attention to periods, commas, parentheses, underlining, quotation marks, and spaces. In MLA style, most en-tries have three principal components, each one followed by a period: the author, the title, and the publication information. The most common oversight is to omit the period at the end of each entry.

9.   **What heading?** Informal bibliographies do not require any special heading. A formal list of works cited, except in short papers with few sources, should begin on a separate page at the end of your paper. Center the heading:

Works Cited

(or *Bibliography,* if you prefer) and double-space (skip one line within and between entries). Do not skip an extra line between the heading and the first entry.

Citing Electronic Sources

Not many years ago, students who wrote research papers encountered almost all of their written sources in print form. Today, many research sources are likely to be gathered electronically. These might include a newspaper article retrieved from an online database, an entry from an encyclopedia on a CD-ROM, a Web page on the Internet, even a play by Shakespeare stored on some distant computer. As with other sources, you are expected to cite electronic sources so as to give credit to their authors and to allow your readers to retrieve and consult them directly.

A problem peculiar to electronic sources, particularly online sources, is that many of them are subject to being updated without notice or moved to another electronic address or even withdrawn altogether, so that someone seeking to consult a source next week may not find it in exactly the same form as another person who consulted it last week—or perhaps may not find it at all. In contrast, a printed work, such as a book, can be cited in the certainty that others who consult it will be able to find exactly the same text that you encountered. Although thousands of copies may be printed, all of them have the same words on the same pages. A book may be updated (e.g., the book you are now reading has been updated five times since its initial publication), but each update is identified with a new edition number. (This is the fourth edition of *Research: The Student's Guide to Writing Research Papers.*)

Being able to identify electronic sources accurately is not a great problem with **portable electronic sources** such as software programs on CD-ROM or diskette, which, like books, are identified with edition or version numbers. **Online sources** such as World Wide Web pages and some databases, however, are subject to frequent updating and revision. For such sources, it may not be possible to provide a citation that will allow others to consult the source in exactly the same form it took when you consulted it. In your citation of such sources, you should give information that is as adequate as possible, as well as the date when you consulted the source. Consult the models that follow for citing both portable and online electronic sources.

■ MODEL ENTRIES—MLA FORMAT

You are likely to encounter many different kinds of sources in your research. When you compile a list of works cited using MLA style, you should find the appropriate model for each source from the samples that follow and copy its format with care. If you still have questions about a source you wish to list, consult the *MLA Handbook for Writers of Research Papers,* sixth edition, which can be found in the reference section of most college libraries, or ask your instructor for assistance.

Examine the following model entries and read the explanatory notes. For quick reference later on, you can consult the model MLA citations printed on the inside front and back covers.

Sources in Books

Citations for books have three main divisions:

```
Author's name. The title of the book. Publication information.
```

For the ***author's name,*** list the last name first, followed by a comma, followed by the author's other names. Abbreviations such as *PhD* and titles such as *The Rev.* are omitted from citations. The ***book title*** is underlined. List the full title, including any subtitle. When there is a subtitle, place a colon immediately following the main title and then list the subtitle. ***Publication information*** is cited in this format:

```
City of publication: publisher, year of publication.
```

You can find this information on the book's title page and its copyright page (usually the page following the title page). Use the shortened version of the ***publisher's name.*** If the ***year of publication*** is not recorded on the title page, use the most recent year on the copyright page. If more than one ***city of publication*** is listed, give the first. If the city is not widely known, you can also list the state (using standard post office abbreviations—two capital letters, no periods) or foreign country.

Books

Following are sample entries for books (accessed in print form). For online books, see Internet and Electronic Sources on pages 110–11.

A Book with One Author

```
Macdonald, James. A Free Nation Deep in Debt: The Financial
     Roots of Democracy. New York: Farrar, 2003.
Wheelock, Arthur K., Jr. Vermeer and the Art of Painting. New
     Haven: Yale UP, 1995.
```

In the first example, a colon is placed between the book's title and its ***subtitle.*** Publishers' names are abbreviated: *Farrar* is short for the publishing company Farrar, Straus and Giroux. *UP* is the standard abbreviation for University Press, as in *Yale UP.* However, you may give the publisher's name in a more complete form, particularly if you are in doubt (*Hill and Wang* rather than *Hill,* to avoid confusion with Ernest Hill Publishing or Lawrence Hill Books).

A Book with Two or Three Authors

Dingman, Robert L., and John D. Weaver. <u>Days in the Lives of</u>
    <u>Counselors</u>. Boston: Allyn, 2003.
Reid, Jo Anne, Peter Forrestal, and Jonathan Cook. <u>Small Group</u>
    <u>Learning in the Classroom</u>. Portsmouth, NH: Heinemann,
    1990.

The first book is written by Robert L. Dingman and John D. Weaver. Note that only Dingman's name is inverted (last name first), since only the first author's last name is used to determine the work's alphabetized placement in the list of sources. In the second book, the three authors' names are not listed alphabetically; they are listed in the order in which their names appear on the title page. You may use the state abbreviation when you consider it helpful in identifying a city of publication that is not well known, such as *Portsmouth, NH.*

A Book with More Than Three Authors

Courtois, Stéphane, et al. <u>The Black Book of Communism: Crimes,</u>
    <u>Terror, Repression</u>. Cambridge, MA: Harvard UP, 1999.

Courtois is one of six authors of this book. The term *et al.* is a Latin abbreviation meaning "and others." It is not italicized or underlined in lists of works cited. You may also list all the authors, if you consider it desirable to acknowledge them by name.

Two or More Works by the Same Author

Asimov, Isaac. <u>Adding a Dimension</u>. New York: Discus, 1975.

---. "Fifty Years of Astronomy." <u>Natural History</u> Oct. 1985:
    4+.

---. <u>The New Intelligent Man's Guide to Science</u>. New York:
    Basic, 1965.

Asimov, Isaac, and John Ciardi. <u>A Grossery of Limericks</u>. New
    York: Norton, 1981.

The first three works (two books and a magazine article) are written by the same author, Isaac Asimov. The fourth work is written by Asimov and another author. When you have used more than one work by the same author, your works-cited list should arrange the works alphabetically by title. (In our example *Adding* comes before *Fifty,* which comes before *New.*) Replace the author's name for all but the first work with three hyphens followed by a period. The reader can then see at a glance that the author is represented more than once and is alerted not to confuse one work with another. Use hyphens only when works have identical authors; notice that Asimov's name is not replaced for the fourth work, since its authors (Asimov and Ciardi) are not identical with the author of the first three works (Asimov alone).

A Book with No Author Listed

Addison Wesley Longman Author's Guide. New York: Longman, 1998.

In the works-cited list, give the book alphabetically according to the first main word of the title.

A Book with a Corporate or Group Author

Sotheby's. Nineteenth Century European Paintings, Drawings and
    Watercolours. London: Sotheby's, 1995.

U of North Carolina at Wilmington. 2002-2003 Code of Student
    Life. [Wilmington, NC]: n.p., [2002].

Cite the group as author, even if it is also the publisher. Publication information that can be inferred but is not printed in the publication is placed in brackets. If publication information is not known, use *n.p.* for "no place" or "no publisher," and use *n.d.* for "no date." Note that these abbreviations do not require italics or underlining.

A Book by a Government Agency

United States. Dept. of Health and Human Services. Substance
    Abuse and Mental Health Services Admin. Center for Mental
    Health Services. What You Need to Know about Youth Violence
    Prevention. Rockville, MD: GPO, 2002.

For a work produced by a government, first state the name of the government (e.g., *United States*), followed by the agency (and subgroup, if any) authoring the work. *GPO* stands for the Government Printing Office.

A Book with a Translator

> Ramos, Julio. Divergent Modernities: Culture and Politics in
>
> Nineteenth-Century Latin America. Trans. John D. Blanco.
>
> Durham: Duke UP, 1999.

Ramos's book was translated into English by Blanco. Note that *translator* is capitalized and abbreviated as *Trans.*

A Book with an Author and an Editor

> Shakespeare, William. Henry V. Ed. T. W. Craik. New York:
>
> Routledge, 1995.

Shakespeare is the author of the play, which is published in an edition edited by Craik. Note that *edited by* is capitalized and abbreviated as *Ed.*

A Book with an Editor

> Stimpson, Catherine R., and Ethel Spector Person, eds. Women:
>
> Sex and Sexuality. Chicago: U of Chicago P, 1980.

Stimpson and Person edited this book, an ***anthology*** of essays by various writers. Note that *editors* is lowercased and abbreviated as *eds.* It should be noted that occasions when you refer to such a collection *as a whole* in your research will be relatively rare. More frequently, you will use material from a selection in the collection, and you will cite that specific work (rather than the collection as a whole) in your list of works cited. See "A Selection from an Anthology" on page 102.

A Book in a Later Edition

> Skinner, Ellen. Women and the National Experience. 2nd ed. New
>
> York: Longman, 2003.

Skinner's book is in its second edition. Use *3rd, 4th,* and so on for subsequent editions. Abbreviate *edition* as ed.

A Book in a Series

> Matthee, Rudolph P. The Politics of Trade in Safavid Iran: Silk
>
> for Silver, 1600-1730. Cambridge Studies in Islamic
>
> Civilization. New York: Cambridge UP, 2000.

Matthee's book is one of several books published by Cambridge University Press in a series entitled Cambridge Studies in Islamic Civilization. Note that the series title follows the book title and is neither italicized or placed within quotation marks.

A Multivolume Book

When an author gives different titles to individual volumes of a work, list a specific volume this way:

> Brinton, Crane, John B. Christopher, and Robert Lee Wolff.
> Prehistory to 1715. Vol. 1 of A History of Civilization.
> 6th ed. 2 vols. Englewood Cliffs, NJ: Prentice, 1984.

When individual volumes do not have separate titles, cite the book this way:

> Messenger, Charles. For Love of Regiment: A History of British
> Infantry, 1660-1993. 2 vols. Philadelphia: Trans-Atlantic,
> 1995.

If you use only one of these volumes, cite it this way:

> Messenger, Charles. For Love of Regiment: A History of British
> Infantry, 1660-1993. Vol. 1. Philadelphia: Trans-Atlantic,
> 1995.

Note that when citing a specific volume, *volume* is capitalized and abbreviated to *Vol.* When citing the number of volumes that exist, *volumes* is lowercased and abbreviated to *vols.*

A Book Published before 1900

> Nightingale, Florence. Notes on Nursing: What It Is, and What It
> Is Not. New York, 1860.

The publisher's name may be omitted for works published before 1900. Note that a comma, instead of a colon, follows the place of publication.

A Paperback or Other Reprinted Book

> Horwitz, Tony. Confederates in the Attic: Dispatches from the
> Unfinished Civil War. 1998. New York: Vintage, 1999.

The book was originally published (in hardcover, by a different publisher) in 1998. Note that the copyright year of the original publication follows immediately after the book title and is punctuated with a period.

Selections from Books

A Selection from an Anthology

> Leifer, Myra. "Pregnancy." Women: Sex and Sexuality. Ed.
>
>   Catherine R. Stimpson and Ethel Spector Person. Chicago:
>
>   U of Chicago P, 1980. 212-23.
>
> Lichtheim, George. "The Birth of a Philosopher." Collected
>
>   Essays. New York: Viking, 1973. 103-10.
>
> Rushdie, Salman. "A Pen Against the Sword: In Good Faith."
>
>   Newsweek 12 Feb. 1990: 52+. Rpt. in One World, Many
>
>   Cultures. Ed. Stuart Hirschberg. New York: Macmillan, 1992.
>
>   480-96.

Leifer's article "Pregnancy" is one of the essays in the collection *Women: Sex and Sexuality* edited by Stimpson and Person. Leifer's essay appeared on pages 212 to 213 of the book. (See the "Page Numbers" box on page 105 for information on how to list pages.) The Lichtheim book in the example does not have an editor; he is the author of all the essays in the book. Rushdie's article originally appeared in *Newsweek;* the person who wrote this listing found it in Hirschberg's book, where it had been *reprinted* (*rpt.*).

Several Selections from the Same Anthology

If several essays are cited from the same collection, you can save space by using *cross-references*. First, include the entire collection as one of the items in your list of works cited, as follows:

> Stimpson, Catherine R., and Ethel Spector Person, eds. Women:
>
>   Sex and Sexuality. Chicago: U of Chicago P, 1980.

Then you are free to list each article you refer to in your paper, followed by an abbreviated reference to the collection—just the last names of the editors and the pages on which the articles appear, as follows:

> Baker, Susan W. "Biological Influences on Human Sex and Gender."
>
>   Stimson and Person 175-91.

Diamond, Irene. "Pornography and Repression: A Reconsideration."

Stimson and Person 129-23.

Leifer, Myra. "Pregnancy." Stimson and Person 212-23.

An Article in an Encyclopedia or Other Reference Work

Harmon, Mamie. "Folk Arts." The New Encyclopaedia Britannica:

Macropaedia. 15th ed. 2002.

"Morrison, Toni." Who's Who in America. 57th ed. 2003.

"Yodel." The Shorter Oxford English Dictionary. 1973.

The *Britannica* is a printed encyclopedia. Pages need not be listed for reference works whose entries are arranged alphabetically (and can therefore easily be found). In many reference works, such as *Who's Who in America,* no authors are named for individual entries. Publishers need not be cited for well-known reference books. Provide publisher information for ***lesser-known reference works:***

Hames, Raymond. "Yanomamö." South America. Vol. 7 of

Encyclopedia of World Cultures. Boston: Hall, 1994.

For a reference work that you have accessed on the Internet, see Internet and Electronic Sources on page 112.

A Preface, Introduction, Foreword, or Afterword

Bradford, Barbara Taylor. Foreword. Forever Amber. By Kathleen

Winsor. 1944. Chicago: Chicago Review, 2000.

The entry begins with the author of the preface, introduction, foreword, or afterword. The book's author follows the title (preceded by the word *by*).

Sources in Periodicals and Newspapers

Following are entries for a periodical and newspaper (when accessed in print form). Periodical entries are also summarized in Figure 6.3. For articles accessed online, see Internet and Electronic Sources on pages 111–12.

An Article in a Magazine

Block, Toddi Gutner. "Riding the Waves." Forbes 11 Sept. 1995:

182+.

Jellinek, George. "Record Collecting: Hobby or Obsession?" <u>Opera</u>
   <u>News</u> Feb. 2003: 85.
Van Zile, Susan. "Grammar That'll Move You!" <u>Instructor</u>
   Jan./Feb. 2003: 32-34.

This format is used for all weekly, biweekly, monthly, or bimonthly periodicals, except for scholarly journals. The Van Zile article appears on pages 32 through 34. The Block article is not printed on continuous pages; it begins on page 182 and is continued further back in the magazine. For such articles, only the first page is listed, immediately followed by a plus sign (+). Although some magazines may show a volume or issue number on the cover, these are not needed in the entry.

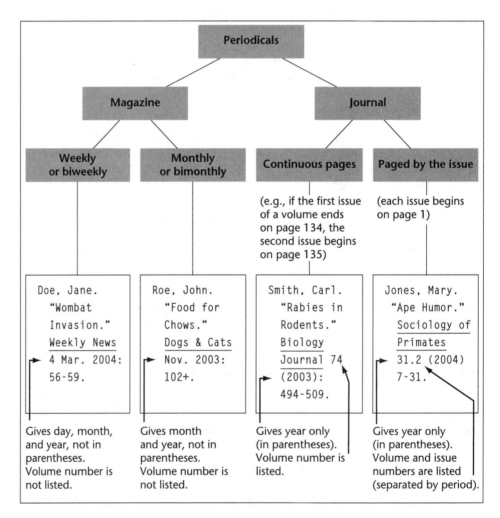

Figure 6.3 Periodical listings for an MLA works cited list.

Page Numbers

Book. Do not give page numbers when citing a book in a works-cited list.

An article or a selection from a book. Give the page numbers on which an essay or article appears within a larger work, such as a book or periodical. List the pages for the *entire* selection, not just pages cited in your paper.

Page number style. In listing page numbers, omit all but the last two digits of the final page number, unless they are different from those of the first page. *Examples:*

  5-7
  377-79 (not -9 or -379)
  195-208
  1006-07 (not -7 or -1007)
  986-1011

Noncontinuous pages. For articles that are continued on pages further back in the publication, list only the first page and a plus sign. For example, for an article that appears on pages 45 to 47 and continues on pages 123–130, list the following:

  45+

Names of months, except for May, June, and July, are abbreviated. Note that there is no punctuation between the periodical's name and the publication date. For a magazine article that you have accessed on the Internet, see various entries under Internet and Electronic Sources on pages 111–13.

An Article in a Journal

Larter, Raima. "Understanding Complexity in Biophysical

  Chemistry." Journal of Physical Chemistry 107 (2003): 415-29.

Journals are usually scholarly publications and are typically published three or four times yearly. Each year begins a new volume. The volume number (107 in this case) is included in the entry for a journal article. It is not necessary to include the seasonal designation (Winter, Spring, etc.). Pages in many journals are numbered according to the volume, not the issue. For example, if the Winter issue of volume 107 of *Journal of Physical Chemistry* ended on page 110, the Spring issue would begin on page 111. The paging of the next volume (108) would begin again with page 1. Some journals, however, begin each issue on page 1; for these, add a period and the issue number following the volume number, as follows:

Mitchell, W. J. T. "The Surplus Value of Images." Mosaic 35.3

  (2002): 1-23.

The number 35.3 tells you that the article appeared in volume 35, issue 3, of *Mosaic*. Periodical listings are also shown in Figure 6.3 on page 104. For a journal article that you have accessed on the Internet, see various entries under Internet and Electronic Sources on pages 111–12.

An Article in a Newspaper

Argetsinger, Amy. "Lobbying Gets Old College Try." <u>Washington</u>
<u>Post</u> 13 Jan. 2003: B2.

Leonhardt, David. "Defining the Rich in the World's Wealthiest
Nation." <u>New York Times</u> 12 Jan. 2003, natl. ed.: sec. 4: 1+.

Ranii, David. "New AIDS Drug Is Step Closer to Approval." <u>News</u>
<u>and Observer</u> [Raleigh] 7 Nov. 1995: 1D+.

The article *The* is omitted from citations of newspapers such as the *Washington Post*. When the newspaper's name does not include the city (e.g., *News and Observer*), provide the city name in brackets; however, do not give a city for national newspapers like the *Wall Street Journal* and *USA Today*. Number pages as they appear in your source. The number on the page of the newspaper where the Argetsinger article appears is B2 (i.e., page 2 of section B), while the newspaper where the Ranii article appeared has the section and page numbers reversed (it begins on page 1D). When both the section and pages are numbered, present them as in the second example (*sec. 4: 1+*). Because the *New York Times* publishes two different editions (called the late and the national editions), it is necessary to specify which edition you used. For a newspaper article that you have accessed on the Internet, see various entries under Internet and Electronic Sources on pages 111–12.

An Editorial

"Six Sigma Schools." Editorial. <u>Wall Street Journal</u> 15 Jan.
2003: A10.

A Letter to the Editor

Rothschild, Michelle. Letter. <u>Kiplinger's</u> Jan. 2003: 14.

A Review

Flanagan, Caitlin. "Get a Job." Rev. of <u>What Should I Do with My</u>
<u>Life?</u>, by Po Bronson. <u>New York Times Book Review</u> 12 Jan.
2003: 4.

Glenn, Kenny. Rev. of <u>Man on the Moon</u> [film]. <u>Premiere</u> Jan. 2000: 20.

Rev. of <u>Going to the Territory</u>, by Ralph Ellison. <u>Atlantic</u> Aug.

    1986: 91.

Stearns, David Patrick. Rev. of <u>The Well-Tempered Clavier</u>, by J. S.

    Bach [CD]. Angela Hewitt, piano. <u>Stereophile</u> Dec. 1999: 173+.

The first and third reviews are of books; the second is of a film; the fourth is of a music recording on CD. Information in review listings appears in this order: the reviewer's name; the title of the review; the work reviewed; its author; performers and performance information, if applicable; and the publication information. Notice that only the first review was published under a title. In the third review, Ralph Ellison is the author of the book reviewed; the review itself is published anonymously. If the medium of the reviewed work is not obvious, it can be added in brackets after the name of the work (e.g., *[CD]*).

Other Sources

An Audio Recording

Dickinson, Dee. <u>Creating the Future: Perspectives on Educational</u>

    <u>Change</u>. Audiocassette. Minneapolis: Accelerated Learning

    Systems, 1991.

Mahler, Gustav. Symphony No. 7. Michael Tilson Thomas, cond.

    London Symphony Orch. CD. RCA Victor, 1999.

Shuster, George N. Jacket notes. <u>The Poetry of Gerard Manley</u>

    <u>Hopkins</u>. LP. Caedmon, n.d.

Audio recordings vary greatly in type and purpose, so do not hesitate to exercise judgment about what information is important. In general, label each recording by medium (CD, audiocassette, LP, etc.), although the label is optional for compact discs, which are assumed to be the standard audio medium. For a musical recording, list first the name of the composer or performer or conductor, depending on what aspect of the recording you are emphasizing. Recordings are produced by print-media publishers as well as traditional record companies, with the line separating them increasingly blurred; list either the manufacturer and year (as in the second example) or city, publisher, and year (as in the first example). Cite jacket or liner notes as in the third example. When a date is unavailable, as in the last example, use *n.d.* for "no date." For a multidisc publication, follow the medium with either the total number of discs included or the specific disc number being cited.

A Film, DVD, or Video Recording

> 25th Hour. Dir. Spike Lee. Screenplay by David Benioff.
>
>   Touchstone, 2003.

For a film, give the title, the director, the distributor, and the year of release. You may include other information you consider pertinent, such as the screenwriter and principal performers. For a film viewed on videocassette, DVD, or videodisc, provide that same information, but also identify the medium, the distributor, and the video release date:

> All about Eve. Dir. Joseph L. Mankiewicz. Perf. Bette Davis,
>
>   Anne Baxter, and George Sanders. Fox, 1950. DVD. Studio
>
>   Classics, 2003.

Cite a nontheatrical video as follows:

> The Classical Hollywood Style. Program 1 of The American Cinema.
>
>   Prod. New York Center for Visual History. Videocassette.
>
>   Annenberg/CPB, 1995.

A Government Document
See "A Book by a Government Agency" on page 99.

A Lecture

> Granetta, Stephanie. Class lecture. English 315. Richardson
>
>   College. 7 Apr. 2003.
>
> Kamenish, Eleanor. "A Tale of Two Countries: Mores in France and
>
>   Scotland." Public lecture. Friends of the Public Library.
>
>   Louisville, 16 Apr. 2003.

A Pamphlet

> Golden Retriever Club of America. Prevention of Heartworm. n.p.:
>
>   GRCA, 2004.
>
> Who Are the Amish? Aylmer, Ont.: Pathway, n.d.

Pamphlets are treated like books. Use these abbreviations for unknown information: *n.p.* for both "no place" or "no publisher," *n.d.* for "no date," and *n. pag.* for "no pagination" (when the source lacks page numbers). Because pamphlets vary widely, you should exercise judgment to make your listing clear.

An Interview

```
Barefoot, Blake. Personal interview. 18 Sept. 2002.

Spacey, Kevin. Interview with Terry Gross. Fresh Air. Natl.

     Public Radio. WHQR, Wilmington, NC. 21 Jan. 2003.

Trump, Donald. "Trump Speaks." Interview with Aravind Adiga.

     Money Feb. 2003: 28.
```

All interviews begin with the name of the person being interviewed, not the interviewer. Label an interview that you conduct as *Personal interview.* Label a broadcast or print interview as *Interview with [interviewer].* Only those print interviews that are presented in a question-and-answer format are listed in this way; other print sources in which a person is quoted are listed in a standard format (author's name first).

A Television or Radio Program

```
The Crossing. Dir. Robert Harmon. Screenplay by Sherry Jones and

     Peter Jennings. History Channel. 1 Jan. 2000.

Stone, Susan. Report on Japanese comic books. All Things

     Considered. Natl. Public Radio. 9 Jan. 2003.
```

An Unpublished Essay

```
Gould, Emily. "Fast Food Comes at a High Price for Workers."

     Essay written for Prof. Katherine Humel's English 12 class.

     Fall semester 2002.
```

An Unpublished Letter

```
Cilano, Cara. Letter to author. 5 Mar. 2003.
```
See also "E-Mail" on page 114.

An Unpublished Questionnaire

```
Questionnaire conducted by Prof. Barbara Waxman's English 103
    class. Feb. 2003.
```

A citation for a project or paper written for a college class needs be no more formal than this. An essay meant for wider circulation, however, would need to include the title of the course and the name of the college. Common sense is your best guide in these matters.

Internet and Electronic Sources

A basic principle for citing a print source found online is to provide the information one would supply for the print source, followed by information about the online source. Unlike citations for books that have three major divisions, a citation for an electronic publication may have up to five:

```
Author's name. "Title of document." Information about print
    publication. Information about electronic publication.
    Access information.
```

Access information include the date of access and the URL. Following are examples of both print and nonprint sources found online.

An Online Book

```
Irving, David. Hitler's War. New York: Viking, 1977. 19 Jan.
    2003 <http://www.fpp.co.uk/books/Hitler/>.
Richards, Hank. The Sacrifice. 1996. 3 Mar. 2003
    <http://www.geocities.com/Area51/Vault/8101/>.
Wollstonecraft, Mary. Vindication of the Rights of Women. 1792.
    Bartleby.com, 1999. 13 Feb. 2003 <http://www.bartleby.com/144/>.
```

For an online book that first appeared in print, such as the first and third examples, provide standard information for the print source of the reproduced text, if available. Then provide the name of the online "publisher" and the date of the online publication (not known in the first example; *Bartleby.com, 1999* in the third). Finally, give the date you consulted the online work, immediately followed (no period) by the online address within angle brackets. If an online address cannot fit completely on one line, you can break it following a slash (/), but do not use a hyphen to show the break. Richards's book did not first appear in print and is available on a personal Web page. Because electronic sources vary widely, you may need to use your judgment about how best to identify your source.

A Part of an Online Book

> Coyle, Edward R. Spies and Their Work. Ambulancing on the French
>
>   Front. 1918. 30 Apr. 2003 <http://www.ku.edu/carrie/
>
>   specoll/medical/Coyle/Coyle04.htm#18>.

Note that if the selection is a standard part of the book such as a chapter, preface, or introduction, the title does not need to be placed within quotation marks. However, when the selection is a poem or essay, then quotation marks are needed. Also note that the URL should indicate the specific location of the part of the book you are citing.

A Print Periodical (Newspaper, Magazine, or Journal) Accessed on the Publication's Web Site

The following works appeared in print but were accessed on the Web sites of the publications. See also "A Work Accessed in an Online Database" below.

> Falsani, Cathleen. "Did Respect for Religion Cloud 'Clone'
>
>   Coverage?" Chicago Sun-Times 10 Jan. 2003. 19 Jan. 2003
>
>   <http://www.suntimes.com/output/falsani/cst-nws-fals10.html>.
>
> Fineman, Howard, and Tamara Lipper. "Spinning Race." Newsweek 27
>
>   Jan. 2003. 19 Jan. 2003 <http://www.msnbc.com/news/
>
>   861383.asp?>.
>
> Young, A. J., A. S. Wilson, and C. G. Mundell. "Chandra Imaging
>
>   of the X-Ray Core of the Virgo Cluster." Astrophysical
>
>   Journal 579.2 (2002): 560-70. 19 Jan. 2003 <http://
>
>   www.journals.uchicago.edu/ApJ/journal/issues/ApJ/
>
>   v579n2/54935/54935.html>.

For online periodical articles that also appeared in print, first provide the same information as for the print article, including the publication, the date of print publication, and the articles' pages, if available. Finally, give the date you consulted the online work, immediately followed (no period) by the online address, within angle brackets.

A Nonprint Periodical Accessed on the Publication's Web Site

```
Clinton, Bill. "The Path to Peace." 10 Sept. 2002. Salon.com 20
    Jan. 2003 <http://www.salon.com/news/feature/2002/09/10/
    clinton/>.
```

The essay was published in the exclusively online magazine *Salon.com.*

A Work Accessed in an Online Database

Use the following format when you access a work in an online database such as EBSCOhost, InfoTrac, LexisNexis, ProQuest, or WilsonWeb.

```
Jovanovic, Rozalia. "Snowmobilers Tied to Rules of the Road."
    National Law Journal Aug. 5, 2002: B1. InfoTrac OneFile. 20
    Jan. 2003 <http://infotrac.galegroup.com/>.
Parks, Noreen. "Dolphins in Danger." Science Now 17 Dec. 2002:
    2-3. Academic Search Elite. EBSCOhost. 20 Jan. 2003
    <http://web3.epnet.com/>.
"Political Inclination of the States." Associated Press 9 Jan.
    2003. LexisNexis Academic Universe. 20 Jan 2003
    <http://web.lexis-nexis.com/universe>.
```

Provide the standard publication information, including the pages of the original publication, if available. Include the name of the database and underline it (in the first example, InfoTrac OneFile) and the name of the database family if not included in the database name (in the second example, EBSCOhost). Because the Internet address of an individual citation is often a very long temporary address that cannot be used on later occasions, give only the general address of the database or of the library where you accessed the database.

An Online Encyclopedia Article

```
"Humpback Whale." Encyclopaedia Britannica 2003. Encyclopaedia
    Britannica Online. 28 Jan. 2003 <http://
    0-search.eb.com .uncclc.coast.uncwil.edu/eb/>.
```

An Online Review

```
Ebert, Roger. Rev. of Identity, dir. James Mangold. Chicago Sun-
    Times Online 25 Apr. 2003. 29 May 2003 <http://
    www.suntimes.com/output/ebert1/wkp-news-identity25f.html>.
```

Eprile, Tony. "'Red Dust': Settling Scores in South Africa."

    Rev. of <u>Red Dust</u>, by Gillian Slovo. <u>New York Times Online</u>

    28 Apr. 2003. 29 May 2003

    <http://nytimes.com/2002/04/28/books/review/

    28EPRILET.html?ex=1051761600&en=0f435a46a2f839eb&ei=5070>.

In Ebert's movie review, the director's name (preceded by *dir.*) follows the movie's title. In Eprile's book review, the name of the book's author (preceded by the word "by") follows the book title.

An Organization's Web Site

<u>The Coral Reef Alliance</u>. "Coral Friendly Guidelines." 21 Jan.

    2003 <http://www.coralreefalliance.org/parks/

    guidelines.html>.

Note that the name of the site is <u>underlined</u>. And, if available, the editor (*Ed.*) of the site immediately follows it.

A Course Web Page

Reilly, Colleen. English 204: Introduction to Technical Writing.

    Course home page. U of North Carolina at Wilmington.

    Spring 2003. 29 Apr. 2003 <http://people.uncw.edu/

    reillyc/204/>.

The course title is not underlined or placed within quotation marks.

An Academic Department Page

Dept. of English home page. U of North Carolina at Wilmington.

    10 Mar. 2003 <http://www.uncwil.edu/english/>.

A Personal Web Page

Hemming, Sally. Home page. 4 Feb. 2003 <http://

    www.sallyhemming.com>.

If the page has a title, it is <u>underlined</u> and placed before the word Home page.

Khan, Genghis. <u>Latest Conquests</u>. Home page. . . . .

E-Mail

Wilkes, Paul. E-mail to author. 29 Dec. 2002.

Computer Software

Atoms, Symbols and Equations. Vers. 3.0. Software. 2002 <http://

ourworld.compuserve.com/homepages/RayLec/atoms.htm>.

Twain's World. CD-ROM. Parsippany, NJ: Bureau Development,

1993.

The first example is of software downloaded from the Internet; the second is software published on a CD-ROM. The boundary between pure software and a book or other work that is published in an electronic medium is not a distinct one. See also "A Work on CD-ROM or Diskette" above.

EXERCISE | **A List of Works Cited**

This exercise practices many types of bibliographic entries. Imagine that (in a temporary lapse from sanity) you have written a paper called "The Shoelace in History" and you have made use of the following sources. Compile your list of works cited, paying close attention to proper MLA format.

As a first step, circle the word in each of the following items that would begin the listing. Second, order the entries alphabetically. Third, put each listing in proper MLA form. (*Warning:* Some listings contain irrelevant information that you will not use in your works-cited list.) Finally, prepare the finished list.

1. The book *Sandals in Greece and Rome* was written by Sally Parish and published in 1997 by Wapiti Press in Omaha.
2. You found Walter Kelly's article "Shoelaces" on page 36 of volume 12 of the 1994 edition of *Encyclopedia of Haberdashery,* published in New York by the Buster Green Company.
3. During World War II, Fiona Quinn wrote *Knit Your Own Shoelaces* as part of the Self-Reliance Series printed in Modesto, California, in 1942 by Victory Press.
4. On page 36 of its July 23, 1977, edition, *Time* magazine published "Earth Shoes Unearthed in Inca Ruins." No author is given.
5. Two days ago, using the Internet, you consulted an online book by Imelda Markoz, *Never Too Many Shoes.* Two years ago, it had appeared in print, published by Converse Press in Wichita. You found the book at the address http://www.shoebooks.umanila.edu.
6. Constance Jowett translated a book by Max Philador and Elisaveta Krutsch, *Shoelaces in Africa and the Far East 1800–1914.* It was published in 1999 by Vanitas Publishers, Inc. Cities listed on the title page for Vanitas are Fort Worth, Texas; Chicago; Amsterdam; and Sydney, Australia.

7. On January 5 of this year Louise K. Frobisher wrote you a letter about her father's shoelace research.

8. You found volume 3 of Fiona Quinn's six-volume work of 1950: *The Shoe in the English-Speaking World*, published by S. T. Bruin & Sons of Boston.

9. On pages 711 and 712 of volume 17 of the *Indiana Journal of Podiatry* (November 1974) appears an essay, "Solving the Loose Shoe Problem" by Earl Q. Butz.

10. Leon Frobisher, Werner Festschrift, Ella Fitsky, and Ian McCrimmer published the twelfth edition of *Shoemaking with a Purpose* in 1996. The publisher, Hooton-Muffin of Boston, has published editions of the book since 1939.

11. The Society of Legwear Manufacturers wrote a book, *Laces, Gaiters, and Spats*, in 1901. Provolone-Liederkranz Publishers, Ltd., of Toronto reprinted it in 1955.

12. Mr. O. Fecteau and Ms. Mary Facenda edited a 1993 anthology, *An Ethnography of Footwear*, published in New Orleans by Big Muddy Publications. You found an article on pages 70–81, "Footloose and Sandal-Free," by J. R. R. Frodobaggins.

13. Norman Zimmer thoroughly explores "The Shoelace Motif in Finno-Latvian Sonnet Sequences" in the Fall 1993 edition (volume 43), pages 202 through 295, of a scholarly journal called *PMLA*.

14. Theodore and Louisa Mae Quinn edited a book written by their mother, Fiona Quinn, shortly before her death. The book, *Old Laces and Arsenic*, is published by Capra Press of Los Angeles. Copyright dates given are 1947, 1952, and 1953.

15. In the February 4, 1968, *Hibbing Herald* newspaper, the article "Lace, Lady, Lace" appeared under Robert Dylan's byline. A week ago today, you printed out a copy of the article online in the MasterFile Premier database by using the EBSCOhost search engine. EBSCOhost's homepage is http://www.epnet.dome/ehost/.

16. You draw on information from a television exposé, "The Shoelace Coverup," which appeared last Sunday on the CBS show *60 Minutes*. Leslie Stahl is the narrator.

17. *Dog's Life* is a monthly magazine published in Atlanta. In volume 16, number 3, of that publication (whose date is August 2000), Walter Kelly's article "Little Laces for Little People" appeared. It began on pages 32 to 37 and continued on pages 188 and 189. You found it using the ProQuest reference service (homepage: http://www.bellhowell.infolearning.com/proquest/).

18. You used the World Wide Web to read an article, "Tasteless Laces" by M. R. Blackwell. It appeared this year in the January issue of *Cyberlace*, which calls itself "the e-zine for the well shod." The address of the article is http://www.knotco.edu/cyberlace/notaste.html.

Congratulations. Having completed this exercise, you are now prepared for almost any situation that you may face as you prepare lists of sources in the future.

Remember, for quick reference, consult the summary of MLA bibliographic models on the inside front covers.

7 *Putting Your Sources to Work: Reading and Taking Notes*

USING YOUR WRITTEN SOURCES

The early stages of your project may have been easier than you expected. You selected a topic, did some preliminary browsing in the library, and assembled a list of sources to work with. So far so good. But now what? Is there some simple technique that experienced researchers use to get ideas and information *out* of their sources and *into* their writing?

In fact, there is a reasonably uncomplicated and orderly procedure for putting your sources to use, but it isn't exactly simple. You can't just sit down before a stack of sources, read the first one and write part of your paper, then read the second one and write some more, and so on until you are finished. Obviously, such a procedure would make for a very haphazard and disjointed paper.

You can't write your paper all at once. Because you have a substantial body of information to sort through, digest, select, and organize, you have to use good management skills in your project. Your course of action needs to consist of manageable subtasks: You need to (1) *read* your sources efficiently and selectively and (2) *evaluate* the information you find there. As you learn more about your topic, you should (3) *narrow your focus* and (4) *shape a plan* for the paper. And to make use of new ideas and information, you need to (5) *take notes* on what seems important and usable in the sources. Only then are you ready to begin the actual drafting of the paper.

This chapter examines each of these tasks in turn, but do not think of them as separate operations that you can perform one after the other. They must interact. After all, how can you know what to read and take notes on unless you have some plans for what your paper will include? On the other hand, how can you know what your paper will include until your reading reveals to you what information is available? In working on your paper, you can never put your brain on automatic pilot. As you read and learn from your sources, you must continually think about how you can use the information and how using it will fit in with (or alter) your plan for the paper.

Emily and Justin received an assignment like the following from their instructors.

Note Cards and a Preliminary Outline	A S S I G N M E N T

Continue your research by reading your sources, evaluating them, taking notes on note cards, narrowing your focus, and shaping a plan (a preliminary outline) for your paper. This is the most time-consuming stage of your research project, so be sure to begin working on it right away. Continue to record your experiences and observations in your research notebook.

Reading Your Sources

At this stage, you need to undertake several tasks, the first of which is to *read your sources.* A research paper should be something new, a fresh synthesis of information and ideas from many sources. A paper that is largely a summary of only one or two sources fails to do this. Become well informed about your topic by reading widely, and use a breadth of information in your paper. Most likely you have found many sources related to your topic, and the sheer volume of available material may itself be a cause for concern. Because your time is limited, you need to use it efficiently. Following are some practical suggestions for efficient reading:

- **Read only those sources that relate to your topic.** Beginning researchers often try to read too much. Do not waste valuable time reading sources that do not relate specifically to your topic. Before reading any source in detail, examine it briefly to be sure of its relevance. Chapter titles in books and section headings or even illustrations in articles may give you a sense of the work's usefulness. If you find dozens of books devoted solely to your topic, that topic probably is too broad to treat in a brief paper, and your focus should be narrowed. (Narrowing your paper's focus is discussed later in this chapter.)

- **Read each source selectively.** Do not expect to read every source from cover to cover; rather, read only those passages that relate to your topic. With a book, for example, use the table of contents in the front and the index in the back to locate relevant passages. Skim through promising sections, looking for passages relating directly to your topic—only these should you read carefully and deliberately.

- **Think as you read.** Ask yourself if what you are reading relates to your topic. Is it important and usable in your paper? Does it raise questions you want to explore further? What additional research do you need to do to answer these questions? Find new sources as needed, discard unusable ones, and update your working bibliography.

- **Read with curiosity.** Do not let your reading become a plodding and mechanical task; don't think of it as plowing through a stack of sources. Make your reading an act of exploration. You want to learn about your topic, and each source holds the potential to answer your questions. Search out answers, and if you don't find them in one source, seek them in another. There are many profitable ways for researchers to think of themselves: as explorers discovering unknown territory, as detectives following a trail of clues, as players fitting together the pieces of an intriguing puzzle.

• **Use your hand as well as your eyes when you read.** If you have photocopied an article or book chapter, underline important passages while reading, and write yourself notes in the margins. (Of course, don't do either of these things unless you own the copy; marking up material belonging to the library or to other people is a grave discourtesy.) Getting your hand into action as you read is a good way of keeping your mind active as well; writing, underlining, and note-taking force you to think about what you are reading. An article from *Human Resources Focus* magazine that Emily photocopied and then annotated is shown in Figure 7.1.

• **Write notes about your reading.** Use your research notebook to "think on paper" as you read. That is, write general comments about what you have learned from your sources and the ideas you have gained for your paper. Use note cards to write down specific information that you might use in writing your paper. (Note cards are discussed in detail later in this chapter.)

Evaluating Your Sources

All sources are not equally reliable. Not all writers are equally competent; not all periodicals and publishers are equally respected; and not all statements from interviewees are equally well informed. Certainly not every claim that appears in print is true. Because you want to base your paper on the most accurate, up-to-date, and authoritative information available, you need to exercise discretion in *evaluating your sources.* Following are some questions you can ask about a source:

• **Is the publication respectable?** If you are researching flying-saucer sightings, for example, an article in an astronomy or psychology journal commands far more respect than an article like "My Baby's Daddy Came from a UFO" in a lurid supermarket tabloid. Between these two extremes are popular magazines, which cover a wide range of territory. Information that appears in a news magazine such as *Newsweek* or *U.S. News & World Report* is more likely to be accepted as balanced and well researched than information taken from a less serious publication such as *People* or *Teen*. You must use your judgment about the reliability of your sources. Because sources differ in respectability and prestige, scholars always identify their research sources so as to allow readers to make their own judgments about reliability. (Acknowledging sources is discussed in Chapters 8 and 9.) As a general rule, works that identify their sources are more likely to be reliable than those that do not.

• **What are the author's credentials?** Is the author a recognized authority? An astrophysicist writing about the possibility of life in other galaxies will command more respect than, say, an amateur flying-saucer enthusiast who is a retired dentist. Expert sources lend authority to assertions you make in your

Employee Turnover: The Hidden Drain on Profits

In today's economy, business owners and managers need to control expenses to increase profits. Employee turnover is one of the most frustrating areas. For many industries—such as fast food, retail, convenience stores, trucking and healthcare—turnover rates exceed 75 percent.

(!)

Although related costs are not always direct or budgeted, turnover drains profits and adversely affects the business' overall efficiency. For example, a company that operates on a 5 percent margin must add about $20,000 in sales for every $1,000 lost to turnover costs.

The U.S. Department of Labor estimates that it costs a company one-third of a new hire's annual salary to replace an employee. Using a wage rate of only $6 an hour, it would cost a company $3,600 for each departing employee. This estimate, however, may be too high. Many fast-food companies, in fact, calculate the cost at $500 to replace one crew person and about $1,500 to replace a manager. Thus, for a fast-food operation with 500 employees and 300 percent turnover, the annual cost would be $750,000 (500 x 1,500 new hires x $500). In the trucking industry, managers estimate the per-driver replacement expense between $3,000 and $5,000.

Cheap labor leads to turnover—but costs are not so cheap.

TANGIBLES AND INTANGIBLES

Tangible costs include time involved for recruitment, selection and training of new personnel. These are real costs in terms of advertising expenses and manpower. The time a manager spends in the hiring process could otherwise be devoted to managing his or her everyday functions. For large companies, high turnover also requires additional staff to process the huge volume of applicants who race through the proverbial revolving door. This further drains profits and indicates a weakness in the selection process.

Other employees pay the price

Intangible costs are reflected in increased workloads as coworkers take up the slack until new employees are hired; the turbulence inherent in companies with high turnover; and the adverse publicity that seems to follow high-turnover businesses.

managers and workers

Although these intangible costs are more difficult to quantify, they definitely have an adverse impact on overall efficiency and worker morale. And unless the cause of the turnover is identified, low morale may lead to more troubles, such as greater tension with management and disruptive behavior.

Hidden cost: morale

Unfortunately, turnover costs often reach critical levels before managers react. One well-known restaurant chain, for example, recently quantified its annual turnover cost at $67 million. Incredibly, these costs had never been tracked until this year.

Figure 7.1 Annotation of a photocopied source.

paper—another reason for the standard practice of identifying your sources to your readers.

• **Is the source presenting firsthand information?** Are the writer's assertions based on primary or secondary research? For example, articles about cancer research in *Reader's Digest* or *Time* may be written with a concern for accuracy and clarity, but their authors may be reporters writing secondhand on the subject—they may not be experts in the field. You can use these sources, but be certain to consider all factors in weighing their reliability.

• **Does the source demonstrate evidence of careful research?** Does the author show by way of notes and other documentation that the statements presented are based on the best available information? Or does it appear that the author's statements derive from unsupported speculation or incomplete research? A source that seems unreliable should either not be used at all or else be cited as an example of one point of view (perhaps one that you refute using more reliable sources).

• **Is the source up-to-date?** Clearly, you do not want to base your paper on information that is no longer considered accurate and complete. For example, a paper on a dynamic field such as nuclear disarmament or advances in telecommunications would be hopelessly out-of-date if it is based on five-year-old sources. If you are writing a paper on a topic about which new findings or theories exist, your research should include recent sources. Check the publication dates of your sources.

• **Does the source seem biased?** Writers have opinions that they support in their writing, but some writers are more open-minded than others. Is the author's purpose in writing to explain or to persuade? Does the author provide a balanced presentation of evidence, or are there other perspectives and evidence that the author ignores? Be aware of the point of view of the author and of the publication you are examining. An article in a magazine of political opinion such as *National Review* can be expected to take a conservative stance on an issue, just as an article in *The Nation* will express a more liberal opinion. Your own paper, even when you are making an argument for a particular viewpoint, should present evidence for all sides. If you use opinionated sources, you can balance them with sources expressing opposing points of view.

• **Do your sources consider all viewpoints and theories?** Because many books and articles are written from a single viewpoint, it is important to read widely to discover if other points of view exist as well. For example, several works have been written claiming that ancient monuments such as the pyramids are evidence of past visits to our planet by extraterrestrials. Only by checking a variety of sources might a student discover that scientists have discredited most of the evidence on which these claims are based. Students writing about such topics as astrology, subliminal advertising, Noah's flood, holistic healing, Bigfoot, or the assassination of President Kennedy should be aware that these areas are controversial and that they should seek out diverse points of view in their research so they can be fully informed and present a complete picture of the topic to their readers.

Narrowing Your Paper's Focus

If you are like most students, the research paper assigned in your composition course may be the longest paper you have had to write, so you may feel worried about filling enough pages. Most students share that concern at this stage, but they soon find so much material that having *too much* to say (not too little) becomes their concern.

The ideal topic for your paper is one to which you can do justice—one you can write about with some thoroughness and completeness—in a paper of the length you are assigned. Most student researchers start out with a fairly broad

conception of their topic and then make it more and more limited as their research and writing progress. As you learn how much information is available
about your topic and as you discover through your reading what aspect most intrigues you, you should ***narrow your paper's focus***—that is, bring your topic into
a sharper and more limited scope.

From your first speculations about a topic until the completion of your final
draft, your topic will probably undergo several transformations, usually with each
new version more narrowly defined than the one before. For example, a student
might begin with the general concept of her major, oceanography, and narrow it
through successive stages as follows:

This narrowing
might occur
during the
brainstorming
phase.

> Oceanography
> |
> Undersea exploration
> |
> Adapting undersea exploration for salvaging sunken ships
> |
> Salvaging the *Titanic*
> |

This further
narrowing
might occur
during the
research and
writing phases.

> The most recent exploration of the *Titanic*
> ↓
> What was learned then about how the ship sank and
> broke apart

The path from the original germ of an idea to the eventual paper topic isn't
always a matter of successive narrowing. As in Emily's case, it sometimes involves
some turns and detours. In her clustering exercise on page 52, we can discern a
narrowing process as she reached the topic of fast food.

Broader topic   Unhealthy food
    | |
    | Effects of poor diet
    | |
    | Obesity
    | |
    | Causes of obesity
    ↓   ↓
Narrower topic   Fast food

As she conducted her research, however, other aspects of fast food besides the
health aspects also attracted her interest. By the time she wrote her prospectus, her

topic had expanded to include the social issues and work issues associated with fast food. She would soon realize, however, that she was attempting too much, and once again her topic narrowed appropriately to just work issues in the fast-food industry. Do not be surprised, or discouraged, if your path to your topic takes similar twists and turns. Just keep in mind that *narrowing* your paper's focus is generally the best advice for making your project manageable and for producing the best result.

EXERCISES | **Narrowing a Topic**

1. Speculate on how each of the following general topics might be successively narrowed during the course of a research project. Write each topic in your notebook, and beneath it give three or four additional topics, each more specific and more narrowly focused than the one above it. (For example, if you were given the topic *oceanography,* you might create a list something like the one given on the preceding page.)

   warfare   music   famous people   luxury goods

2. Now take your own research topic and make a general-to-specific list of its successive stages. First list the most general idea you started with and show how it narrowed to your present topic. Then speculate on how your topic might be narrowed even further as you complete work on your project.

Formulating and Refining a Plan

Writing is never an exact science or a tidy procedure, and the business of planning and organizing is the untidiest part of all. It would be nice if you could start by creating a full-blown outline of your paper, then take notes on the areas you have outlined, and finally write your paper from your notes, exactly as first planned. However, any writer can tell you it rarely if ever works that way.

Research papers evolve as you do research, and they continue to evolve as you write them, so it is important to remain flexible. As you learn more about your subject—as you read and take notes, and even as you begin writing—new directions will suggest themselves to you. Be prepared to adjust the focus and organization of your paper at every stage, right up to your final revision. Many a student has expected to write one paper, only to discover something quite different actually taking shape on the page. There is nothing wrong with making these changes—they are a natural part of the writing process. Writing is as much a process of discovery for the writer as it is a medium for communicating with readers.

As you start examining your sources, you may have only a hazy notion of the eventual contents of your paper, but the beginnings of a plan should emerge as you learn more and more. Shortly into your research you should be ready to pause and sketch a very general ***informal preliminary outline*** of where your paper seems to be going. Emily's first rough outline, shown in Figure 7.2, makes no pretense of being complete or final or even particularly pretty—nor should it at

Figure 7.2 **Emily's rough outline.**

this stage. Emily was "thinking on paper," making sense of her own thoughts and trying to bring some vague ideas into focus. She was doing it for her own benefit, not trying to impress any outside readers. Having established some sense of her paper's parts, Emily was then able to resume reading and taking notes with greater efficiency. She now had a clearer idea of what she was looking for. She was also aware that the organization of her paper would probably change as she continued writing.

Begin with a very general outline, perhaps listing just a few of the main topics you expect your paper to include. As you continue reading, taking notes, and thinking, your outline may become more fleshed out, as you continue to refine your preliminary plans. Remember that an informal outline is an aid to you in organizing and writing your paper. It is not a part of the paper and does not need to be in any kind of polished, orderly form. A formal outline, if you do one, can be written as one of the last steps of your project. (Formal outlines are discussed on pages 238–43.)

Taking Notes on Note Cards

Clearly, you cannot put into your paper everything you read during the course of your research. Some sources will be more useful than others, but still you will use only a small portion of any one source. Note-taking is a way of selecting what you can use. It is also a way of aiding your memory and storing the information and ideas you find in a convenient form for use when you write the paper.

Good notes, then, have the virtue of being both selective and accessible. You could take notes in your notebook, but a notebook is far less easy to work with than *note cards,* which have the advantage of flexibility. Unlike entries in notebooks or on long sheets of paper, notes on index cards can be easily sorted, rearranged, and weeded out. When you are ready to write, you can group note cards according to topics and arrange them in the order in which you expect to use them in the paper. This greatly simplifies the task of writing.

Besides being selective and convenient, good notes have another quality—accuracy. You are obliged as a scholar to be scrupulously accurate in reporting and acknowledging your sources. In research writing, you must quote your sources accurately and paraphrase them fairly. (Quoting and paraphrasing sources are discussed more fully in Chapter 8.) Moreover, you should give credit to sources for their contributions and make it clear to your readers which words in the paper are your own and which are taken directly from sources. You can use your sources fairly and accurately only if you write from notes that you have taken with great care.

For an example of how a writer takes notes, look first at this passage that Emily read in one of her sources, "Virtues of Work vs. Finishing Homework," an article by Yvonne Zipp that appeared in the *Christian Science Monitor*:

> More than in other developed countries, in the US donning a McDonald's cap or Blockbuster khakis is a teen rite of passage as universal as driver's ed. Surveys show 4 in 5 American teens hold some kind of job during the school year, and half those who work are manning cash registers and flipping burgers more than 20 hours a week.
>
> Everyone can rattle off the benefits of a job: It can instill a solid work ethic, build self-confidence, and teach teens responsibility, time management, and the value of the dollar—not to mention socking funds away for college.
>
> But even though teen work is a proud American tradition—one that has held steady since the 1970s—many are now arguing that the cost to kids is too high.
>
> Students who work more than 20 hours a week are less likely to get enough sleep and exercise, less likely to go on to higher education, and more likely to use alcohol or drugs, according to a recent report by the National Research Council and the Institute of Medicine in Washington.

Figure 7.3 is the note card that Emily made for this passage. Later, when Emily wrote her paper, she used this card to write the following:

    . . . Yvonne Zipp of the Christian Science Monitor observes
    that such jobs have become "a teen rite of passage as

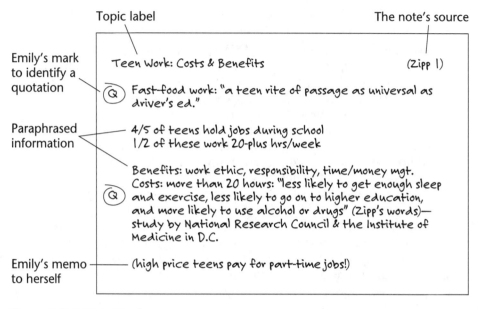

Topic label

The note's source

Emily's mark to identify a quotation

Teen Work: Costs & Benefits   (Zipp 1)

Ⓠ Fast-food work: "a teen rite of passage as universal as driver's ed."

Paraphrased information

4/5 of teens hold jobs during school
1/2 of these work 20-plus hrs/week

Benefits: work ethic, responsibility, time/money mgt.
Costs: more than 20 hours: "less likely to get enough sleep
Ⓠ and exercise, less likely to go on to higher education, and more likely to use alcohol or drugs" (Zipp's words)—
study by National Research Council & the Institute of Medicine in D.C.

Emily's memo to herself

(high price teens pay for part-time jobs!)

Figure 7.3 A Note Card

universal as driver's ed." They are ideal for teens because they require no special skills, and many believe that such jobs provide the educational benefit of teaching responsibility and good time and money management. These benefits may be more than offset by costs, however. Zipp cites a study by the National Research Council and the Institute of Medicine in Washington that teens who work more than twenty hours a week are "less likely to get enough sleep and exercise, less likely to go on to higher education, and more likely to use alcohol or drugs." These findings are disturbing, since four-fifths of American teens work at least part-time during the school year, and of these, half work more than twenty hours weekly (Zipp 1).

There are various systems for taking notes on cards, and you should use consistently a system that meets your needs. All good note-card systems have several features in common. In making note cards, you should follow these guidelines:

• **Put only related information on a note card.** That is, use one card for each important fact or idea. If you try to economize by crowding many unrelated notes from a source onto a single card, you will sacrifice flexibility later when you try to sort the cards by subjects. Some cards may contain long notes, whereas others may contain only a word or two. One source may provide you with notes on a dozen different cards, whereas another may give you only a single note (or no notes at all).

- **Label each card by topic.** A topic label helps you remember what a note card is about so that after you have finished taking notes from all your sources, you can easily arrange your cards according to topic. Emily selected the label *Teen Work: Costs & Benefits,* writing it in the upper left corner of the card. Similar labels appeared on two other cards that Emily prepared while reading different sources. When she was ready to organize her notes, Emily gathered these three cards together, discarded one of them that she knew she would not use, and arranged the remaining two in the order she was likely to use them in a first draft of her paper.

You should consider following a procedure similar to Emily's. Whenever you take a note, consider where within your subject the information might fit and give the note a label. The label may correspond to one of the divisions in your preliminary outline. If it does not, this may suggest that the organization of your paper is developing and changing and that you need to expand or revise your outline to reflect those changes.

- **Identify the source of each note precisely.** In the upper right corner of her note card, Emily identified her note's source: *(Zipp 1).* This is an example of a parenthetical note (explained in Chapter 9), and its purpose is to tell Emily that the information on the card comes from page 1 of the article written by Zipp. Emily had recorded the full information about that source in her working bibliography, so she needed only the author's last name to identify it.

It is important for each note card to contain all the information you will need in order to cite its source when you write your paper—so you can give the source credit in a parenthetical note. You will find nothing more frustrating as a researcher than having to search through sources at the last minute to find a page reference for a passage that you forgot to identify on a note card. It is smart to identify each source, as Emily did, just as you will identify it in the paper itself—with a parenthetical note. For that reason, you should consult Chapter 9 before you begin taking notes.

- **Clearly identify the kind of information your note contains.** Three principal kinds of information can appear on note cards; you must make it clear which is which, so you do not get confused later if you use the card in writing the paper:

   Direct quotations. The passage "teen rite of passage . . ." on Emily's card is quoted directly from the author, Yvonne Zipp. *Any time you put a source's own words on a note card, place them within quotation marks.* Do so even if everything on the card is a quotation. It is essential that when you read a note card later, you can tell whether the words are a direct quotation or your own paraphrase of the source. For this reason, you might even use a backup procedure for identifying quotes, as Emily did. She put a circled Q next to each quotation on her cards to be doubly sure she knew these were her source's exact words.

Your own comments. When you write a note from a source, it may inspire some additional thoughts of your own that you will want to jot down. You may also want to remind yourself later of how you intend to use the note in your paper. *Put your own comments in parentheses.* For example, at the bottom of Emily's note card, she wrote a note to herself about where she might use the material in her paper: "(high price teens pay. . .)." She placed these comments in parentheses to alert herself that these were her own ideas, not those of her source.

Paraphrase. Like Emily's, your cards should consist largely of paraphrases of what you have found in your sources. *Anything on a card that is not in quotation marks or in parentheses is assumed to be your paraphrasing of the source.* To paraphrase, recast the source's words into your own language, using your own phrasing and style.

* **Be selective in your note-taking.** Because many beginning researchers fear they will not have enough material to use in writing their papers, they often take too many notes. When it comes time to write the paper, they soon discover that if they were to make use of every note, their paper would be dozens of pages long. In fact, for each student who cannot find enough source material for a paper, many others discover to their surprise that they have more than enough.

With experience, researchers learn to be selective, restricting their note-taking to material they stand a good chance of using. Of course, no one makes use of every note card. Especially in the early stages of reading, a researcher does not have a clear notion of what the paper will include or of what information is available. As reading continues, however, hazy notions become more substantial, and the researcher can take notes more selectively.

Figure 7.4 shows two cards that Emily wrote when she read the article in *Human Resources Focus* magazine shown in Figure 7.1 on page 119.

■ AVOIDING PLAGIARISM

To ensure that you use your sources fairly and accurately, you should observe one additional guideline when you take notes: *Do your paraphrasing on the note card, not later.* If you do not intend to use a source's exact words, do not write those words on your card. (When you should and should not quote a source directly is discussed on pages 154–59.) It is wise to translate important information into your own words right after you read. This will save time and help you avoid unintentional *plagiarism*—using the source's words without quotation marks—when you begin to write from your notes. Paraphrasing and summarizing your sources now will also give you more focused notes, as well as force you to read and analyze your sources more carefully.

Since you cannot use everything in your sources, no matter how interesting, it is often necessary to boil down what you find into brief summaries of what is

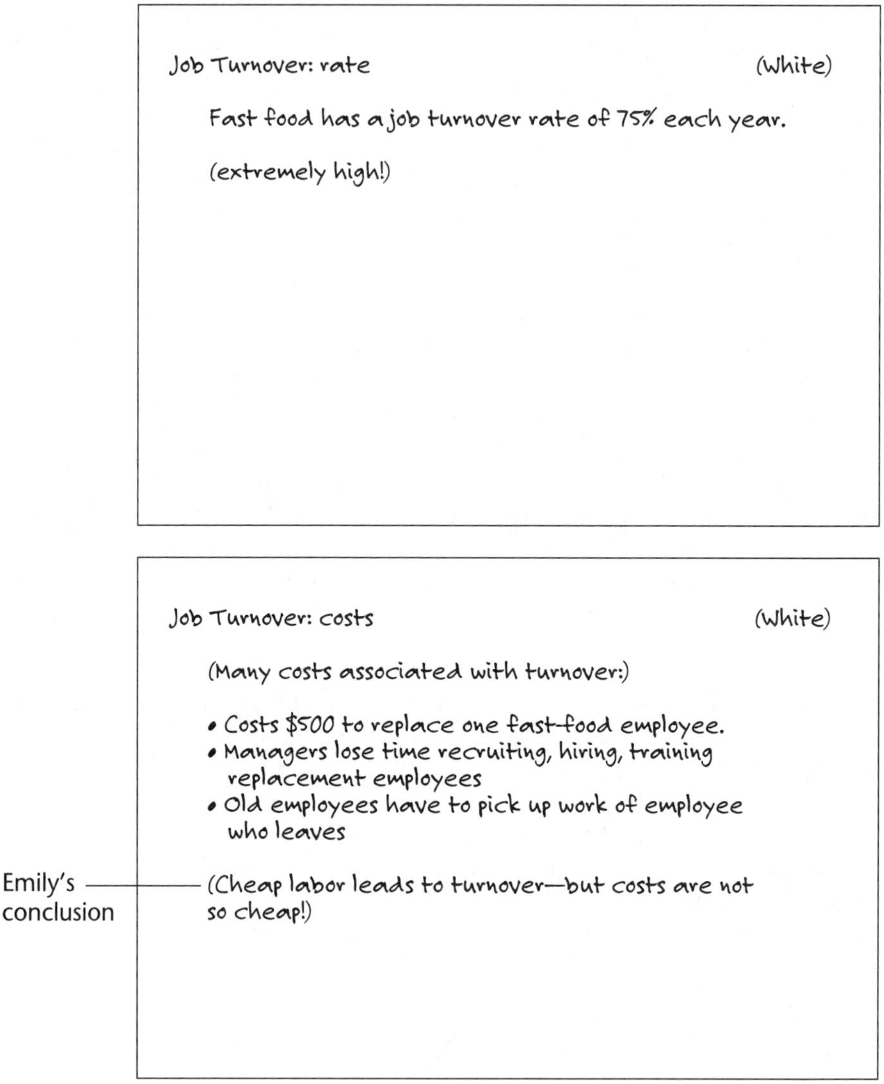

Job Turnover: rate   (White)

    Fast food has a job turnover rate of 75% each year.

    (extremely high!)

Job Turnover: costs   (White)

    (Many costs associated with turnover:)

    • Costs $500 to replace one fast-food employee.
    • Managers lose time recruiting, hiring, training
      replacement employees
    • Old employees have to pick up work of employee
      who leaves

Emily's ——————— (Cheap labor leads to turnover—but costs are not
conclusion   so cheap!)

Figure 7.4 Two additional note cards.

important. In general, the procedure for paraphrasing and summarizing a source is as follows:

1. When you have discovered a passage that you may want to use in your paper, reread it with care.

2. After you have reread it, put it aside and think about the essential idea you have learned. Then write that idea on your card in a brief version, using your own words and style. It is often best not to look at the passage while you write the note, so as to be less likely to plagiarize the original language.

Do not forget to indicate on your note card the specific source of the paraphrase.

Consider how Emily used material from one of her sources. First she read this passage from Eric Schlosser's book *Fast-Food Nation:*

> Although the McDonald brothers had never encountered the term "throughput" or studied "scientific management," they instinctively grasped the underlying principles and applied them in the Speedee Service System. The restaurant operating scheme they developed has been widely adopted and refined over the past half century. The ethos of the assembly line remains at its core. The fast-food industry's obsession with throughput has altered the way millions of Americans work, turned commercial kitchens into small factories, and changed familiar foods into commodities that are manufactured.

The original source

If Emily had written a note like the following, she might have plagiarized the passage when she used the note card to write her paper:

> The McDonald brothers grasped the "throughput" concept instinctively and applied it in their cooking system. The scheme they developed has been copied and improved upon over the past fifty years. It relies on an assembly-line mentality. An obsessive concern for "throughput" has changed the way countless Americans work, made restaurants into factories, and turned restaurant food into a manufactured commodity.

Note too close to the original

Notice how this passage—while it selects from the original, changes some words, and rearranges phrases—relies too closely on Schlosser's original wording. Now look at the note Emily wrote from this passage:

> McDonalds' founders revolutionized fast-food kitchens by introducing assembly-line techniques and "changed familiar foods into commodities that are manufactured."

A legitimate note

In this note, Emily succinctly summarized her understanding of Schlosser's ideas in her own words. Where Schlosser's words were memorable and could not easily be paraphrased, she quoted them exactly.

Putting source information into your own words does *not* mean substituting a few synonyms now and again as you copy your source's sentence onto your note card. For example, consider how it would be possible to misuse the following sentences from an article in *Good Housekeeping* by Patrick Kiger:

> Twenty-five percent of teenage deaths in the workplace are caused by violence, mostly in the commission of a robbery. Yet, though more than half of all teen employees work in retail jobs, only about a third of young workers are given any training on what to do if they're confronted by an armed robber.

The source's words

> One quarter of all teen deaths at work are the result of violence, mostly when robberies are committed. Even though more than fifty percent of teenage workers have retail jobs,

A plagiarized note

only a third of them are trained in any way about how to act
if they encounter an armed robber.

Observe that this is really the Kiger passage with a few word substitutions (*one quarter* for *twenty-five percent, at work* for *in the workplace*, etc.). Putting sources aside when you write note cards is one way to avoid this plagiarism by substitution. It also ensures that your paraphrase will be a genuine expression of your own understanding of a source's idea. Of course, if the exact words are particularly memorable or effective, you may wish to copy them down exactly, within quotation marks, for possible use in your paper.

The foregoing can be summed up as follows:

GUIDELINES for Avoiding Plagiarism

1. Whenever you use ideas or information from a source but do not intend to quote the source directly, paraphrase the source. You must restate the material in your own words, using your own phrasing and style. Merely substituting synonyms for the source's words or phrases is not acceptable. Do your paraphrasing at the time you take notes.

2. Whenever you intend to use the source's words, copy those words exactly onto a note card and place them within quotation marks. To be doubly sure that you will not later mistake the author's words for your own, place a circled letter Q (or some other prominent device) on the card next to the quotation.

3. For any borrowed material—whether a direct quotation or your paraphrase of it—carefully note the source and page number(s) on your note card so that you can cite them in your paper.

4. In your paper, you will give full credit to the sources of all borrowed material, both those you quote directly and those you paraphrase. The only exception is for commonly available factual information. (For further guidelines, see the section "When Are Notes Needed?" in Chapter 9.)

5. Observe the rules for acknowledging sources in your paper by providing acknowledgment phrases, parenthetical notes, and a list of works cited. (Further information about giving credit to sources can be found in Chapters 8 and 9.)

EXERCISES   **Note-Taking**

Imagine that, in doing a research project on the subject of urban legends, you discovered the following sources. Using the guidelines provided in this chapter, write notes from these sources. On your note cards, you may want to paraphrase some passages, quote others, and offer your own comments or responses. You may take more than one note from a passage.

1. The following appeared on page 175 in an essay by Richard A. Reuss titled "Suburban Folklore." Write one note card that captures an explanation of what is meant by the term "urban legend." Then write a second card whose heading is "Urban legend: example." Include at least one passage that you might want to quote in your paper.

    Another major component of the verbal lore of contemporary suburbia is the so-called urban legend, which perhaps deserves equal billing in the folklorist's lexicon as the "suburban legend," since so large a percentage of these narratives are set, either explicitly or implicitly, in a suburban locale. These narratives typically are brief accounts of anonymous people caught up in bizarre and traumatic, occasionally supernatural or humorous, circumstances because of the violation of some unspoken community or social norm. They are most intensively communicated among teenagers but are widely disseminated throughout the rest of the suburban population as well. One cycle of these stories revolves around babysitters left alone with their young charges. In one narrative the parents call to notify the sitter of a later returning time only to be informed by the teenager spaced out on LSD that all is well and "the turkey is in the oven." Knowing no such food is in the house, the parents speed home to find their baby roasting in the oven.

2. Darcy Lockman wrote an article titled "What Fuels Urban Legends?" for *Psychology Today.* The following paragraph appeared on page 21. Write a note card that summarizes the researchers' discovery about what causes urban legends to succeed.

    Psychologists at Stanford and Duke universities had another theory. "We proposed that ideas are selected and retained in part based on their ability to tap emotions that are common across individuals," explains Chip Heath, Ph.D., an associate professor of organizational behavior at Stanford. Heath and his colleagues decided to examine anecdotes that inspire disgust (some 25 percent of urban legends fit the bill). They took 12 urban legends and presented undergraduates at Duke University with three increasingly revolting versions of each story. . . . Amused undergrads consistently repeated the version that elicited the most disgust. "Emotion matters," says Heath. "It's not informational value alone that causes these things to succeed."

Before reading your sources and taking notes, you should consult Chapter 8, where conventions of quoting and paraphrasing are more fully explained. Chapter 9 demonstrates appropriate ways of acknowledging sources with parenthetical notes.

8 Reporting on Sources: Paraphrase and Quotation

Mostly when you *do* research on sources, you find out what other people have thought, discovered, said, or written. When you *report* on your research, you tell your readers what you have learned. The following very different passages could all be called examples of reporting on research sources:

1. My old man says he can lick your old man.

2. "If man does find the solution for world peace," wrote General George C. Marshall in 1945, "it will be the most revolutionary reversal of his record we have ever known."

3. Senator Woodling made it clear today that she would shortly declare herself a candidate for the presidency.

4. The first words ever transmitted by telephone were spoken by Bell to his assistant: "Mr. Watson, come here, I want you."

5. The Stoics argued that it was the highest wisdom to accept triumph without elation, tribulation without regret.

6. V. O. Key, Jr., a leading political scientist, offered this positive assessment of the role played by interest groups in American politics:

   > At bottom, group interests are the animating forces in the political process. . . . The chief vehicles for the expression of group interest are political parties and pressure groups. Through these formal mechanisms groups of people with like interests make themselves felt in the balancing of political forces. (Qtd. in Lowery 63–64)

These six passages all report on sources, since each of them communicates what has been learned from someone else. They certainly do so in different ways and with different effects. The first statement, you might guess, is spoken by one child to another, reporting on what he learned from his father. As for its authority, a listener might be wise to doubt that his father said any such thing. The last statement, in contrast, is surely an example of writing, not speech, since it has all the earmarks of a passage from a scholarly paper or article. Its very form, its direct quotation, its acknowledgment of its source and claim for his expertise (*V. O. Key, Jr., a leading political scientist*), and its careful source citation (*Qtd. in Lowery 63–64;*

i.e., the quotation was found on those pages in a work by Lowery) all lend it an impressive authority. The four middle passages could be either spoken or written.

There are other differences among them as well. Passages 2, 4, and 6 all present their sources' words through **direct quotation,** with the original language repeated in a word-for-word copy. Passages 1, 3, and 5, on the other hand, *paraphrase* their sources, with the source's ideas and information recast in different words. The identity of the sources in each statement is generally clear, although we are not told where the author of passage 5 learned about the Stoic philosophy; still, it is evident that the ideas presented are those of the Stoics and not the author. Of all these passages, however, only number 6 with its **parenthetical note** gives a careful **citation** of its source, the exact location from which the quotation was taken.

▮ THE CONVENTIONS OF REPORTING

Like the reporting of journalists, the reporting of scholars aims to get at and present the truth. To ensure accuracy and clarity, both types of writing follow careful rules and procedures.

Often these practices are identical in both fields. Both journalism and scholarship, for example, require that sources be acknowledged and identified. Both pay scant attention to unsupported opinions. On the other hand, both pay great respect to expert testimony. In reporting on sources, both fields observe the same time-honored conventions, including rules for paraphrasing, quoting, and even punctuating quotations. If there is one outstanding difference between scholarship and journalism, however, it is that scholarly writing, with its careful conventions of documentation, follows even more stringent procedures for identifying the precise sources from which ideas and information are taken.

This chapter is in large part devoted to these conventions. While some of it involves technicalities (e.g., does a comma go to the left or right of a quotation mark?), even they are important extensions of the care that researchers take to be accurate and truthful. While you are expected to become familiar with most of the conventions here, you should also regard this chapter as a resource that you can turn to often throughout your college career for guidance in presenting the results of your research.

▮ OPTIONS FOR PRESENTING SOURCES

Whenever you report on your research, you need to find a way of presenting to your readers what you have learned from your sources. Sometimes the appropriate method will be paraphrase; at other times, quotation. In fact, you have several options.

Imagine, for example, that in an introductory anthropology course, your instructor has assigned a research paper in which you are to analyze some aspect of American culture. You have chosen to write about the way Americans express their emotions, and in your research you come upon the following passage from page 248 of Ashley Montagu's book, *The American Way of Life*:

To be human is to weep. The human species is the only one in the whole of animated nature that sheds tears. The trained inability of any human being to weep is a lessening of his capacity to be human—a defect which usually goes deeper than the mere inability to cry. And this, among other things, is what American parents—with the best intentions in the world—have achieved for the American male. It is very sad. If we feel like it, let us all have a good cry—and clear our minds of those cobwebs of confusion which have for so long prevented us from understanding the ineluctable necessity of crying.

The passage expresses an interesting opinion—that American men have been trained, unnaturally, not to cry—and you want to use it in your paper. You can do so in many ways; the following are examples of your options.

Paraphrase

You can restate an author's ideas in your own words:

```
Montagu claims that American men have a diminished capacity
to be human because they have been trained by their culture
not to cry (248).
```

Direct Quotation of a Sentence

You can quote an author's exact words, as in these three examples:

```
In his book, The American Way of Life, Ashley Montagu writes,
"The trained inability of any human being to weep is a
lessening of his capacity to be human--a defect which usually
goes deeper than the mere inability to cry" (248).

According to Montagu, "To be human is to weep" (248).

"If we feel like it," writes Ashley Montagu, "let us all have
a good cry--and clear our minds of those cobwebs of confusion
which have for so long prevented us from understanding the
ineluctable necessity of crying" (248).
```

Quoting Part of a Sentence

You can incorporate part of an author's sentence into a sentence of your own:

```
One distinguished anthropologist calls the American male's
reluctance to cry "a lessening of his capacity to be human"
(Montagu 248).
```

```
Montagu finds it "very sad" that American men have a "trained
inability" to shed tears (248).
```

Quoting Longer Passages

You can quote more than one sentence:

```
Anthropologist Ashley Montagu argues that it is both
unnatural and harmful for American males not to cry:
            To be human is to weep. . . . The trained
            inability of any human being to weep is a
            lessening of his capacity to be human--a defect
            which usually goes deeper than the mere inability
            to cry. . . . It is very sad. (248)
```

In this chapter, we will study these options in some detail. We will first examine the precise methods of presenting sources through paraphrase and quotation. Afterward, we will look at strategies for using sources: when and where to use the options at our disposal. Chapter 9 considers the techniques for citing these sources in parenthetical notes.

■ ACKNOWLEDGING SOURCES

Whether you paraphrase or quote an author, it is important that you make it clear that it is the author's ideas, not your own, you are presenting. This is necessary for the sake of clarity and fairness—so that the reader knows which words, ideas, and discoveries are yours and which are your source's. Parenthetical notes, which cite a page reference and, if needed, the author's name, do that. Notice, too, that each of the preceding examples makes its indebtedness to its source clear through an ***acknowledgment phrase,*** such as "Montagu claims that. . . ." Other acknowledgment phrases that we might have used include the following:

```
Ashley Montagu maintains that . . .
Ashley Montagu, author of The American Way of Life,
        says that . . .
Montagu also believes that . . .
Professor Montagu argues that . . .
According to Ashley Montagu, the eminent
        anthropologist, American men . . .
```

Acknowledgment phrases

A quotation should never be placed in a paper without acknowledgment. Even a parenthetical note is not enough to identify a quotation. You must always introduce a quotation, telling your readers something about it. Avoid writing passages like this with a "naked" quotation in the middle:

Bad: un-
acknowledged
quotation

```
When my grandfather died, all the members of my family--men and
women alike--wept openly. We have never been ashamed to cry.
"To be human is to weep" (Montagu 248). I am sure we are more
human, and in better mental and physical health, because we are
able to express our feelings without artificial restraints.
```

Even though the parenthetical note identifies the source, readers find it awkward to read a quotation without knowing its origin in advance. Forcing them to skip ahead to find the note creates an undesirable interruption of the flow of the paper. These problems would not arise if the writer had used a simple phrase (e.g., *As anthropologist Ashley Montagu observed,*) to introduce the quotation:

Better:
acknowledged
quotation

```
When my grandfather died, all the members of my family--men
and women alike--wept openly. We have never been ashamed to
cry. As anthropologist Ashley Montagu observed, "To be human
is to weep" (248). I am sure we are more human, and in better
mental and physical health, because we are able to express
our feelings without artificial restraints.
```

Not only does the reader better understand the quotation's function with the introductory phrase, but the quotation has more impact as well because it has been attributed to a recognized authority.

Always give your readers enough information to identify your sources. The first time you refer to a source, give both the person's first and last names. Unless the source is a well-known figure, identify him or her so that the reader can understand why this particular person is being quoted.

```
Winston Churchill said, . . .
```

First references

```
Cynthia Bathurst, author of The Computer Crisis,
          believes that . . .
```

```
According to Valerie Granville, British ambassador to
          Bhutan during the Sherpa Riots, . . .
```

```
Rock star Mick Jagger gave a flip answer: . . .
```

After the first reference, the source's last name is sufficient:

```
Churchill said that . . .
Later Jagger remarked, . . .
```

Although acknowledgment phrases almost always introduce quotations, they are sometimes unnecessary with paraphrased material. As a general rule, use an acknowledgment phrase when the paraphrased material represents an original idea or opinion of the source, when the source's credentials lend the material authority, or when you wish to distance yourself from opinions with which you disagree.

```
Anthropologist Ashley Montagu argues that crying is a
distinctively human activity--as appropriate and necessary
for males as for females (248).
```

However, an acknowledgment phrase is not needed for largely factual information, as in these passages:

```
At one point in his life, even Alex Haley, the author of
Roots, possessed only eighteen cents and two cans of sardines
(Powell 179).

One study has found that firstborns score better in
achievement tests that measure language and mathematics
skills (Weiss 51).
```

In such cases, the parenthetical notes provide adequate recognition of sources. (Parenthetical notes are discussed in Chapter 9.) Use your best judgment about whether an acknowledgment phrase is called for with paraphrased material. When in doubt, however, provide the acknowledgment phrase. It is better to err on the side of *over-* rather than *under-*recognition of your sources.

RELYING ON EXPERTS

Besides being fair, acknowledging the contribution of a source can also add force to your own writing. In most cases, the sources you present will have greater expertise than you on the subject; a statement from one of them can command greater respect than an unsupported statement from you, a nonexpert. To illustrate this, assume that, in writing a research paper, you quote Montagu on the subject of crying and identify him to your readers as an eminent anthropologist. Could you have made the point equally effectively if instead you had written the following?

```
I think it is wrong that men in America have been brought up
to think it is not manly to cry. Crying is natural. Our
macho-man mentality takes a terrible toll on our emotions.
```

While you are entitled to your opinions, a reader who doubts your expertise on the subject is likely to question whether you have considered all aspects and implications of your position. After all, what reason does the reader have to trust you? However, when an expert such as Montagu is quoted, many of the doubts are removed and the statement carries greater weight.

This is not to say that experts are automatically right. Experts do not always agree with each other, and progress in humanity's quest for truth often comes as new ideas are introduced to challenge old ones. What it does mean is that experts are people who have studied their subjects thoroughly and have earned the right to be listened to with respect. Since you will not often begin with a thorough knowledge of the subjects you write about in research papers, your writing will rely heavily on what you have learned from expert sources.

■ PARAPHRASING SOURCES

Most of the time when you present ideas or information from sources, you will paraphrase them. To *paraphrase* a statement or a piece of writing is to recast it into different words. Paraphrase is the least cumbersome way of communicating what a source has said, as well as the easiest to read. Often the source is too technical for your readers or too wordy; you can present the source's point more clearly and succinctly using your own words. When you paraphrase a source, be accurate and faithful to what your source wrote, but use your own style and phrasing. Imagine, for example, that you wished to make use of this passage as a research source:

> Nearly forty years ago Damon Runyon nearly collapsed in laughter when he covered the trial of George McManus, a gambler, who was accused of shooting Arnold Rothstein, another gambler, who thereupon died. The cause of Damon Runyon's mirth was the sight of the witnesses and jurors in the case running out into the halls during court recesses to place bets with their bookies—even as they considered the evils of gambling in the city.
>
> —Edwin P. Hoyt, *The Golden Rot*

You can paraphrase this information in a briefer version, using your words:

Good

```
According to Edwin P. Hoyt, Damon Runyon was highly amused
that both witnesses and jurors in a gambling trial would
place bets with their bookies during court recesses.
```

What you must *not* do is simply change a word or two while keeping the structure of the original intact:

```
Edwin P. Hoyt writes that about forty years ago Damon Runyon        Bad

almost fell down from laughing when he was a reporter for the

trial of gambler George McManus, accused of murdering another

gambler, Arnold Rothstein.
```

You can avoid word-substitution paraphrase, as well as unintentional plagiarism, if you paraphrase from memory rather than directly from the original copy. Chapter 7 describes the best method as follows: *Read the passage so that you understand it; then put it aside, and write your recollection of its meaning on a note card, in your own words.* Be certain to observe the guidelines for avoiding plagiarism (see pages 127–30).

Paraphrasing a Source

EXERCISE

Imagine that each of the following is a source for a research project. Write a paraphrase of important information from each quotation as you would on a note card. Then write it as you would in the paper itself, giving credit to your source with a suitable acknowledgment phrase. *(Note:* You do not need to present all of the information from each passage in either your paraphrases or your acknowledgments.)

a. *Source:* Linus Pauling. He won Nobel Prizes for both Chemistry (1954) and Peace (1962).

  Quotation
  Science is the search for truth—it is not a game in which one tries to beat his opponent, to do harm to others. We need to have the spirit of science in international affairs, to make the conduct of international affairs the effort to find the right solution, the just solution of international problems, not the effort by each nation to get the better of other nations, to do harm to them when it is possible.

b. *Source:* Edwin P. Hoyt. This quotation is from his book, *The Golden Rot: A Somewhat Opinionated View of America,* published in 1964.

  Quotation
  Let there be no mistake, the pressures on government for destruction of wilderness areas will grow every time the nation adds another million in population. The forest service has been fighting such pressures in the West for fifty years. Any national forest visitor can gauge the degree of success of the "multiple use program" of the forest service very nicely by taking a fishing rod and setting out to catch some trout. He will find mile after mile of the public waters posted by private landowners who do not allow fishing or hunting on their property—or on the government property they lease. Inevitably this includes the best beaver dams and open stretches of water along the streams.

c. *Source:* Marvin Harris. He is an anthropology professor and author of several books on human behavior throughout the world.

    Quotation
    The trouble with the "confessions" is that they were usually obtained while the accused witch was being tortured. Torture was routinely applied until the witch confessed to having made a pact with the Devil and having flown to a sabbat [a witches' meeting]. It was continued until the witch named the other people who were present at the sabbat. If a witch attempted to retract a confession, torture was applied even more intensely until the original confession was reconfirmed. This left a person accused of witchcraft with the choice of dying once and for all at the stake or being returned repeatedly to the torture chambers. Most people opted for the stake. As a reward for their cooperative attitude, penitent witches could look forward to being strangled before the fire was lit.

d. *Source:* Jessica Mitford. She was a well-known muckraker, an investigative journalist who specialized in exposing scandals and abuses.

    Quotation
    True, a small minority of undertakers are beginning to face the facts and to exhibit more flexibility in their approach to customers, even to develop some understanding and respect for people who as a matter of principle do not want the full funerary treatment ordinarily prescribed by the industry. But the industry as a whole, and particularly the association leaders, are unable to come to grips with the situation that confronts them today because their whole operation rests on a myth: the assumption that they have the full and unqualified backing of the vast majority of the American people, that the costly and lavish funeral of today, with all its fabulous trimmings, is but a reflection of American insistence on "the best" in all things. It is particularly hard for them to grasp the idea that a person who has lived well or even luxuriously might *prefer* the plainest disposition after death.

▣ QUOTING SOURCES

In research writing, sources are quoted less often than they are paraphrased, but quotation is more complicated and requires more explanation.

Punctuating Quotations

The conventions of punctuation have driven many a student nearly to distraction. They seem arbitrary and often illogical. If you were to set about tinkering with the rules of punctuating, you could very likely make some worthwhile improvements in the current system. Nonetheless, the system as it stands is well established and unlikely to change. Your consolation is that, even if it is complicated, it can be mastered, and it does serve its purpose of giving readers helpful signals that make reading easier. In the case of quotations, punctuation makes it clear just which passages are your own and which belong to your sources.

The following are the most important punctuation conventions for presenting sources. You should learn these guidelines and follow them carefully.

1. *Use double quotation marks (" ") before and after a source's words when you copy them directly.*

At the Battle of Trafalgar, Admiral Nelson exhorted his

fleet: "England expects every man to do his duty."

The phrase "bats in the belfry" was coined by the writer Eden

Phillpotts.

Double quotation marks

2. *Use single quotation marks (' ') before and after quoted material when it occurs within other quoted material—that is, when it occurs inside double quotation marks.*

Charles and Mary Beard contend that the American government

was not established as a democracy: "The Constitution did not

contain the word or any word lending countenance to it,

except possibly the mention of 'We, the people,' in the

preamble."

We used this example earlier in the chapter: "According to

Ashley Montagu, 'To be human is to weep.'"

Single quotation marks

3. *Indent a quotation that takes up more than four lines in your paper.* In typing, indent one inch (ten spaces) from the left margin. Do not indent any additional spaces from the right margin. If you are quoting a single paragraph or less, do not indent the first line of the quotation any additional spaces:

The millionaire Andrew Carnegie believed that free enterprise

and private charity, not government social programs, offered

the best solution to the problem of poverty:

   Thus is the problem of Rich and Poor to be

   solved. The law of accumulation will be left

   free; the laws of distribution free.

   Individualism will continue, but the millionaire

Indent the left margin one inch (ten spaces). Do not indent the right margin.

```
will be but a trustee of the poor; entrusted
for a season with a great part of the increased
wealth of the community, but administering it
for the community far better than it could or
would have done for itself.
```

However, if the indented quotation consists of two or more paragraphs, indent the first line of each paragraph an additional quarter inch or three spaces:

Indent
paragraphs an
additional
quarter inch
(three spaces)

```
Florence Nightingale questioned the unequal treatment of
men and women in Victorian England:
        Now, why is it more ridiculous for a man
    than for a woman to do worsted work and drive
    out everyday in the carriage? Why should we
    laugh if we see a parcel of men sitting around
    a drawing room table in the morning, and think
    it all right if they were women?
        Is man's time more valuable than woman's?
    Or is the difference between man and woman
    this, that women have confessedly nothing to do?
```

These passages demonstrate other guidelines as well:

- **An indented quotation is never placed within quotation marks.** Quotation marks are unnecessary since the indenting already makes it clear that the passage is a quotation.
- **When typing, do not skip extra lines before or after an indented quotation.** The entire paper, including such quotations, is double-spaced.

4. *Accuracy is essential in quoting a source.*
   - **Copy a quoted passage exactly as it is printed.** The only exception is for obvious typographical errors, which you should correct. Otherwise, make no changes in a quoted passage, even if you disagree with its wording or punctuation. For example, if you, rather than Andrew Carnegie, had been the author of the quotation that concludes on the top of this page, you might have used a colon or dash after the word *poor* instead of a semicolon. But since Carnegie used a semicolon, that is the way it must appear when you copy it.

- **Insert *[sic]*, the Latin word meaning "thus," in brackets, immediately after an apparent error.** Do so only if you feel it necessary to identify it as your source's error, not your error in copying the passage.

```
The régime posted a proclamation on every streetcorner:

"Amnesty will be granted all mutineers who lay down their arms.

Die-heart [sic] traitors who persist in rebellion will be shot."
```

This device should be used only rarely. Avoid using *sic* to belittle a source with whom you disagree.

5. *Use punctuation to separate a quotation from an acknowledgment phrase or sentence.*

- **Use a comma or colon when the phrase comes before the quotation. A comma is preferred when the introduction is not a complete sentence:**

```
Jacques Delille wrote, "Fate chooses our relatives, we

choose our friends."
```
The introduction is not a complete sentence

```
As Al Jolson remarked, "You ain't heard nothin' yet, folks."
```

- **A colon is preferred when the introduction is a complete sentence:**

```
Edmund Burke believed that sadism is a component of human

nature: "I am convinced that we have a degree of delight and

that no small one, in the real misfortunes and pains of others."
```
The introduction is a complete sentence

```
The last words in Act II are spoken by Hamlet: "The play's

the thing / Wherein I'll catch the conscience of the King."
```
Colon

- **Use a colon to introduce an indented quotation:**

```
From his jail cell Martin Luther King wrote about the law:
        An unjust law is a code that a numerical or power
        majority group compels a minority group to obey
        but does not make binding on itself. This is
        difference made legal. By the same token, a just
```

```
                    law is a code that a majority compels a minority
                    to follow and that it is willing to follow
                    itself. This is sameness made legal.
```

- However, no punctuation is needed when a quotation is a continuation of the introductory sentence:

No colon

```
                    According to the Library Bill of Rights, libraries are
                    forums for information and ideas, and they have
                        . . . the responsibility to provide . . .
                    all points of view on all questions and issues
                    of our times, and to make these ideas and
                    opinions available to anyone who needs or wants
                    them, regardless of age, race, religion,
                    national origin, or social and political views.
```

- Use a comma when the acknowledgment phrase comes after the quotation, unless the quotation ends in a question mark or exclamation point:

Comma

```
                    "When you have nothing to say, say nothing," wrote Charles
                    Caleb Colton.
```

But:

No comma

```
                    "Who can refute a sneer?" asked William Paley.
```

- When the acknowledgment phrase is inserted within a quoted sentence, begin and end it with commas:

Commas

```
                    "Politics," said Bismarck, "is not an exact science."
```

- Use no punctuation at all (other than quotation marks) when you make quoted words part of your own sentence:

No comma

```
                    Robert E. Rogers's advice to the Class of 1929 at MIT was to
                    "marry the boss's daughter."
```

The word *that* incorporates a quotation that follows it into your sentence. Note carefully the difference in punctuation among the following three sentences:

–**Quotation treated as an independent sentence:**

Henry Ford said, "History is more or less bunk."   Comma

–**Quotation incorporated into the sentence:**

Henry Ford said that "history is more or less bunk."   No comma

–**Quotation paraphrased:**

Henry Ford said that history is nonsense.   No comma

6. *Capitalize the first word of a quotation when it is treated as an independent sentence. Do not capitalize it when it is incorporated into your own sentence.*

Margaret Hungerford gave us the famous saying, "Beauty is in the eye of the beholder."   Uppercase letter

Like Margaret Hungerford, many psychologists believe that "beauty is in the eye of the beholder."   Lowercase letter

7. *The trickiest rules apply to punctuation at the close of a quotation. Refer to the following examples whenever necessary.*

- **Commas and periods are always placed inside a closing quotation mark:**

"From the sublime to the ridiculous is but a step," wrote Napoleon.   Comma inside the quotation mark

Martin Joseph Routh offered timeless advice over a century ago: "You will find it a very good practice always to verify your references, sir."   Period inside the quotation mark

Period inside
single and
double
quotation
marks

Judge Learned Hand wrote, "I should like to have every court
begin, 'I beseech ye in the bowels of Christ, think that we
may be mistaken.' "

- **Colons, semicolons, and dashes are placed outside a closing quotation mark:**

Colon outside
the quotation
mark

"Blood, toil, tears and sweat": these were the sacrifices
Churchill promised to his country.

Semicolon
outside the
quotation mark

On his deathbed, O. Henry said, "Turn up the lights--I don't
want to go home in the dark"; then he expired.

- **Questions marks and exclamation points go inside the closing quotation mark when they belong to the quotation, but outside when they do not:**

Question mark be-
longs to quotation

Macbeth asked, "What is the night?"

Question mark does
not belong to quo-
tation

Who said, "Cowards die many times before their deaths"?

Exclamation point
belongs to quotation

Colonel Sidney Sherman first shouted, "Remember the
Alamo!"

Exclamation point
does not belong to
quotation

How dare you respond, "No comment"!

- **For punctuation following a parenthetical note, see pages 164–66 or the quick reference guide on the inside back cover.**

8. *Follow these conventions for quoting poetry:*
   - **Use a slash with a space before and after it to divide quoted lines of poetry:**

Space, slash,
space

Ogden Nash wrote, "Candy / Is dandy / But liquor /
Is quicker."

- Longer passages of poetry are indented:

```
Emily Dickinson wrote

        "Faith" is a fine invention

        When Gentlemen can see--

        But Microscopes are prudent

        In an Emergency.
```

Indent the left
margin ten
spaces

Like other indented passages, poetry is not placed within quotation marks. The word *"Faith"* is in quotation marks because Dickinson punctuated it that way in her poem.

Punctuating Quotations

EXERCISES

1. The following passages that appear in brackets are quotations, printed with their original capitalization and punctuation. Remove the brackets and add whatever punctuation is necessary. Make whatever additions and changes are necessary to put each sentence into proper form.

   a. Anne Morrow Lindbergh wrote [The wave of the future is coming and there is no fighting it.].

   b. Rachel Carson was among the first to warn against the pollution of the environment [As crude a weapon as the cave man's club, the chemist's barrage has been hurled against the fabric of life.].

   c. [Gentlemen of the old régime in the South would say, "A woman's name should appear in print but twice—when she marries and when she dies."] wrote Arthur Wallace Calhoun in 1918.

   d. [Gentlemen] wrote Anita Loos [always seem to remember blondes.].

   e. How many students today believe with James B. Conant that [He who enters a university walks on hallowed ground.]?

   f. William Morris called this a [golden rule] [Have nothing in your houses that you do not know to be useful, or believe to be beautiful.]; a rather different conception of what a house should be is presented in a statement of architect Le Corbusier [A house is a machine for living in.].

   g. Freud never underestimated the role of religion in human culture [If one wishes to form a true estimate of the full grandeur of religion, one must keep in mind what it undertakes to do for men. It gives them information about the source and origin of the universe, it assures them of protection and final happiness amid the changing vicissitudes of life, and it guides their thoughts and motions by means of precepts which are backed by the whole force of its authority.].

h. Poverty is not portrayed as romantic in Keats's poem "Lamia"
[Love in a hut, with water and a crust,
Is—Love, forgive us!—cinders, ashes, dust.]

i. Gloating on his pact with the devil, Doctor Faustus asked [Have not I made blind Homer sing to me?].

j. [We was robbed!] shouted manager Joe Jacobs into the microphone in 1932, when the decision went against his fighter, Max Schmeling.

2. Create sentences that incorporate quotations according to the following guidelines:

a. Use this quotation by Mark Twain in a sentence that begins with an acknowledgment phrase:

Man is the only animal that blushes. Or needs to.

b. Use the following quotation by Havelock Ellis in a sentence that ends with an acknowledgment phrase:

The place where optimism most flourishes is the lunatic asylum.

c. Use the following quotation by George Santayana in a sentence with an acknowledgment phrase inserted within it:

Fanaticism consists in redoubling your efforts when you have forgotten your aim.

d. Incorporate a paraphrase of this quotation into a sentence that acknowledges its author, Congressman Grimsley Buttersloop:

My opponents have accused me of embezzlement, drinking, fooling around, and falling asleep during committee meetings. The only thing they haven't accused me of is not loving my country, and that they can never do.

e. When you quote the following, let the reader know that its author, Frank Winslow, deliberately misspelled the word *souperior* in a letter to his aunt, Martha Fleming:

All I can say of your clam chowder is that it was positively souperior.

Altering Quotations

Sometimes when you write about your research, you will want to use a quotation that does not precisely fit. Either it lacks a word or a phrase that would make its meaning clear to your readers, or else it contains too much material—unnecessary words that are not relevant to your point. For example, imagine that you found this quotation from a person named Vanessa O'Keefe:

I absolutely long to prove to the world, as I said in an interview yesterday, that a perpetual motion machine is not an impossibility.

Assume you wanted to introduce it with the phrase *Vanessa O'Keefe announced that she. . . .* Fortunately, there are methods that allow you to alter such a quotation to fit your needs. By using them, you can write

```
Vanessa O'Keefe announced that she "absolutely long[ed] to
prove to the world . . . that a perpetual motion machine is
not an impossibility."
```

As you can see, you can make certain alterations in quotations to suit your needs. When you do so, however, you must obey these two guidelines:

1. You must make it completely clear to your readers precisely what changes you have made.

2. Your alterations must not distort the meaning or essential phrasing of a quotation or make it appear to say something other than what the author intended.

The following methods may be followed to alter quotations.

Adding to Quotations: Brackets [ ]

Whenever a word, phrase, or suffix needs to be added to a quotation to make its meaning clear, you may insert it within **brackets.** Brackets are most commonly used to explain a reference. For example, it would not be evident to a reader of this quotation that it was the United States that José Martí was referring to as "the monster":

```
I have lived in the monster and I know its insides; and my
sling is the sling of David.
```

By using brackets when you quote this sentence, you can make the reference clear:

```
In a letter to Manuel Mercado, Martí wrote, "I have lived in
the monster [the United States] and I know its insides; and
my sling is the sling of David."
```

Insertion in brackets

Similarly, you can insert modifiers in brackets. The following insertion makes it clear which frontier is being referred to:

```
Churchill said, "That long [Canadian-American] frontier
from the Atlantic to the Pacific Oceans, guarded only by
```

```
neighborly respect and honorable obligations, is an example

to every country and a pattern for the future of the world."
```

Another use for brackets is to provide brief translations of foreign or archaic words:

```
Chaucer wrote, "A fol [fool] can not be stille."
```

Unusual terms may also require explanation. For example, if you used the following quotation in writing about doctors performing unnecessary operations, you might need to explain the term *arthroscopic surgery* to your readers.

```
According to Dr. Robert Metcalf, who teaches orthopedic

surgery at the University of Utah, the problem exists in

his field as well: "There's considerable concern that

arthroscopic surgery [a technique for repairing damaged

knees] is being overutilized and is sometimes being done in a

manner damaging to healthy cartilage."
```

When the unclear term is a simple pronoun, you can replace it altogether with the noun it refers to. For example, in the following quotation, instead of "They [the Americans] are the hope of the world," you can write

```
Baron de l'Aulne expressed a more favorable opinion in 1778:

"[The Americans] are the hope of the world."
```

Instead of brackets, however, sometimes the simplest solution is to incorporate the unclear portion into your own sentence:

```
Writing about Americans in 1778, Baron de l'Aulne expressed the

more favorable opinion that "they are the hope of the world."
```

Or better still:

```
In 1778, Baron de l'Aulne expressed the more favorable

opinion that Americans are "the hope of the world."
```

The best rule is to use brackets when they provide the simplest way of making the source's meaning clear to your readers. As you can see, bracketing is a useful tool that can solve several writing problems. At the same time, it should not be overused. As with other devices, when brackets appear again and again in a paper, readers will find them distracting.

Subtracting from Quotations: Ellipsis Dots (. . .)

You can omit irrelevant parts of a quotation and replace them with *ellipsis dots,* three typed periods separated by spaces. The part you omit can be a word, a phrase, one or more sentences, or even a much longer passage. As with everything you alter, there is one important condition: You must not distort the author's meaning or intentions.

Good writers edit their writing, paring away what is unnecessary, off the point, or distracting. Quotations are used most effectively when you select them carefully and when you keep only the pertinent parts and omit what is not needed. As an example, consider again the passage by Ashley Montagu quoted earlier:

> To be human is to weep. The human species is the only one in the whole of animated nature that sheds tears. The trained inability of any human being to weep is a lessening of his capacity to be human—a defect which usually goes deeper than the mere inability to cry. And this, among other things, is what American parents—with the best intentions in the world—have achieved for American males. It is very sad. If we feel like it, let us all have a good cry—and clear our minds of those cobwebs of confusion which have for so long prevented us from understanding the ineluctable necessity of crying.

As interesting as this passage is, you might be best able to make your point if you quote only parts of it. For example:

```
Anthropologist Ashley Montagu argues that it is both

unnatural and harmful for American males not to weep:

          To be human is to weep. .  .  .  The trained

     inability of any human being to weep is a lessening

     of his capacity to be human--a defect which usually

     goes deeper than the mere inability to cry. . . .

     It is very sad.
```

Ellipsis dots indicate a deletion

Whole sentences have been removed from the passage and replaced with ellipses. Parts of a sentence can also be omitted, as follows:

```
Montagu feels that "the trained inability . . . to weep is a

defect which usually goes deeper than the mere inability to cry."
```

As with brackets, there is a danger in overusing ellipses. Not only can they become distracting to the reader, but they can also defeat your purpose in quoting, as with this monstrosity:

Montagu feels that "the . . . inability . . . to weep is
a defect which . . . goes deeper than the . . . inability
to cry."

The preceding sentence makes so many changes in the original quotation that it can no longer be said to communicate Montagu's phrasing, and the point of using direct quotation is lost. Paraphrase would make much more sense; for example:

Montagu feels that the inability to cry is a more significant
defect than many realize.

Ellipsis dots are not needed when it is already obvious that the passage you have quoted is only a part of the original:

Ellipsis dots are
not needed

A man's inability to cry, according to Montagu, is a
"lessening of his capacity to be human."

You should use ellipses, however, when it is not obvious that you are quoting only a portion of the source's complete sentence:

Montagu wrote, "The trained inability of any human being to
weep is a lessening of his capacity to be human. . . ."

When the omission comes at the front of a quoted sentence, you may capitalize the first word if you put the first letter in brackets:

Montagu offered this advice: "[L]et us all have a good
cry. . . ."

Using Brackets and Ellipsis Dots

1. The following is part of the transcript of a reporter's interview with a political candidate, Paul Shawn. Read it and comment on the quotations that follow.

Q: Your opponent, Darla Stowe, says you hunger for money. Is that true?

A: If you mean, do I want to earn enough for my family to live decently, then yes, I hunger for money. I think that's true of almost everyone. But I hunger for other things as well: peace, justice, brotherhood, and national prosperity.

Q: Your opponent also says you are using this race as a stepping-stone to higher office. Is this true?

A: Actually, I'm quite certain I have no more desire for higher office than she has.

Which of the following quotations can be justified on the basis of this interview? Explain why each of them is fair or unfair, and discuss its use of brackets, ellipses, and paraphrase.

a. Paul Shawn says he "hunger[s] for . . . peace, justice, brotherhood, and national prosperity."

b. Shawn admitted, "[Y]es, I hunger for money."

c. Shawn's opponent accuses him of using this race to seek further political advancement, but he responds, "I have no more desire for higher office. . . ."

d. Shawn believes that a "hunger for money" is "true of almost everyone."

e. Quick in responding to an opponent's accusation, Shawn retorted that he has "no more desire for higher office than [Darla Stowe] has."

f. While admitting he has the same interest as most people in earning a comfortable living for his family, Shawn says he has other goals as well: "peace, justice, brotherhood, and national prosperity."

2. Use quotations from the following passages according to the instructions given for each. Introduce each quotation with an acknowledgment phrase.

a. Quotation

I always dreamed of it as being a kind of earthly paradise where no troubles ever intruded.

Speaker: Linnea Aycock

Instructions:
(1) Introduce the quotation with the acknowledgment phrase *Linnea Aycock said,* and use brackets to show that Aycock is talking about Tahiti. (2) Write another version, this time quoting only part of her sentence. Without using brackets, show that she is talking about Tahiti.

b. Quotation

Our inspiration was a cartoon that appeared in a children's magazine.

Speaker: A NASA scientist

Instruction:
Use brackets to indicate that the cartoon inspired the design of a new space helmet.

c. Quotation

My generation never thought of college in terms of making ourselves employable. It was OK to be interested in Plato or T. S. Eliot or Freud, but never in IBM or General Mills. It was easy then to regard jobs with contempt since there were so many of them. It is very different with today's job-conscious generation. The response to Shakespeare now is likely to be, "How will he help me in my job?"

Writer: Ronni Jacobsen

Instruction:
Quote two or three sentences that communicate the main idea of this passage. Use ellipsis dots to represent what you omit.

d. Quotation

My message to all you students is that hard work and self-discipline are the keys—and you should never forget this—to success in your college and business careers.

Speaker: Cyrus T. Pierpont

Instruction:
Begin with *Cyrus T. Pierpont told students that.* Omit unnecessary parts of the quotation, including the first eight words and the part that is surrounded by dashes. Although it is not necessary, you can change *your* to *their.*

e. Quotation

If idiots drive motor vehicles when they are drunk, this should happen: they should lose their licenses and be sent to jail—for 90 days or longer.

Speaker: Sergeant Robert Symmes

Instruction:
Introduce the quotation with the words *Sergeant Robert Symmes said that.* Alter the quotation by deleting the word *if,* inserting *who* after *idiots,* omitting *this should happen:,* and making whatever other changes are necessary.

■ WHEN TO QUOTE AND WHEN TO PARAPHRASE

One of the questions beginning research writers often ask their instructors is: "How many quotations should I put in my paper?" Their uncertainty is not usually allayed by the appropriate answer: "It depends." What it depends on are the circumstances of the individual case—and your own good judgment. While there is no easy answer to the question, some useful guidelines can help you decide how to use your sources.

1. *Do not overquote.* In fact, do not quote very much at all. Most beginning researchers quote far too much in their papers. Quotations should be saved for special occasions, and with good reason: Readers find papers that are filled with quo-

tation after quotation unpleasant and hard to read. (By now you are probably tired of reading quotations in this chapter!) When they encounter a great many quotations, readers will often skim them or skip them entirely. No one likes to read a passage like this:

"Early [Roman] amphitheaters," according to Fredericks, "were temporary wooden structures that often collapsed under the weight of spectators, with the result of great loss of life" (40). Bennett reports:

Bad (too many quotations)

> The most famous of all buildings of this kind was
> the Flavian Amphitheater in Rome. Also called the
> Colosseum because of its size, it was begun by the
> emperor Vespasian and dedicated by his son Titus
> in A.D. 80. . . . After the 6th century it was
> used as a fortress and a quarry. (101)

Fredericks says, "Although accounts of the time report it held more than 80,000 spectators, modern estimates place its capacity at 50,000" (42). The architectural historian Anne Ramsey wrote:

> Structurally and functionally, the Roman Colosseum
> has been rivaled by no comparably sized arenas
> until the most recent age. Even today it remains a
> model of planning for rapid crowd access and
> exit and for unobstructed spectator sight lines.
> (17-18)

Of these four quotations, piled one on the other, all but the last, which expresses the opinion of an authority, should be rephrased in the writer's own words. The passage then becomes much more readable:

The first Roman amphitheaters were temporary structures built of wood. Because they could not long support the great crowds who attended the spectacles, they often collapsed in terrible disasters (Fredericks 40). Later they were replaced

Better

by permanent facilities, the most famous of which was the
Flavian Amphitheater, better known as the Colosseum. Begun by
the emperor Vespasian, it was dedicated in A.D. 80 by his
son, Titus. It served as a sports and gladiatorial arena with
a capacity of 50,000 spectators until the sixth century. It
was then allowed to deteriorate, being used occasionally as a
fortress and frequently stripped of its stone for use in
other buildings (Bennett 101). Nevertheless, it survived and
remains today one of the most widely admired Roman buildings.
Architectural historian Anne Ramsey writes:

> Structurally and functionally, the Roman
> Colosseum has been rivaled by no comparably sized
> arenas until the most recent age. Even today it
> remains a model of planning for rapid crowd
> access and exit and for unobstructed spectator
> sight lines. (17-18)

The rule can be restated as follows: *If you have a choice between quoting and paraphrasing a source, paraphrase it.*

2. *Always paraphrase a source, except when a direct quotation is needed.* You should paraphrase most of your sources most of the time, especially under the following conditions.

- **Paraphrase if the source provides factual information.** Avoid quotations like the following:

Unnecessary
quotation

The collapsing of bridges was a considerable problem in the
past: "In the latter half of the 19th century, American
bridges were failing at the rate of 25 or more per year!"
(Worth 29).

Instead, state this factual information in your own words:

Better

A century ago American bridges were far more dangerous
than today, collapsing at an annual rate of 25 or more
(Worth 29).

• **Paraphrase if you can say it more briefly or clearly in your own words.**

Sun worshiper Andrea Bergeron claims that "Solists face   Wordy
grave and persistent discrimination, not the least of which
is that which prohibits a fair hearing for our beliefs.
Because our beliefs are not traditional we are dismissed as
cultists" (202).

Very likely, you would need nothing more elaborate than this brief paraphrase to make your point:

Andrea Bergeron feels that she and her fellow Solists (sun   Better
worshipers) are discriminated against and their religious
views are not taken seriously (202).

3. *Quote a source directly when the source's words work better than your own.*
If you use them sparingly, quotations can be effective in your research writing.
Use them in the following cases:

• **Quote when the source's words are phrased in a particularly eloquent
  or memorable way.** Paraphrase could not do justice to the following quotations:

General Patton wrote, "A pint of sweat will save a gallon
of blood" (987).

In 1947, physicist J. Robert Oppenheimer expressed the
unease felt by many scientists about their role in
developing the atom bomb: "In some sort of crude sense
which no vulgarity, no humor, no overstatement can quite
extinguish, the physicists have known sin; and this is a
knowledge which they cannot lose" (1055).

You may not always find it easy to decide whether a statement from a
source is so well phrased that it should be presented to readers directly. Use
your best judgment. In cases where you are in doubt, the wisest course is to
paraphrase.

- **Quote when you are writing about the source or the source's words:**

Ginter was never modest in his self-descriptions:
"When I was born 42 years ago to a family of humble
asparagus farmers, none suspected I would one day be
the world's leading transcriber of baroque music for
the banjo" (37).

The advertisement promised "luxury villas with a
spectacular ocean view," but only by leaning far out
the windows of our ancient bungalow could we gain even a
distant glimpse of the sea.

Victor Hugo called Jean Henri Fabre "the Homer of the
Insects" with good reason. Few naturalists wrote such
vivid metaphors as Fabre does in this description of the
praying mantis:

> To judge by the term Prègo-Diéu, we should look
> to see a placid insect, deep in pious
> contemplation; and we find ourselves in the
> presence of a cannibal, of a ferocious spectre
> munching the brain of a panic-stricken victim.
> (Qtd. in Lynch and Swanzey 51)

- **Quote when the source is an expert whose exact words will lend authority to a claim that you make:**

Paratrupus schusterensis, the common swamp frogwort, is a
delicacy among scavenger gourmets. Florence Demingo, author
of A Field Guide to Edible Weeds, exclaims: "Ah, the frogwort! No other plant offers such a thrill to the palate
while fortifying the liver with such potent dosages of
Vitamin B-8" (188).

The public is often outraged when technicalities decide the
outcome of important court cases, but as Justice Felix
Frankfurter observed in 1943, "The history of liberty has
largely been the history of the observance of procedural
safeguards" (37).

As anthropologist Ashley Montagu observed, "To be human is
to weep" (248).

Usually, however, you can paraphrase an authority with the same good results:

Florence Demingo, author of A Field Guide to Edible Weeds,
finds the frogwort both tasty and rich in Vitamin B-8
(188).

And one final consideration for quotation in research papers:

- **Do not restrict your quoting to already quoted material.** Many students
  quote only passages that appear within quotation marks in their sources;
  that is, they quote writers they have found quoted by other writers. It
  never occurs to them to quote their sources directly. Of course, you should
  not overquote, but on the other hand, do not be afraid to quote your
  sources themselves. If, for example, you were using this very paragraph as
  a research source, you could quote from it:

Veit advises, "Do not restrict your quoting to already
quoted material" (428).

Judging When to Paraphrase and Quote   EXERCISE

Decide if any of the quotations in the following passages should instead have been
paraphrased by the writers. For those quotations, write a paraphrase that could be
substituted for the inappropriate quotation. Omit any notes that you decide are unnecessary.

a. Pott's disease is "tuberculosis caries of the vertebrae, resulting in curvature of the spine. It was named after the physician who described it, Percival Pott (1714–88)" (Gleitman 110).

b. Geologists and seismologists are uncertain how to interpret the cryptic note found in McPhilibar's hand after the cave-in: "Major discover [sic]—8th strata, fault line demarcation—earthquake predictor. Eureka!" (Donnelly 192).

c. Harris argues that the animal-powered agriculture of India is not necessarily a problem to be corrected:

> To convert from animals and manure to tractors and petrochemicals would require the investment of incredible amounts of capital. Moreover, the inevitable effect of substituting costly machines for cheap animals is to reduce the number of people who can earn their living from agriculture. . . . Less than 5 percent of U.S. families now live on farms, as compared with 60 percent about a hundred years ago. If agribusiness were to develop along similar lines in India, jobs and housing would soon have to be found for a quarter of a billion displaced peasants. (12)

d. Humans are not entirely logical creatures. Often we take our guidance from emotional and spiritual voices within us. As the philosopher Pascal observed, "The heart has its reasons which reason knows nothing of" (40).

e. "The word *ain't*," says Phillips, "has generated its share of controversy" (64). Frelling writes, "*Ain't* is widely accepted in casual conversation. It is rarely used in formal discourse and in writing" (6). A controversy arises especially over its use as a contraction for *am not.* Dwight Macdonald speaks in its behalf, noting that "there is no other workable contraction, for *amn't* is unpronounceable and *aren't* is ungrammatical" (144). Theodore Bernstein, on the other hand, says, "There can be no doubt that *ain't I* is easier to say than *aren't I* and *amn't I,* and sounds less stilted than *am I not.* Nevertheless, what should be not always is" (13–14).

▓ A FURTHER NOTE ON PLAGIARISM

Undoubtedly, the most often repeated exhortation in this book is your obligation as a scholar to acknowledge your sources. The message is so important that we don't want to risk its being missed. Feel free to make use of sources (after, all, that is what research is all about), but give them full credit when you do so. Failure to acknowledge a source, thereby making someone else's work appear to be your own, is plagiarism.

The most glaring cases of plagiarism are deliberate acts of cheating: students handing in papers that they did not write or copying articles from magazines and passing them off as their own work. These are dishonest acts that rank with library vandalism as among the most serious breaches of the code of scholarship. They are dangerous as well, since penalties for them are understandably severe, and instructors are much better than most plagiarists realize at spotting work that is not a student's own.

A less serious offense, but also one to be avoided, is an unintentional act of plagiarism. Most of the time when students plagiarize, they do so innocently, unaware that they are violating the rules of scholarship. They copy a sentence or two from an article, not knowing that they should either quote or paraphrase it. They change a few words in copying a sentence, sincerely believing that they are paraphrasing it. They do not provide a parenthetical note because they do not know that one is needed. They are not trying to cheat; they are not even aware that they are cheating. It is just that no one ever told them to do otherwise. Perhaps when they were in the fifth grade, they wrote papers that consisted of copying out passages from encyclopedia articles. That may have gone unreprimanded in grade school. It is never tolerated in college.

There is certainly no need to plagiarize, because you are allowed to use sources provided that you acknowledge them. In fact, there is no advantage in it either: Papers based on expert sources, fairly acknowledged, are what is wanted of scholars. They are exactly what instructors are looking for.

9 *Using Parenthetical Notes*

Research writing has two principal devices for giving detailed information about sources: lists of works cited and notes. The former is a *general,* alphabetized list of all the sources you used in your writing. A ***note,*** in contrast, acknowledges the *specific location* within a source of a *specific quotation* or bit of information in your paper. For example, if you quoted this very sentence in a paper you were writing, you would include the fourth edition of *Research: The Student's Guide to Writing Research Papers* in your list of works cited. A note, however, would also be needed with the quotation to tell your readers that it came from page 162 of this book.

■ TYPES OF NOTES

Notes are of three principal kinds: parenthetical notes, footnotes, and endnotes. Parenthetical notes are by far the simplest kind of notes to use, and they are the standard method for documenting sources in MLA style. Footnotes and endnotes, however, are sometimes used by scholars in such fields as history, theology, and the fine arts. The following case illustrates the differences among these three types of notes.

Imagine that you included the following source in your list of works cited:

A works-cited listing

Sternberg, Robert J., and Todd I. Lubart. Defying the Crowd:

Cultivating Creativity in a Culture of Conformity. New

York: Free, 1995.

Suppose you made use of the following passage about the invention of Post-it® Notes, which appeared on page 4 of that book:

A passage from that source

Consider, for example, the Post-its on which many people jot reminders of things they need to get done. These "stick-ums" were created when an engineer at the 3M Company ended up doing the opposite of what he was supposed to. He created a weak adhesive, rather than the strong one that was the goal of his working division. But instead of throwing out the weak adhesive, he redefined the problem he was trying to solve: namely, to find the best use for a very weak adhesive. . . . Some of the greatest discoveries and inventions happen when people do just the opposite of what they have been told to do!

162

Assume you paraphrased material from this passage in your paper as follows:

```
Creativity consists in seeing possibilities where others see
only dead ends. For example, the discovery of a weak adhesive
by an engineer who was actually looking for a strong adhesive
led to the invention of Post-it® Notes.
```

Your
paraphrase
of the source

It is your obligation to identify the specific source you used in writing this paraphrase. Here it is done with a *parenthetical note:*

```
Creativity consists in seeing possibilities where others see
only dead ends. For example, the discovery of a weak adhesive
by an engineer who was actually looking for a strong adhesive
led to the invention of Post-it® Notes (Sternberg and Lubart
4).
```

A parenthetical
note

The note tells your readers that you discovered this information on page 4 of the Sternberg and Lubart book, the complete citation for which can be found in your list of works cited.

By contrast, if you use the footnote or endnote system, you mark your paraphrase with a raised number:

```
Creativity consists in seeing possibilities where others see
only dead ends. For example, the discovery of a weak adhesive
by an engineer who was actually looking for a strong adhesive
led to the invention of Post-it® Notes.[1]
```

Reference to a
footnote or
endnote

The raised number refers the reader to the following note:

```
[1] Robert J. Sternberg and Todd I. Lubart, Defying the
Crowd: Cultivating Creativity in a Culture of Conformity (New
York: Free, 1995), 4.
```

A footnote or
endnote

As a *footnote,* it would be typed at the bottom of the page on which the reference appeared. As an *endnote,* it would be typed in a list of notes at the end of the paper.

Unless you are using a word processor that automatically formats and arranges your footnotes for you, you will find endnotes easier to type than footnotes. Both, however, involve redundancy; notice that the sample footnote repeats all the information already found in the works-cited listing. In contrast, parenthetical notes are far simpler and more economical than either footnotes or endnotes. In this chapter, we will focus on the MLA parenthetical style, but a full discussion of footnotes and endnotes can be found in Appendix B, and still other styles of notation are explained in Appendix A.

▉ PARENTHETICAL NOTES

The rationale for parenthetical notes is that a note should give the least amount of information needed to identify a source—and give it within the paper itself; readers who want to know more can consult the list of works cited for further information. Different academic fields use slightly different formats for parenthetical notes. We consider here one general-purpose format, but you should be aware that papers written for other classes may require some adjustment in their note form. Always ask your instructor for format information if you are in doubt.

In the style used here as a model—the MLA style—a note is placed in the paper at the point where it is needed to identify a source. A typical note consists of two bits of information, in this format: (author pages). That is, the author's last name and the pages from which the information is taken are placed in parentheses. Here is an example of how a parenthetical note is used with a quotation:

> One textbook defines <u>false arrest</u> as "an intentional,
> unlawful, and unprivileged restraint of a person's liberty,
> either in prison or elsewhere, whereby harm is caused to the
> person so confined" (Wells 237).

Observe that the note follows the quotation and that the period is placed *after* the parentheses, not at the end of the quotation. In other words, the note is treated as a part of the sentence. If a quotation ends with a question mark or exclamation point, add a period after the note, as follows:

Period follows
the note
> Schwitzer taped a quotation from Thoreau to the wall above
> his desk: "I have never yet met a man who was quite awake.
> How could I have looked him in the face?" (Johnson 65).

If the author's name already appears in your sentence, it can be omitted from the note. For example:

> Wells writes that "a false arrest or false imprisonment is an
> intentional, unlawful, and unprivileged restraint of a
> person's liberty, either in prison or elsewhere, whereby harm
> is caused to the person so confined" (237).

For a longer, indented quotation, the note can be placed immediately following the acknowledgment phrase, as follows:

```
Historians of the last century maintained a firm belief in

human progress, according to British historian Edward Hallett

Carr (324):

     The liberal nineteenth-century view of history had a

     close affinity with the economic doctrine of laissez-

     faire--also the product of a serene and self-confident

     outlook on the world. Let everyone get on with his

     particular job, and the hidden hand would take care of

     the universal harmony.
```

Alternatively, the note can be placed at the quotation's end, as in this example:

```
Although the earth is a small planet in a remote corner of a

minor galaxy, there are reasons for arguing its importance:

     One should not be impressed too much by mere quantity;

     great dimensions and heavy mass have no merit by

     themselves; they cannot compare in value with

     immaterial things, such as thoughts, emotions, and

     other expressions of the soul. To us the earth is the

     most important of all celestial bodies, because it has

     become the cradle and seat of our spiritual values.

     (Öpik 9)
```

Period pre-
cedes the note
in an indented
quotation

Notice one oddity of the parenthetical style: When a note is placed after an indented quotation, it follows the final period. (In the other cases we have seen, the
period follows the parenthetical note.)

Many students mistakenly assume that notes are used only for quotations,
but they are used for paraphrased ideas and information as well. For example:

```
John Huston's first movie, The Maltese Falcon, is a faithful

adaptation of Dashiell Hammett's novel (Fell 242).
```

Note for
paraphrased
material

Fell's book is the source of the information, but the sentence is not a direct quotation. This point is important and needs to be stressed: *Use notes whenever you make*

use of a source's ideas and information, whether you quote the source's words directly or paraphrase them. Since your research paper will contain more paraphrasing than direct quotation, most of your parenthetical notes will follow information written in your own phrasing.

The beauty of parenthetical notes is their simplicity: They provide the *least* amount of information needed to identify a source from the list of works cited, and the same form is used whether the source is a book, a periodical, or a newspaper. Only a few special cases require any variation from this standard form.

Some Special Cases

Notes should be as unobtrusive as possible; therefore, they should contain the least information needed to identify the source. In the following special cases, you will have to include additional information in your notes.

An Anonymous Work (Unidentified Author)

For works where no author is given, substitute the title (the item that comes first in the entry for that work in the list of works cited; remember that the point of notes is to refer your readers to the list of works cited if further information is needed). For example, consider a note for an anonymous article listed like this:

> "An Infant's Cries May Signal Physiological Defects." <u>Psychology
> Today</u> June 1974: 21-24.

A parenthetical note referring to this article might look like this:

> ("An Infant's" 22)

Notice that when a title is long, only the first word or two should be given in the note, with no ellipsis dots. Also notice another difference: The list of works cited locates the complete text of the article, pages 21 through 24, whereas the note lists only page 22. The reason is that a list of works cited gives *all the pages* on which an article appears, whereas a note refers to the *specific page* or *pages* from which a quotation or piece of information is taken.

Works with Two or More Authors

Notes for works with multiple authors list their names just as they appear in your list of works cited. (You can find the works-cited entries for these two sources on page 98.)

> (Reid, Forrestal, and Cook 52-54)
>
> (Courtois et al. 112)

Two or More Works by the Same Author

When two or more works by the same author appear in your list of works cited, add the first word or two from the title to your note to distinguish one work from another. For example, if your paper uses both a book by Isaac Asimov, *Adding a Dimension,* and a magazine article by him, "Happy Accidents," notes for those two sources might look like this:

(Asimov, Adding 240-43)

(Asimov, "Happy" 68)

Two Authors with the Same Last Name

When two authors with the same last name are cited in a paper, include their first names in notes so as to distinguish between them. For example:

(George Eliot 459)

(T. S. Eliot 44)

A Multivolume Work

If you are citing a book published in more than one volume, you do not need to list the volume number in the note if it is shown in the list of works cited.

Take, for example, the following entry:

Agus, Jacob Bernard. The Meaning of Jewish History. 2 vols.

London: Abelard, 1963. Vol. 2.

Since your list of works cited shows that only this one volume is used in your paper, your notes should not list the volume number. For example:

(Agus 59)

If, on the other hand, your paper uses more than one volume of a work, each note needs to specify the volume as well, as in these examples:

(Agus 1: 120)

(Agus 2: 59)

A Reference to an Entire Work

When you refer to a work as a whole, rather than to a specific passage, no page numbers are needed, as in this example, which refers readers to three different sources found in the list of works cited:

```
At least three full-length biographies of Philbin have

been written since his death (Brickle; Baskin;

Tillinghast).
```

More often, when a work as a whole is referred to, the author's name is mentioned in the paper itself, so no note is needed. For example:

```
Fermin's book on wine-making is sold only by mail-order.
```

A Reference to More Than One Work

Sometimes a note needs to refer to more than one work. You can list multiple sources in a note, separated by semicolons:

```
Broadwell's controversial theory about the intelligence of

lizards has been disputed by eminent herpetologists

(Matsumoto 33; Vanderhooten 7; Crambury 450).
```

A Reference to Discontinuous Pages

When you have taken source material from discontinuous pages of a work, list the pages, separated by commas:

```
(Witanowski 47, 103)
```

An Interview or Other Source without Pages

Many sources, such as recordings, television programs, and interviews, have no pages. For example, suppose you have conducted an interview for your paper and have this entry in your list of works cited:

```
Philcox, Arthur C. Personal interview. 17 Oct. 2003.
```

Information from the interview can be cited simply with the interviewee's name:

```
During World War II, children in Hadleyville played at being

civil defense spotters on the levee, searching the skies for

German aircraft (Philcox).
```

If the interviewee's name appears in the passage, no note at all is needed, as shown here:

```
Retired teacher Arthur Philcox says that ballpoint pens did

not replace fountain pens in Hadleyville's grade schools

until the mid-1950s.
```

References with Other Forms of Page Numbering

Page references in parenthetical notes should use the same numbering system as in the text being referred to. For example, a reference to pages with Roman numbering would look like this:

```
(Bullock iv-viii)
```

Reference to a newspaper article uses the system employed by that newspaper:

```
(Carlton B17-B18)
```

An Electronic Source

Some electronic texts look much like their printed versions, and the text appears on numbered pages. An example is David Irving's book *Hitler's War,* which you would list on a works-cited page like this:

```
Irving, David. Hitler's War. New York: Viking, 1977.

    20 Jan. 2000 <http://www.focal.org/books/hitler/

    HW.pdf>.
```

Because page numbers are visible on screen, you would cite a reference to this book as you would to any other—for example:

```
(Irving 166)
```

Some works, however, display no page numbers on screen, such as Kenneth Robinson's online book *Beyond the Wilderness.* Consequently, a parenthetical note referring to that work as a whole or to any part of the work would simply be:

```
(Robinson)
```

The same is true for periodical articles that you have not consulted in their original print forms but only as reproductions, without page numbers, in an electronic database. For example, the newspaper article in the following works-cited listing was consulted online through the Newspaper Source database, where it was reproduced without page numbers:

Yue, Lorene. "Economists Expect Federal Reserve to Leave

    Rates Unchanged." <u>Detroit Free Press</u> 20 Dec. 1999.

    <u>Newspaper Source</u>. EBSCOhost. 14 Jan. 2000 <http://

    www.epnet.com>.

Since it was consulted online and not in its original print form, a parenthetical note would not list page references:

(Yue)

One Source Cited in Another

Sometimes you wish to quote a source whom you have found quoted in *another* source. In such a case, your note should cite the actual source from which you take the material you are using. Imagine, for example, that in reading a book by an author named Robinson, you encounter a quotation from an article by another author named Amoros. Robinson provided a note (*Amoros 16*), to cite the quotation's location in Amoros's article. However, unless you actually then go to Amoros's article to look up the quotation, you would list Robinson as your source, preceded by *qtd. in* (an abbreviation for "quoted in"):

Quoting a print source found in another source

Amoros writes that "successful politicians, like successful

    actors and teachers, always stay in character" (qtd. in

    Robinson 199).

Also use *qtd. in* for notes when the person being quoted was an interview source. For example, if Robinson had interviewed and then quoted someone named Reese, you would give Robinson as your source for the Reese quotation:

Quoting an interview source found in another source

Reese said, "The secret to life is learning how to write off

    your losses" (qtd. in Robinson 208).

However, if you paraphrased Reese, you would omit *qtd. in:*

Paraphrasing one source found in another source

Reese believes that people should not dwell on past setbacks

    (Robinson 208).

Once you have practiced citing sources in your own research writing, you will quickly become familiar with the techniques involved. Observe the way notes are used in the works that you read, as in Emily's and Justin's papers on pages 11–42. In writing your own research papers, refer to the Quick Reference Guide on the inside back covers of this book as needed, and use this chapter for fuller explanations. When unusual situations arise and you are uncertain how to cite a source, the wisest course may be to improvise, guided by your common sense. Always keep in mind that the purpose of notes is to acknowledge your sources in a clear, brief, consistent, and unobtrusive way.

Using Parenthetical Notes

EXERCISE

Assume that the following passages are all taken from the same research paper. Parenthetical notes have been omitted, but information about their sources is given in brackets following each passage. First, write the list of works cited that would appear at the end of the paper (assuming that these are the paper's only sources). Second, insert parenthetical notes in the passages.

1. The world's most advanced bicycle was invented in 1977 by

Swiss inventor Ugo Zwingli.

[You discovered this information on page 33 of Vilma Mayer's book, *101 Offbeat Ideas*, published by the Phantom Company of Chicago in 1994.]

2. When he first encountered Zwingli's invention, cyclist Freddie

Mercxx exclaimed: "This will either revolutionize road racing

or set it back a hundred years!"

[Mercxx wrote this on page 44 of his column, "New Products," which appeared on pages 44 and 45 of the November 1978 *Cyclist's World.*]

3. According to Rupert Brindel, president of the International

Bicycle Federation, "The cycling world was in a tizzy about

the Zwingli frame. Supporters called it 'the bike of the

future,' while detractors said it removed the sport from the

sport of cycling."

[You found this in Melba Zweiback's book, *Two Wheels,* on page 202. She is quoting from Brindel's article, "The Zwingli Fiasco," which appeared on page 22 of the *Sporting Times* newspaper, April 13, 1993. *Two Wheels* was published in Montreal by Singleday in 2000.]

4. Zwingli had discovered a revolutionary way to reinforce tissue

paper. The result was a frame so lightweight that it would

actually gain speed while coasting uphill.

[This too was taken from Mayer's book, page 36.]

5. In his <u>Memoirs</u>, Zwingli wrote, "I was overjoyed by how strong
the tissue-paper frame was. The first prototype held up well
under every test--until the first rainstorm."

[He wrote *Memoirs* in 1988; the quotation is from the bottom of page 63 and the top of page 64. Zigurat Press of Zurich published it.]

6. Zwingli's bicycle was a mere curiosity until the following
year, when he made his second brilliant discovery: waterproof
tissue paper.

[You paraphrased this from "And Now: Non-Absorbent T.P.," an anonymous brief article on page 416 of the July 1978 *Applied Chemistry Bulletin* (volume 28), a journal with continuous paging.]

7. The twin brother of Freddie Mercxx, also a world-class
cyclist, wrote:

> With all other bicycles, the strongest and
> fittest cyclist wins the race. With the Zwingli
> bike, the lightest racer wins. I'm tired of
> being wiped off the track by skinny guys on tissue
> paper.

[Otto Mercxx wrote this in a letter to his brother dated 28 January 1980.]

8. The fate of the Zwingli bicycle was sealed in 1985 when it
was outlawed for competition by a vote of 70 to 3 of the
International Bicycle Federation.

[You found this information on page 54 of Melba Zweiback's magazine article, "IBF Disposes of Tissue Paper 10-Speed," published on pages 54, 55, and 56 of the August 1985 *Newsmonth*.]

9. Although the following week's Tour de Finland race was marred
by protests from newly unemployed lightweight riders, the
cycling world soon returned to normal.

[This information appeared on page C17 of the *New York Times-News-Post* newspaper dated August 22, 1980, in an article by Greg LeMoon under the headline "Featherweight Furor in Finland." You read the article last Tuesday in the AllSports-News online database, using the BOSCOworld online reference service at http://www .BOSCO.com.]

When Are Notes Needed?

It is your privilege as a scholar to make use of the scholarship of other people in your writing. It is your obligation as a scholar to make it clear to your readers which words and ideas in your writing are your own and which ones came from your sources. The general rule for when notes are needed is this: *Provide notes for all quotations; provide notes for all paraphrased information that is not commonly available knowledge.* The examples that follow illustrate this rule.

A frequent mistake made by beginning scholars is to give notes only for quotations. Remember that you need to acknowledge your debts to your sources, whether you quote their exact words or only borrow their ideas. You should give a note for information you have used, even if you have phrased it in words entirely your own. For example, assume you are writing an article on the Black Death, the plague that devastated medieval Europe, and one of your sources is Barbara Tuchman's book *A Distant Mirror.* Imagine that you found this passage on page 94:

> . . . Although the mortality rate was erratic, ranging from one fifth in some places to nine tenths or almost total elimination in others, the overall estimate of modern demographers has settled—for the area extending from India to Iceland—around the same figure expressed in Froissart's casual words: "a third of the world died." His estimate, the common one at the time, was not an inspired guess but a borrowing of St. John's figure for mortality from plague in Revelation, the favorite guide to human affairs in the Middle Ages.
>
> A third of Europe would have meant about 20 million deaths. No one knows how many died. Contemporary reports were an awed impression, not an accurate count.

If you wrote any of the following sentences based on this passage, you would need to give credit to Tuchman in a note.

```
It is widely accepted that about one third of Europe's

population died from the Black Death (Tuchman 94).
```

```
Although a mortality of 20 million Europeans is usually

accepted for the Black Death, no accurate figures exist to

confirm this estimate (Tuchman 94).
```

```
Even if the usual mortality estimate of one third of Europe

(Tuchman 94) is not accepted, the Black Death still exacted a

horrendous toll of the population.
```

None of these passages is a direct quotation, but since they are based on your source, they require notes. In the first two examples, by placing the note at the end of the sentence, you signal that all the information is from Tuchman's book. In the third example, by placing the note in the middle of the sentence, you indicate that only the material preceding the note is from that source.

You do not need to note information from a source if it is widely available and generally accepted. For example, you might have learned this information in an encyclopedia or almanac: *Oklahoma became a state in 1907.* Although you did not know this fact before you looked it up, it is such common information that it is in effect public property, and you need not acknowledge a source in a note. The facts on the Black Death in Tuchman's article, on the other hand, represent her own research findings, and she deserves full acknowledgment when her ideas are used.

The distinction being drawn here may not always be an obvious one. As is often the case with research writing, your best practice is to let common sense be your guide. You can usually tell when information is public property and when a source deserves credit for it in a note. But when you are in doubt, the safest course is to provide the note.

How Many Notes Are Enough?

In writing a research paper, you are creating something new, even if almost all the ideas and information in it are from your sources. At the very least, your contribution is to synthesize this information and to present it in a fresh way. For this reason your research paper will be based on a variety of sources. A long paper based on only one or two sources serves little purpose since it does nothing new. Consequently, your research papers are likely to have a number of notes, indicating the contributions of your various sources.

Sometimes you will have to use many notes to acknowledge a complex passage that is developed, quite legitimately, from several different sources. For example:

```
Herbal folk remedies have been imported to the West with
mixed results. An East African tea seems to be effective
against cholera ("Nature's" 6), while moxibustion, a
Chinese remedy for diarrhea, is still largely untested
("Burning" 25). A Chinese arthritis medicine called "Chuifong
Toukuwan," on the other hand, is a positive danger to health
(Hunter 8).
```

The second sentence requires two notes because it is based on two separate sources.

On the other hand, there can be a danger in overloading your paper with notes. One reason the format of notes is so brief is to keep them from getting in the way of what you are saying in the paper. When a paper is filled with note after note, even brief notes call attention to themselves, and they distract and annoy readers. With notes—as with quotations, brackets, and ellipsis dots—there can be too much of a good thing. Avoid passages like this in your writing:

```
In 1948, Isaac Stork ran for president (McCall 80) on the

Anti-Vice ticket (Sullivan 42). His platform included a

prohibition on all sweetened or alcoholic beverages (McCall

80), fines for wearing brightly colored outfits (Stokes 124),

and the clothing of naked cats, dogs, and horses (McCall 81).
```

Bad (too many notes)

The notes here are annoying, not only because they interrupt the passage so often but also because they are unnecessary. It is evident that the writer has done some research and is eager to show off. The writer is deliberately juggling three sources, all of which contain the same information. The first sentence would seem to state commonly available information that does not require acknowledgment. Information in the second sentence might also be considered public property, but to be safe, the writer might provide a single joint note after the final sentence like this:

```
. . . cats, dogs, and horses (McCall 80-81; Stokes 124).
```

Judging When Notes Are Needed

EXERCISE

Imagine that it is some time in the near future and that you are writing a brief research report. Imagine too that, having found the following six passages in your research, you have then written the report that follows them. What remains for you to do is to supply notes for the report.

1. Horseradish (*Armoracia lapathifolia*), a plant of the mustard family, is grown for its pungent, white fleshy root. [*Source:* Elizabeth Silverman's book, *Common Plants of North America,* page 208.]

2. I first met Mr. Finnahey when I stopped by his farm to get forms filled out for his medical benefits. When I asked him his age, he said, "I forget the exact year I was born. It was the same year the Brooklyn Bridge was built." Naturally I didn't believe him since he didn't look a day over 40, and his wife, Becky, was 26. Imagine my surprise when he brought out his birth certificate. [*Source:* social worker Marlys Davenport, quoted on page 35 of a newspaper article written by Lester Grady.]

3. The Brooklyn Bridge was built in 1883. [*Source:* an anonymous article in *Encyclopedia Galactica,* volume 4, page 73.]

4. When I arrived to examine Julius Finnahey, he was eating a lunch of peanut butter and horseradish sandwiches. "Best thing for you," he said. "I eat 'em every day—always have." This was my first clue to the cause of his longevity. My research into his diet led to a discovery that may provide humans of the future with lifetimes lasting perhaps two centuries. [*Source:* Chester Vinneman writing on page 19 of his article, "Radish-Legume Combination Slows the Aging Process," in the *New England Medical Report.*]

5. Chester Vinneman discovered that the combination of the trace element *vinnemanium,* which occurs in the common horseradish root, with amino acids in the common peanut retards the decay of the cell wall lining in human tissue. To

Vinneman, the increased longevity which his discovery will provide is a mixed blessing: "I find the prospect both thrilling and frightening. The questions and problems that it raises stagger the mind." [*Source:* an unsigned article, "Life Everlasting Now a Reality?" in *Timely* magazine, page 78, continued on page 80.]

6. Chester Vinneman won the Nobel Prize for medicine for his discovery of the miracle age retardant. He is a professor of biochemistry at the University of Manitoba. [*Source: Who's Who,* page 993.]

Here is a section of your report, which is based on the preceding list of sources. Supply the appropriate parenthetical notes.

Important discoveries are often the result of chance occurrences. If it had not been for a routine inquiry by social worker Marlys Davenport, Chester Vinneman might never have won the Nobel Prize for medicine. It was Davenport who confirmed Julius Finnahey's amazing statement that he was born in 1883, "the year the Brooklyn Bridge was built."

Professor Vinneman made the connection between Finnahey's extraordinary youthfulness and his diet of peanut butter and horseradish sandwiches. Horseradish (Armoracia lapathifolia) was not previously thought to have benefits beyond the flavor of its pungent root. Through extensive tests, however, Vinneman discovered a previously unreported trace element in horseradish, which he named vinnemanium. This element, when combined with amino acids such as those found in peanuts, prevents human cell walls from decaying.

Vinneman predicts that as the result of his discovery, human lifetimes may extend in the future to as many as two centuries. He finds the prospect of such longevity "both thrilling and frightening. The questions and problems that it raises stagger the mind." It remains to be seen how wisely humankind will cope with greatly extended lives.

Finally, explain why you placed notes where you did and why you provided notes for some statements and not others.

How Much Material Can One Note Cover?

A parenthetical note comes after borrowed material, but how can a writer make clear *how much* of the preceding material is referred to by the note? The following passage illustrates the problem:

Haagendazs was considered one of Denmark's premier eccentrics.
He continually wore the same heavy woolen sweater, regardless
of the occasion or season. Former colleagues attest that he
worked in near darkness, and he reportedly kept exotic spiders
and beetles as pets (Noland 18).

The extent of the reference is not clear. Is Noland the source for all three examples of Haagendazs's eccentricities or just the latter two (or the last one)? The ambiguity could be avoided, perhaps, by placing a note after each paraphrased sentence. But the paper would then be overloaded with notes, and readers would find it annoying to meet with identical notes sentence after sentence.

A somewhat clearer way to define a long borrowed passage is to mark its beginning with an acknowledgment phrase. For example:

Noland reports that Haagendazs was considered one of
Denmark's premier eccentrics. He continually wore the same
heavy woolen sweater, regardless of the occasion or season.
Former colleagues attest that he worked in near darkness, and
he reportedly kept exotic spiders and beetles as pets (18).

The acknowledgment phrase marks the beginning of the borrowed passage

The note marks the end of the passage

Here it is clear that the entire passage is taken from page 18 of a work by Noland. However, acknowledgment phrases are not commonly used with factual information, and an excess of acknowledgment phrases can be as distracting to readers as an excess of parenthetical notes. Alas, some ambiguity in the scope of your references is probably unavoidable. Rely on your judgment about whether a borrowed passage is adequately marked, but if you are in doubt, supply the acknowledgment phrase. You may also ask your instructor for advice.

Judging When Borrowed Material Is Adequately Marked

EXERCISE

Examine the parenthetical notes in the research papers by Emily and Justin on pages 11–42. For each parenthetical note, is it clear how much material is borrowed from the source? If not, can you suggest a way to make it clearer?

■ INFORMATION FOOTNOTES

Even when you use parenthetical notes to acknowledge sources, you can still use footnotes to supply information that you feel does not belong in the text of your paper. To mark an *information footnote,* place a raised asterisk (*) in the place where you invite the reader to consult the note, like this:

```
. . . domesticated animals such as dogs, cats,* and . . .
```

At the bottom of the same page, type ten underline bars and present your footnote on the next line, beginning with a raised asterisk, like this:

```
          ————————
     * Witherspoon does not classify the common house cat as

a "domesticated" animal but as a "wild" animal that merely

"coexists" with humans (16).
```

Typing footnotes can be cumbersome. Fortunately, most word-processing programs can place footnotes automatically at the bottom of the proper page.

If you use a second information footnote on the same page, mark it with a double asterisk (**) or dagger (†). You should, however, use information footnotes rarely. Almost always when you have something to tell your readers, it is better to say it within the paper itself. This is in line with the general rule that anything which interrupts the reader or makes reading more difficult should be avoided.

10 *Writing and Revising the Research Paper*

GETTING ORGANIZED

Once Emily Gould and Justin Stafford had gathered material from their sources and taken notes on index cards, they were ready for the next step: the actual writing of their papers. While writing proved less time-consuming than source-gathering, it was no less important, and, like earlier stages of the research process, it consisted of several substeps. Emily and Justin each received an assignment similar to the following for the first of these substeps:

Preparing to Write   ASSIGNMENT

Do the following before our next class meeting in preparation for writing your first draft:

- Complete your note-taking on index cards.

- Formulate a thesis statement; that is, state in a sentence or two your concept of the main idea of your paper.

- Sort your note cards by topic.

- Prepare an updated informal working outline for your first draft.

- Put new topic titles on your note cards as necessary, arrange them in the order suggested by your outline, and put aside (but do not discard) the ones you do not expect to use.

Formulating a Thesis Statement

When Emily began her project, she was afraid she would not have enough to say about her topic. However, halfway through her first source, she had fifteen cards' worth of notes. Aware that she was taking too many notes, Emily concluded that she would need to be more selective. Like almost every other student researcher, she found that a shortage of material would not be a problem for her after all. She sharpened her focus and began to take fewer but more carefully chosen notes. Even so, she ended up taking notes on over a hundred cards, several dozen more than she would end up using.

When Emily began her search for sources, the topic she had in mind was a broad one, issues related to fast-food restaurants. These included health issues, such as the effect of a fast-food diet on America's health; social issues, such as the loss of diversity as national chains replaced local establishments; and employment issues, such as the impact of fast-food jobs on teens. She began to take notes, but before long she saw that her original topic was leading in too many different directions that were far too diverse for one research paper. Her topic, she realized, needed to be more specific, and she soon narrowed it to just work-related issues, a decision made easier by the abundance of sources she found on that topic. Even so, she discovered many different aspects to this topic, and she did not become entirely sure of her paper's thesis or organization until she was well into an early draft of the paper itself. She was then able to formulate a *thesis statement*, a brief summary of what she expected to be her main focus:

> Thesis: Fast-food restaurants provide many thousands of jobs, but the quality of the jobs is poor and the workers are exploited.

Emily's thesis indicates a point of view, an opinion about fast-food jobs that not everyone would be expected to share. Another writer with less clearly developed opinions might have written about the topic by providing a balanced exposition of two sides of a controversial issue, but Emily's research had led her to a definite opinion, and she made her viewpoint clear from the beginning. She was still learning about her topic, however, and her thesis was, at this point, sufficiently generalized to allow room for her topic to develop.

Student writers are sometimes misled by the advice to *start* a research project with a thesis that is clear, unified, and restricted. Like an outline, a thesis ought to assist the process of searching, thinking, and composing; it should never become a straightjacket. As we have seen, Emily's preliminary research caused her to narrow her focus. Justin, however, was quite certain of his topic, and formulating a thesis statement presented little difficulty. He simply expressed in plain language the goals of his project:

> Thesis: I want to find out if a career in pharmacy fits my abilities, interests, and career objectives and, if so, what I need to do to pursue this career.

As we have seen, premature commitment to a thesis can become a hindrance to thorough, objective inquiry. Nevertheless, many writers prefer to develop a cohesive theme during the early stages of research. They have found that keeping such a theme in view—often in the form of a preliminary thesis statement—can help focus their work. If you have difficulty finding such a focus, try the following procedure:

Tips for Formulating a Thesis Statement

1. **Think about your project in general terms.** In your notebook, write a quick informal paragraph describing what you expect your paper to say and do. It may help to respond to these questions: What main topic have your efforts become focused on? What question(s) have you been trying to answer? What have you learned from your research? Do you now have a point of view about your topic—a conclusion or insight that you want to express in your paper?

2. **Make your general idea specific.** Review the paragraph you have written, and see if you can summarize its main idea in a single sentence.

As you continue your work, you should think often about how each part of your paper supports your focus. Be prepared to eliminate any sections that stray from the main topic. You may, of course, adjust your focus as you proceed with your project. In the final draft of her paper, Emily introduced her readers to her subject with this summary of her thesis:

```
Convenience and value have come at a price, however, and many
believe that benefits to the public are outweighed by the
costs that this giant industry imposes on its workers.
```

Sorting Your Note Cards

With an evolving conception of her topic, Emily recorded in her notes material that she thought was usable. While her note cards were a distillation of all she had learned from her reading, they still represented a formidable mass of data. She now had to select and arrange her cards in an order she could use. She read through them and sorted them by topic.

Since Emily had written a topic label at the top of each note card, she was able to group many of her cards together by subject. She found that most of her cards fell into a half-dozen general categories: "background—statistics," "teen employment," "minimum wage," "unionization," and so on. As she sorted, she also set aside many discards—notes it was now clear she could not use. There were also many strays—single cards that did not fit conveniently into categories with any others. Emily had to decide if these belonged in her paper and, if so, how she might use them. In some cases, she would not know for sure until the actual writing.

Even with a good plan and a working outline, the final form of a paper can rarely be predicted in advance. Like Emily, you might follow this procedure:

1. **Read through and sort your note cards.** Sorting your cards into piles on a large table or on the floor can be helpful. Be sure you sort the cards by *topic* (not by any other principle, such as by source). Some piles will contain note cards from several different sources.

2. **When your cards are sorted, think about how they can be used and arranged.** Write about your ideas in your research notebook; think as you write,

using the opportunity to work out ideas for organizing your paper. But do not be dismayed if you encounter loose ends at this stage. You will make many further decisions about your paper's organization as you write it.

3.   Put aside any cards you do not expect to use. The best way to create an organizational plan for a paper is to think first in terms of the most general categories. The following is one of several excerpts from Emily's research notebook that reveals her thoughts about shaping and organizing her project:

> On the one hand, fast food makes many jobs available for students. On the other the jobs are generally poor ones. Many different aspects to work picture: nonthinking robot work, poor wages, lack of unionization. There are also case histories of workers being cheated out of overtime. . . . There is much about teens but also much about immigrants and poor (disadvantaged groups) who are exploited. How do I ~~make~~ these deal with both of these which have different needs? Teens generally work for spending money, but the poor need to feed their families. Probably put emphasis on teens . . .

Emily did not yet have a clear organization in mind for her paper, but we can see her mind working here—even making decisions as she wrote. She was confident she had good materials to work with, and she had enough ideas for at least a tentative organization that she could try out.

Updating Your Outline

Having thought about the parts of her paper and how she might put those parts together, Emily needed a clearer idea—a diagram of what her paper might look like. That is, she needed an *informal working outline,* an updated plan for organizing her paper.

When you create an outline, the headings you use will correspond, in theory, to the topic labels on your note cards. In reality, though, you will need to make adjustments to both the cards and the outline as a clear conception of the shape of your paper gradually forms in your mind. Try to put your ideas on paper in a handy visual form: A working outline is nothing more than a way of making these ideas visible and concrete.

Checking and rechecking her note cards, Emily developed the parts of an outline and, after several revisions, created an informal scheme, shown in Figure 10.1, to use in writing her first draft. Although some of the details would change in the final version of her paper, Emily found this outline helpful as she wrote, especially in getting started.

During her next class, Emily showed her outline and note cards to the other students in her editing group. She discussed her plans, received suggestions, and—even more valuable—answered questions. Explaining and defending her outline helped Emily notice strengths and weaknesses in her plan. An added

```
Emily Gould
Thesis and Working Outline
                 Fast-Food Follies
Thesis: Fast-food restaurants provide many thousands of
jobs, but the quality of the jobs is poor and the workers
are exploited.


Introduction
     Statistics about usage
     Image of fast food: cheap, friendly, popular
     Reality: not a good workplace (thesis)
Nature of job
     Low pay
     Mindless, decision-free routine
     Unskilled staff: teens, immigrants, others without skills
Legislation
     Protections
        Child-labor laws
        Minimum-wage laws
     Violation of laws
Exploitation
     Overtime not paid
     Workers sent home during slow hours
Conclusion: need for reform
     Union organization of workers
     Respect from employers
```

Figure 10.1 Emily's thesis and working outline.

benefit of the session was that it familiarized everyone in each editing group with classmates' projects.

 # WRITING THE FIRST GOOD DRAFT

Having a tentative plan for organizing their papers, Emily and Justin received an assignment like the following from their instructors:

ASSIGNMENT	Writing the Paper

You are now ready to write a careful draft of your paper. Do so, and revise it until you are satisfied that it is as clearly written, well organized, interesting, and informative as you can make it. Be sure to document your sources carefully with parenthetical notes and include an updated list of works cited. You should also consult the guidelines for editing and revising that begin on page 192.

Research Writing: General Guidelines

Emily soon discovered that her outline was only a starting point. In fact, she made changes in her organization from almost the moment she began her actual writing. She encountered difficulties with her opening, and, as her rough drafts would show, she went through at least six versions of the introductory section before she felt ready to move on. Her preliminary outline rapidly became obsolete, but it had served its purpose. It had forced Emily to think about her paper as a whole—about how the individual parts might work together. Once she had made the outline, her concept of what she would accomplish in her writing became considerably less vague.

Although later parts of her draft went more smoothly, Emily discovered there is more to writing a paper than following a plan. Certainly, it is not just a matter of first writing about note 1, then about note 2, and so on throughout the paper. It will help to consider the following guidelines in writing your paper:

1. **Keep your goals in mind.** Novices can easily be overwhelmed by the procedures and details of research writing. Because of the many steps—all the procedures for assembling a list of sources and making note cards, outlines, and parenthetical notes—it is easy to lose sight of what a research paper is really about. The goal of your research is to learn something, to discover truth. In writing your paper, your goal is to present what you have learned so that your readers can also become informed. It follows that your writing should be readable and honest, informative and interesting. Never lose sight of these important goals as you write. Do not be blinded by procedures for their own sake.

2. **Remember that principles of good writing apply to research writing, too.** Like any other type of paper, a research paper should be clear and lively, not

stodgy and pompous. It should be written so it can be read with enjoyment and without difficulty. Quotations and other source material should be neatly integrated into your writing so they are not obtrusive or awkward.

Like any other author, you have a responsibility to make the reader's job easier. Use topic sentences to help the reader know what to expect. Provide paragraph breaks to signal changes in topic or emphasis. Where appropriate, use transitional words and phrases (such as *on the other hand, also, for example,* and *consequently*) to make clear the relationship between successive sentences and paragraphs.

3. **Most of your paper should be you, not your sources.** While your sources may provide you with most of the information that you present, in your paper *you* are the one writing it. Write in your own voice. Your research paper should communicate what you have to say—just like any other paper you write. Remember, too, that your use of sources is simply a means of reaching the goal of informing your readers; it is not an end in itself. Don't let your paper become simply a vehicle for presenting sources. Don't let your sources get in the way of clear writing.

4. **Don't be a slave to your note cards and outline.** Whenever you use a note from one of your cards, think about how it contributes to the point you are making. If a note isn't useful, don't include it. If it isn't clear, explain it. If you realize that your paper would be improved by adding new topics or rearranging your outline, by all means do so.

5. **Don't rely too heavily on one or two sources.** Inevitably, a few of your sources will have proved more helpful than the rest, and you will rely on these more than the others in writing your paper. Remember, however, that it is not your paper's purpose to restate what has already been said by another source or two. A research paper should present something new, a fresh synthesis of information and ideas from many sources. A paper that is largely a summary of only one or two sources fails to do this. A variety of sources should make substantial contributions to your paper. On the other hand, the opposite extreme—where it becomes an end in itself to squeeze in material from every source you find—should also be avoided. Let common sense guide you between these two extremes.

Some Practical Writing Tips

Following are some practical tips on the act of writing itself.

Don't Put Off Your Writing

Although the pressure of an impending deadline may stimulate great energy, it is unwise to begin writing your paper the night before it is due. You will produce a far better paper if you allow time for careful writing and revision. Start writing as soon as possible. Finishing ahead of your deadline will allow you the valuable opportunity to put the paper aside for a day or so, at which time you can take it up again, read it with fresh eyes, and gain new perspectives for improving it further.

Adopt Methods That Work for You

All writers are different. Use your past experience to decide what writing practices give you the best results.

Write in a place you find comfortable. A quiet library setting may free you from distractions and give you ready access to additional sources. On the other hand, you may prefer sitting at your computer keyboard at home. Or perhaps settling into a comfortable easy chair, writing with a pad on your lap and with your note cards on a table by your side, may allow you to do your best work.

Find ways to overcome obstacles. When you get stuck in your writing, perhaps it may help you to pause for a snack or a brief break to recharge your mental batteries—or you may find it best to shift gears, perhaps rereading what you have written or redirecting your attention to another part of the paper.

Adopt Positive Attitudes

Recognize that writing is hard work. Good writers work hard enough to make it *look* easy. Don't be discouraged by the snags that inevitably arise, and be prepared to give your project the time and energy it deserves.

Be persistent in writing. During the hard work of writing, writers are often visited with thoughts of more pleasant things they could be doing. At such times it is tempting to put down the pen or turn off the computer, promising yourself to resume writing later. Such temptations pose stern challenges to one's character and moral fiber. To be a successful writer is to develop self-discipline and to continue when one would rather not. As with any discipline you develop (from quitting smoking to mastering the cello to training for a triathlon), it is important to set realistic goals and to stick with them. At each writing session, set a goal of writing a certain number of pages or working for a certain number of hours—and meet it faithfully. Writing isn't usually fun, although at times it can be. But writing *is* very satisfying, especially when you know you have worked hard and produced a work you are proud of.

Have confidence in yourself. Even if this is your first research project, there is no reason to think you can't achieve admirable results. Remember, there are no secret formulas that others know and you don't. A paper is nothing more complicated than this: You have learned some information and are simply explaining it to readers who are much like yourself. Keep that in mind, tell your story clearly, let your own interest in the topic come through—and you will write a successful paper.

Getting Started

By the time you are ready to write, the hardest work should be behind you. You have plenty to say, as well as a plan for how you want to say it. You have a stack of note cards, arranged in the order in which you expect to use them. Once you are a page or two into your writing, the work should start to flow more smoothly. After students get past the initial unfamiliarity of working with source material, they usually find research writing little different from any other kind. In fact, because they are so well prepared, it is often easier.

Frequently, the most difficult part is simply getting started. In writing her first draft, Emily began by composing her opening section. She decided to establish the pervasive role of fast food in our lives with statistical information. After several drafts, she produced a paragraph that she expected to begin her paper:

> In his book <u>Fast-Food Nation</u>, Eric Schlosser provides statistics to illustrate just how much fast food has revolutionized America's eating habits. In 1970, Americans spent $6 billion on fast food. By the year 2000, that figure soared to $110 billion. That is more than the amount Americans spend buying movies, magazines, newspapers, books, videos, and recorded music, combined. Every day, about a quarter of the U.S.'s adult population eats some type of fast food (3).

An early draft of Emily's opening

As she received feedback from other readers and then revised her paper in subsequent drafts, Emily realized that, while certainly intriguing, the numbers didn't give the reader a context in which to consider them. She decided that this statistical information would have more impact if it followed an opening paragraph in which she introduced the paper's theme. Her revised opening can be seen on page 11.

Struggling with an opening is not uncommon. Often it is best to wait until after you have drafted the body of a paper before even attempting to write the beginning. Writers sometimes waste time by overlooking the fact that the parts of a paper do not have to be written in the order in which they are to be read. If you are having difficulty getting started or are unsure about where to begin, start with a section that especially interests you or that seems easiest to write. Once you are successfully under way, composing the rest of the paper may be easier.

Writing the Opening

After you have written a draft of the body of your paper, you are in a better position to see what type of opening is most effective. An introductory section can serve many purposes: to inform readers of what your paper is about and where it is going, to generate interest, and to create a smooth transition into the body of the paper. There are many ways to begin a research paper; the following strategies are among those most frequently used.

Option 1: Begin with a Summary of the Paper's Main Idea

The purpose of beginning with a summary of the main idea is to tell your readers immediately what the paper is about. A version of your thesis statement will figure prominently in the opening, which serves as a summary of the entire paper to come.

This is the way Emily opened the final draft of her paper:

> McDonald's, Burger King, KFC, Wendy's, and other popular chains have brought countless innovations to the restaurant

> industry, delivering food fast and at low cost year after
> year. Convenience and value have come at a price, however,
> and many believe that benefits to the public are outweighed
> by the costs that this giant industry imposes on its workers.

While Emily's first sentence introduces the general topic of fast-food restaurants, her second sentence succinctly states the thesis of her paper. The readers' job is made easier because she has given them a clear expectation of what will follow in the paper.

Option 2: Begin with Background

Because your readers may not be well informed about your topic, you can provide them with information that will provide a context for your thesis. For example, Emily might have begun with information to show how widespread teen jobs are in fast-food restaurants:

> One-third of all American workers under the age of 35
> got their first jobs working for restaurants (Yum! Brands),
> and about one-eighth of all workers have, at some point,
> worked for McDonald's (Schlosser 4). Yvonne Zipp of the
> Christian Science Monitor observes that such jobs have become
> "a teen rite of passage as universal as driver's ed." Hiring
> teenagers to prepare and serve us food in a fast-food setting
> has become "so natural, so normal, and so inevitable that
> people . . . think little about it," says Stuart Tannock, a
> lecturer in social and cultural studies at the University of
> California at Berkeley (qtd. in Ayoub A20). The topic is well
> worth considering, however, and we should ask if workers
> benefit or are harmed by work in the fast-food industry.

In this paragraph, the background information leads to a statement of the paper's thesis in the final sentence.

The background you provide may also consist of a history of the topic or a summary of occurrences leading up to the events you describe. For example, if Emily had chosen to focus on the plight of teenage workers, she could have opened her paper with historical background:

> The Fair Labor Standards Act of 1938 set limits on the
> number of hours teens under the age of 16 can work and the
> kinds of work they can do. At 14 or 15, students may work no
> more than three hours on a school day, but when they reach
> 16, all limits on their working hours are removed. At the
> time when our current child-labor laws were passed, most
> teens left school at 16 to become full-time workers earning
> their livelihood. Today, however, 90% of teens graduate from
> high school at 18, and most work primarily for extra spending

money or luxuries such as new cars. Relatively few now work
to help support their families (Zipp 1). Many observers
believe that existing legislation to protect young workers is
no longer suitable to current societal realities.

Option 3: Begin with an Interesting Anecdote

Starting with a specific story not only can capture your readers' interest immediately, but also can be used to lead into your thesis statement. Emily might have begun her paper with a specific story about the dangers of fast-food work:

> On a busy Friday evening, 17-year-old Brittany Krollman
> was working the counter of a fast-food restaurant in West
> Seneca, New York. A few feet away another worker was
> filtering the grease used to cook french fries. Without
> warning, the hot grease exploded, covering Brittany and
> setting her uniform on fire. Her second- and third-degree
> burns on her arms and torso required skin grafts and left
> permanent scars that affect her appearance. The restaurant
> was cited for safety violations and fined $5,000 (Kiger).
> Brittany's story is not an isolated one, as all too many
> teens face dangers in the workplace.

The anecdote not only arrests the readers' attention and emotions, but also leads to a more general statement of theme in the final sentence.

Option 4: Begin by Explaining Your Purpose for Writing

A personal research paper often begins with a section headed "Why I Wrote This Paper" or "What I Wanted to Find Out." Justin began his paper with a statement of his purpose:

> Next to finding the person I will marry, selecting the
> profession that will occupy me for the rest of my life is
> the most important decision I am likely to make. At various
> times as a boy and a teenager, I dreamt about exciting jobs,
> such as being an astronaut, a soldier, a senator, and a rock
> star. Lately, however, my plans have become more practical,
> and for the last year I have given serious thought to a
> career with considerably less sex appeal. Rather than
> piloting the space shuttle or winning a Grammy, I have begun
> to think that I can be successful and happy by becoming a
> pharmacist.
> Because the consequences are so great, I do not want to
> make a hasty decision, and this assignment has given me an
> opportunity to learn if pharmacy is the right choice and, if
> so, what I will need to do to pursue this career path.

Many scientific papers also begin by stating specifically what is to come in the rest of the paper. Conventional research papers, however, generally avoid direct statements by the author about purpose. A rule of thumb in writing for the liberal arts is that papers should avoid talking about themselves. That is, they should not contain statements such as "In this paper I will . . ." or "The rest of this paper will examine. . . ." (Note how the other sample beginnings make the theme evident without any such statements.) The personal research paper is an exception to this rule.

Writing the Conclusion

Sometimes, although rarely, a writer explores a topic in a research paper but does not come to any conclusions about it until the end. The writer uses the final section to reveal what is, in effect, the paper's bottom line. Justin's paper, for example, explored the pros and cons of a pharmacy career and only at the end reveals his decision:

> My research into pharmacy has made me enthusiastic about my future. Although several momentous decisions lie before me, I am now increasingly hopeful and confident that this profession offers me the best prescription for my happiness and success.

More often, however, the paper's thesis has already been made clear to the readers, and so the form a concluding passage should take is anything but obvious. After all, once you have said what you have to say, what else remains to be done? Fortunately, it is not as hopeless as that. The principal purpose of a conclusion is not to say something new but to draw the ends of the paper together and to leave the reader with a satisfying sense of closure. Simply put, an ending should feel to the reader like an ending.

One strategy, appropriate for a long paper, is to tie together what you have written by summarizing the paper's content. This may be effective if you can summarize the paper in a fresh and insightful way. A summary serves no purpose, however, if it merely rehashes what has already been made evident to the alert reader.

Emily gave her readers a fresh way of looking at her subject in her final paragraph. The body of her paper was principally devoted to exploring the negative aspects of work for fast-food companies. For her ending, she decided to first remind readers of the positive public image projected by the restaurants in their advertising and then contrast it, in her last two sentences, with a brief summary of her thesis:

> Ads for fast-food companies always show smiling, well-scrubbed, contented workers, and the corporations boast of their employee-friendly policies. Restaurants recruit workers with slogans such as "Everybody's Somebody at Wendy's" (Wendy's) and "A Subway restaurant is a really neat place to work" (Subway). On its Web site, McDonald's

```
proclaims, "We're not just a hamburger company serving
people; we're a people company serving hamburgers," and it
claims that its goal is "to be the best employer in each
community around the world" (McDonald's). While many
thousands of teenagers who annually accept work serving fast
food find the experience rewarding, many others regard the
job as anything but friendly. As author Eric Schlosser
concludes, "The real price [of fast food] never appears
on the menu" (9).
```

A word of caution: Strategies such as these are offered as helpful possibilities, not as rules or boundaries. Good writing resists formulas, and good writers continually find original ways of achieving their goals. Adopt whatever strategies work for you, and consider new approaches. That is the best way to extend your range as a writer.

Giving Your Paper a Title

Giving your paper a title may be the final stage of your project. Ideally, your title should both indicate to your readers what your paper is about and arouse their interest. In her first draft, Emily gave her paper the title "Fast-Food Follies." She thought the title reflected her theme of problems in the fast-food workplace, but a classmate who read the draft remarked that from the word "follies" he expected a relation of comic events. He also suggested that her title should reflect her paper's focus on work-related issues. With some regret for the loss of alliteration, Emily gave her final draft the more prosaic but clearer title, "Fast Food Comes at a High Price for Workers." For his paper about his career search, Justin considered the simple title, "Should I Be a Pharmacist?" but finally chose instead the more playful title, "Becoming a Pharmacist: Prescription for Success?"

Arresting, clever, or witty titles are not easy to create—and not always desirable, as there is a fine line between originality and cuteness. Start with a simple, direct title that captures your theme. If later on you are inspired with a better choice, fine, but if not, no one should object to a plain but clear title.

▮ EDITING AND REVISING

Writers differ in their work habits. Justin is a constant reviser. Composing, rearranging, and editing at the keyboard of his computer, Justin tends to write a little, pause to read what he has produced, make changes, and then move on. Emily, on the other hand, is more of an all-at-once reviser: She generally writes long passages straight through, forging ahead while ideas are still fresh in her mind. Only after she has written several pages will Emily pause to reread and make changes.

Because of their different work habits, Emily and Justin produced very different kinds of preliminary drafts. Emily wrote several complete drafts, each more polished than the previous one. Justin, on the other hand, emerged with something very close to a final draft after having gradually reached the conclud-ing section of his paper. To call Justin's final paper a single "perfect" draft, how-ever, would be very misleading. Since Justin was constantly rereading, revising, and editing earlier parts of his paper, these parts had actually gone through sev-eral drafts by the time he reached his conclusion. His success was due partly to productive work habits and partly to the fact that Justin kept the structure of his paper clearly in view from the outset.

Both writers achieved success by using methods that worked for them. You, too, should feel free to adopt practices that work for you. Basically, though, you can be an effective editor of your own work if you approach it like a reader. Put aside what you have written for a day or more until you can read it with a fresh perspective. Put yourself in your readers' place, trying to anticipate whether they will find it clear, readable, and effective. You may find it helpful to consult the checklist that begins below, considering each question as if you were responding to a paper someone else has written.

Reworking Your Paper

After completing preliminary drafts, both writers put aside what they had written for a while, then came back and reread them with a pencil in hand. A page from Emily's early draft in which she made particularly extensive changes appear in Figure 10.2. Although Emily makes handwritten corrections on pages composed at a word processor, other writers prefer working entirely on paper, while still oth-ers make all their revisions directly at the computer keyboard.

Checklist for Editing and Revising

Topic, Focus, and Support

- Is it clear what the topic of the paper is? Does the writer provide a thesis statement or otherwise make it evident, early in the paper, what the paper is about? Is any further help needed for the reader to see the paper's point?

- Is the topic adequately narrowed—that is, neither too broad nor too lim-ited for the writer to do it justice in a paper of this length?

- Has the writer kept the promises made by the thesis statement? That is, does the paper remain focused on its thesis? Does it stick to the point?

- Is the thesis supported with a variety of details or evidence?

- Is this support clear and convincing?

- In reading the paper, have you learned what you were expecting to learn from it? What questions remain in your mind? What needs to be devel-oped more? What seems to be missing?

Audience, Style, and Readability

- Is the writing style appropriate for its intended audience? What passages do you have trouble understanding?

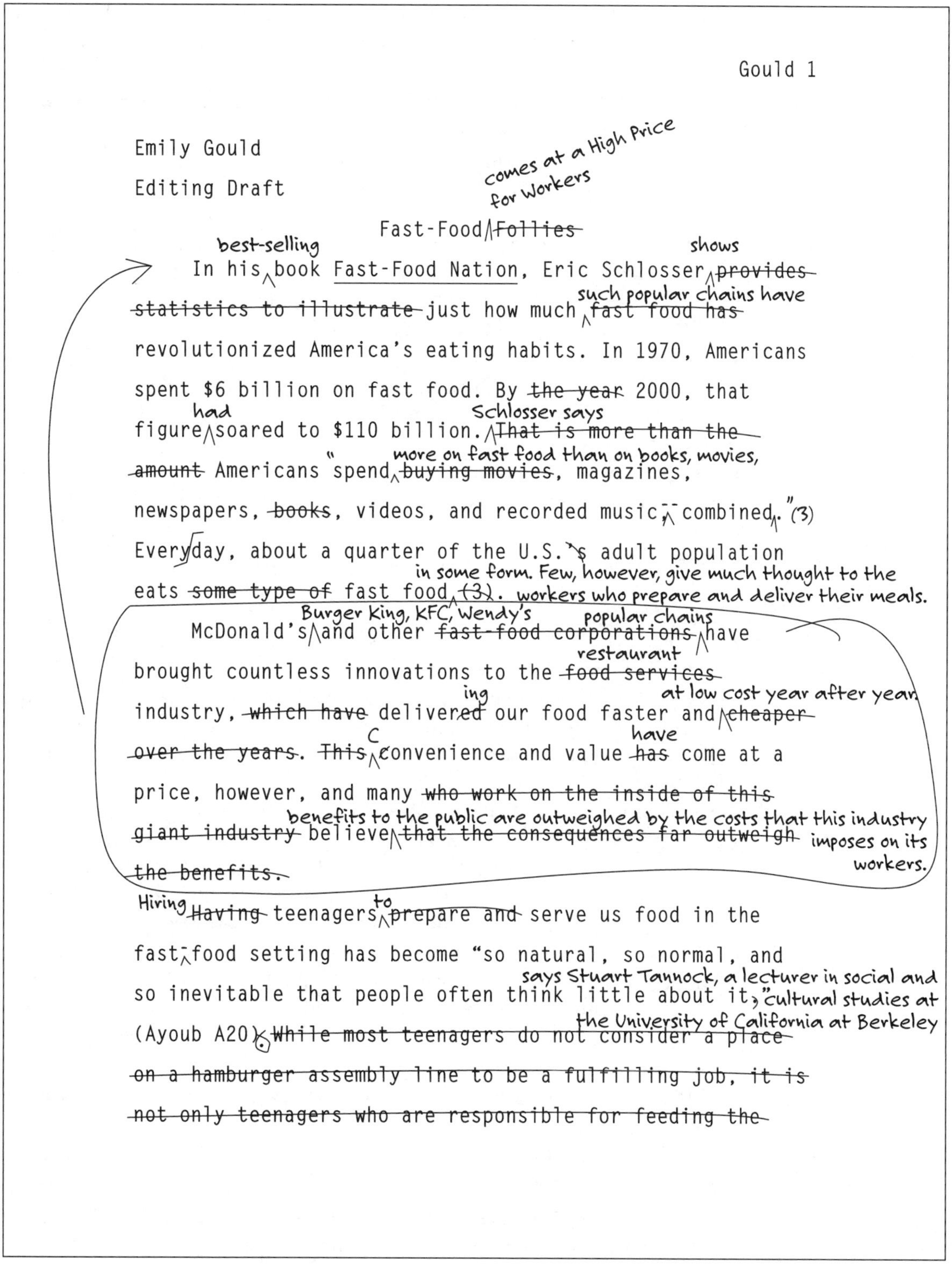

Gould 1

Emily Gould

Editing Draft

Fast-Food ~~Follies~~ comes at a High Price for Workers

In his ^best-selling book <u>Fast-Food Nation</u>, Eric Schlosser ~~provides statistics to illustrate~~ shows just how much ^such popular chains have ~~fast food has~~ revolutionized America's eating habits. In 1970, Americans spent $6 billion on fast food. By ~~the year~~ 2000, that figure ^had soared to $110 billion. ~~That is more than the amount~~ Schlosser says Americans spend ^" ~~buying movies~~ more on fast food than on books, movies, magazines, newspapers, ~~books~~, videos, and recorded music ^, combined ^." (3)

Everyday, about a quarter of the U.S.'s adult population eats ~~some type of~~ fast food ^in some form. ~~(3).~~ Few, however, give much thought to the workers who prepare and deliver their meals.

McDonald's ^Burger King, KFC, Wendy's and other ~~fast-food corporations~~ popular chains ^have brought countless innovations to the ~~food services~~ restaurant industry, ~~which have~~ deliver^ing our food faster and ^cheaper ~~over the years.~~ at low cost year after year. ~~This~~ ^C convenience and value ~~has~~ have come at a price, however, and many ~~who work on the inside of this giant industry~~ believe ^benefits to the public are outweighed by the costs that this industry ~~that the consequences far outweigh~~ imposes on its ~~the benefits.~~ workers.

Hiring ~~Having~~ teenagers ^to prepare ~~and~~ serve us food in the fast ^- food setting has become "so natural, so normal, and so inevitable that people often think little about it," says Stuart Tannock, a lecturer in social and cultural studies at the University of California at Berkeley (Ayoub A20) ~~While most teenagers do not consider a place on a hamburger assembly line to be a fulfilling job, it is not only teenagers who are responsible for feeding the~~

Figure 10.2 Emily's editing of a draft.

- Does the paper read smoothly and easily? Does the paper's use of sources and quotations ever become distracting or interrupt the smooth flow of your reading?

- Is the paper free from awkward phrasing, misspellings, typographical errors, and other mechanical flaws?

- Does the paper conform to MLA format (see Chapter 11)?

Organization

- Is the paper organized in a way that makes sense? Can you understand why topics come where they do in the paper? Could any parts be rearranged for greater logic and clarity? Are there passages in different parts of the paper that should be brought together?

- Does the paper begin with a helpful general introduction to the topic? Can you tell from the introduction where the paper is going? Does the paper capture your interest right from the beginning? Could it be made more lively and interesting?

- Does the writer provide smooth and helpful transitions between subjects? Can you always tell how the part you are reading fits into the paper as a whole?

- Does the paper end with a satisfying conclusion?

Use of Sources

- Is the paper based on a variety of sources? Is the use of sources balanced, or is most of the information taken from only one or two sources?

- Is most of the information from sources paraphrased, rather than quoted directly? Are quotations used excessively? When sources are quoted, is there a reason for doing so? (See pages 154–59 for the proper use of quotations.)

- Does the writer avoid "naked quotations"? That is, is each quotation introduced by a phrase or sentence? When sources are referred to in the paper, are they adequately identified in acknowledgment phrases? That is, are you given enough information about them so that you can tell who they are and whether they are experts on the subject? (See pages 135–37)

- Are sources documented? Does the paper credit its sources within parenthetical notes? Does it credit paraphrased material as well as direct quotations? (Consult the Quick Reference Guides on the inside covers of this book.)

- Does the writer avoid overnoting (unnecessary notes for commonly available information) as well as undernoting (paraphrasing a source's ideas without providing a note)?

- Is it clear what each note refers to? That is, can you tell what information goes with what note?

- Are the sources listed in a works-cited page following the paper? Are the number and types of sources adequate for the paper?

- Does each note provide the least amount of information needed to refer you to the works-cited page and to identify the specific pages being referenced by the note?

- Except for longer, indented passages, are the notes placed inside the sentences with the period after, not before, the note?

- Does the punctuation in each note and in each entry in the works-cited page follow the prescribed format exactly? (Check the Quick Reference Guides on the inside covers.) Are items in the works-cited page listed in alphabetical order? Has the writer remembered that in MLA format these items should not be numbered?

Getting Advice from Other Readers

No matter how good a job writers do at editing their own writing, they can always benefit from outside help as well. Writers become so closely involved with their work that they can lose the ability to observe it from the reader's perspective. For that reason, good editing often requires advice from a reader who can point out flaws and possibilities that have escaped the writer's notice.

When she was satisfied with her revisions, Emily brought her printed paper to class for editing. (Students in Justin's class met with partners outside of class time to edit each other's papers.) Emily and her classmates were given the following assignment:

Group Editing   ASSIGNMENT

Read the papers written by members of your editing group and offer them the most helpful advice you can give.

Your Role as Editor

- Read each paper with care and interest, as if it were written with you as its intended audience.

- In responding to the paper, think of yourself as a friend trying to help, not as a judge providing a grade or evaluation.

The Editing Procedure

Read each paper at least twice, first for a general impression, then for specific details.

- The first time, read it straight through to gain a general impression. Do not stop to ask questions or write comments. When you have completed your first reading, pause to write a paragraph or two about the paper in general, including the following:

—State what the paper's main idea seems to be.
—Describe your general reaction to the paper. What did you learn from it?

—Tell the author how the paper worked for you. Where was the best writing in the draft? Did the paper develop as you expected it to? As you were reading, did questions arise in your mind that the author answered or failed to answer? Did you ever have trouble following it?

—Ask any other questions and make any other general comments about the paper as a whole.

• Now read the paper a second time, paying greater attention to specifics. Pause at any time to write comments, according to the following guidelines:

—Write comments, questions, or ideas in pencil in the margins of the paper. Put checkmarks by passages that you want to talk with the writer about.

—Point out the paper's strengths (note passages you especially like) as well as weaknesses, but be honest. You will not be much help to the author if you say that everything is wonderful when you think the paper might be improved. You are not insulting the writer by offering ideas to improve it. Specific suggestions are much more helpful than vague comments like "?" or "Needs work."

—If you are in doubt about an editing or proofreading matter, consult with your instructor.

• Finally, talk with the paper's author. Explain your comments. Describe your response to the paper, what problems or questions you had while reading it, and what suggestions you have for making it better.

Emily received editing suggestions from the two other students in her editing group. The following pages show the comments of Sean, one of her peers.

Gould 1

Emily Gould

Editing Draft

From your title, I expected some comic stories.

Fast-Food Follies

In his book <u>Fast-Food Nation</u>, Eric Schlosser provides statistics to illustrate just how much fast food has revolutionized America's eating habits. In 1970, Americans spent $6 billion on fast food. By the year 2000, that figure soared to $110 billion. That is more than the amount Americans spend buying movies, magazines, newspapers, books, videos, and recorded music, combined. Everyday, <u>about a quarter of the U.S.'s adult population eats some type of fast food</u> (3). *That's an amazing statistic!*

McDonald's and other fast-food corporations have brought countless innovations to the food services industry, which have delivered our food faster and cheaper over the years. <u>This convenience and value has come at a price, however, and many who work on the inside of this giant industry believe that the consequences far outweigh the benefits.</u> *If this is your thesis, should it go in the first paragraph?*

Having teenagers prepare and serve us food in the fast-food setting has become "so natural, so normal, and so inevitable that people often think little about it." *Period after the note, right?* (Ayoub A20) While most teenagers do not consider a place on a hamburger assembly line to be a fulfilling job, it is not only teenagers who are responsible for feeding the

Gould 2

nation. The number of immigrants arriving in the United States is growing, and many of them start life in the United States with a job in fast food. While fast-food workers have become an essential component in the service industry, employment in the fast-food industry is viewed as an undesirable, "dead-end" job. Most teenagers who work in fast food are only seeking part-time or summer jobs to get extra cash; however, many of the immigrants to the United States depend on these jobs to support themselves and their families. Trends over the past thirty years have indicated that the quality of fast-food jobs is steadily decreasing.

I'm confused. This sentence doesn't seem to fit with the rest of the paragraph.

About one-eighth of all workers in the United States have, at some point, worked for McDonald's (Schlosser 4).

Another amazing statistic

Fast-food jobs have become such a common occupation for teenagers that they are often considered to be a rite of passage into the American workforce. Jobs in fast food are ideal for teenagers because they require no special skills, and they teach basic, but vital life lessons to young people, such as responsibility, teamwork, and the value of a dollar. Studies conducted by the National Academy of Sciences showed that part-time jobs, up to twenty hours a week, were generally a positive experience for teenagers, giving them an increased sense of responsibility and self-esteem. Working more than twenty hours had nearly the opposite effect. Students who worked

This is balanced.

Gould 3

more than twenty hours a week were more likely to have
problems in school, cut classes, drop out, or develop
substance abuse problems (Zipp 1).

Child labor laws govern the number of hours teens can
work and what kinds of work they can do. Children 14 to 15
years can work up to three hours on a school day and eight
hours on non-school days; they may work eighteen hours
during a school week, and up to forty hours during a non-
school week. They can work during the hours 7/am to 7/pm,   *Spaces*
except from June 1 to Labor Day, when the hours are
extended to 9pm. Children ages 14 to 15 are not allowed to
cook and are limited to jobs such as cashier, bagger, or
Teens? cleanup crew. Children 16 to 17 years are not limited to
the number of hours they can work, and while they are
allowed to cook in fast food and restaurant kitchens, they
are not allowed to use hazardous machinery such as
automatic slicers, hamburger patty forming machines,
grinders, or choppers (www.dol.gov).   *Is this the right format?*

Even though there are laws to protect children in the
workplace, many fast-food employers do not abide by these
laws. During Schlosser's visit to Colorado Springs, he
interviewed many high school students who worked excessive
hours, beyond what was permitted by law. In addition, some
teenagers that he interviewed claimed that they regularly

Gould 4

This seems to be hearsay, not solid evidence.

used hazardous machinery that, by law, they should not have been using. Schlosser notes, however, that none of these teens were opposed to working long hours or using hazardous materials simply because they enjoyed getting a paycheck (82). With so many young fast-food employees willing to let their employers violate labor laws by keeping them for double shifts or until closing, it seems unwise to refuse to do so, especially when one is easily replaceable.

Do you mean they're afraid they'll be fired?

Fast-food corporations have worked hard to make their employees easily replaceable, so that when a worker quits or is fired, there is little or no interruption in the restaurant's productivity. The fast-food industry seeks out part-time, unskilled workers, who have traditionally been young people, because they are more willing to accept lower pay (Schlosser 68). Today, fast-food restaurants frequently hire disabled persons, elderly persons, and recent immigrants as well, for similar reasons (70).

I'm not sure I see the relationship

Are you saying they make the job simple so they can hire cheap, unskilled people?

Fast-food corporations are steadily moving towards a goal of "zero training" for their employees, by developing more efficient methods and using the most advanced kitchen technology. The fast-food kitchen is like an assembly line in a factory. Food arrives at the restaurant frozen, and its preparation involves very little actual cooking; it is a process performed in the kitchen and is regimented according

Good examples

Gould 5

to a manual, including how the hamburger patties are to be arranged on the grill to the thickness of the fries. Workers are told what to do, and how to do it. They have menus in both English and Spanish in order to spend less time training the more than one-third of the non-native English speakers in the fast-food industry who speak no English at all. All of these factors have contributed to the "deskilled" nature of fast-food jobs, which is in the best interest of the corporations because it increases output, and costs them less in training and in wages (68- *— Schlosser?* 72). *He seems to be your main source.*

The lack of skill required to be a fast-food worker has made fast-food jobs one of the worst paying in the United States. The fast-food industry pays minimum wage to a higher proportion of its workers than in any other industry. While a minimum wage job is an excellent source of additional income to a teenager still living at home, it is nearly impossible to live off of a minimum wage job, much less support a family. Between the years of 1968 and 1990, during the boom of fast-food restaurants, the "real" value of minimum wage dropped forty percent, and even in the late nineties, despite increases in the federal minimum wage, the value *of the?* minimum wage still remains about 27 percent lower than in 1968. At the same time, the value of restaurant executive earnings has gone up in the past

Gould 6

thirty years (73). The National Restaurant Association is opposed to an increase in minimum wage, however, and some large fast-food chains, such as Wendy's, have backed legislation that would allow states to ignore federal minimum wage laws.

Does this sentence need a note? ←

Critics of a raise in minimum wage are afraid of what increased labor costs will do to the restaurant industry. In response to a possible federal minimum wage increase in 2001, Scott Vincent, director of government affairs for the National Council of Chain Restaurants feared that the industry would be unable to bear a projected 300 percent increase in minimum wage. According to Vincent, "A lot of chains are franchised, which means they're small businesses with thin profit margins that can't handle more labor costs," which would most likely result in reduced hiring, layoffs, or even closings. The only way to accommodate these higher labor costs would be a price increase, which might result in some unsatisfied customers (Van Houten). Schlosser claims that an increase in the minimum wage by one dollar would hardly have any affect on food prices; a fast-food restaurant would only need to increase the price of a hamburger by two cents to finance the extra labor costs. A spokesperson for the Coalition on Human Needs claims that, based on previous increases in minimum wage, there would be no serious labor problems or

You seem to favor a higher wage, but I'm glad you give two sides.

Gould 7

consequences to the restaurant business. Furthermore, he claims that benefits from a minimum wage increase would be seen in low income neighborhoods (Houten).

This is not the only controversy over wages that has plagued the fast-food industry. In 1998, a jury in Washington found Taco Bell guilty of cheating as many as 13,000 workers out of overtime pay (Broydo). According to federal law, overtime is any time an employee works beyond the standard forty hours in a week; overtime pay must be at least one and a half times the normal hourly wage per hour in overtime (www.dol.gov). In the Taco Bell case, the jury found that managers had forced workers to wait until the restaurant got busy to punch in, had them work after punching out, and failed to correctly record hours worked by employees. One worker claimed that she regularly worked 70 to 80 hours in a week but was only paid for 40. While the Taco Bell case is one of the most extreme to date, there is evidence that Taco Bell is not alone when it comes to cheating workers out of overtime pay. The Employment Policy Foundation estimates that employees lose about $19 billion in wages every year, and some critics of the fast-food industry claim that this is a conservative estimate (Broydo).

Fast-food restaurants use several tactics to avoid paying extra labor costs associated with overtime. Workers

You give several good, specific examples.

Gould 8

are employed "at will," meaning that they are only employed as needed, so if a restaurant is not busy, a manager can send them home early. Managers try to keep all workers employed for less than thirty hours per week, and try to maintain large crews so that this is possible. Fast-food chains often reward managers who keep labor costs down, and this can lead to abuses such as the ones in the Taco Bell case, such as compensating workers with food instead of money and requiring workers to clean the restaurant on their own time (Schlosser 74-75). In the case that abuses do occur, large fast-food corporations try not to let themselves get involved. For example, the McDonald's corporation has no formal wage policies, so when abuses do occur, the company as a whole can deny involvement.

Does this need a note?

Hourly workers are not the only ones who claim they have been cheated out of overtime pay; managers and other salaried employees of service companies claim that outdated language in wage laws allow them to be cheated out of overtime pay (Star News). Managers and assistant managers in the service industry, which includes fast-food companies, often work up to thirty extra hours a week, and sometimes more. Overtime pay laws state that salaried workers in administrative or professional positions are not included among workers subject to overtime pay;

Gould 9

however, some salaried workers feel as though they are being shortchanged for the work they are putting in. Managers and salaried workers from RadioShack, Wal-Mart, and Eckerd filed lawsuits with their employers claiming overtime payments, and many of them have been successful. RadioShack vice president has called this the issue "du jour," and because of this, one may expect similar lawsuits to crop up among fast-food restaurant managers.

I'm a little confused by this.

In other industries, labor unions have been an effective way for employees to voice concerns and dissatisfaction with company policies and procedures. Union representation at fast-food restaurants has been rare, however. Attempts to unionize McDonald's restaurants have been the most notorious because of the scandal associated with these attempts. The corporation's seemingly anti-union attitude has made unionization difficult; John Cook, the US labor relations chief for McDonald's during the 1970s once said "Unions are inimical to what we stand for and how we operate" (Royle). The company no longer publicizes this sort of anti-union stance, but the continued lack of union success indicated that corporate executives have not changed their opinion. During the 1960s and 70s, there were several attempts to unionize McDonald's restaurants across the country. Corporate executives responded by holding "rap sessions"

Gould 10

with employees so that they could express their grievances. The company's sudden interest in accommodating their desires kept many of the unionization attempts from moving forward, but it has not always worked.

In 1973, during a union drive of a McDonald's in San Francisco, a group of employees claimed that they had been threatened with dismissal if they did not agree to take polygraph tests, and answer questions regarding union activities. The company was found to be violating state law by administering lie detector tests, and were ordered to stop, but the unionization attempt was still unsuccessful (Schlosser 76).

Labor unions trying to gain representation in fast-food restaurants have not had much success in the United States, especially with attempts to unionize McDonald's restaurants. Unions have turned their attention to Canada in particular, where unionized workers are more common with around thirty percent of workers belonging to a union. In British Columbia, the location of the first McDonald's to be unionized in recent years, when a majority of the employees at a business sign union cards, the remainder of the certification process is completed without much trouble from the management end.

One of the most notorious unionization attempts in recent years occurred with a McDonald's in Saint-Hubert,

Gould 11

Quebec, when the restaurant closed with only a short time before a union would gain certification there (Wall Street Journal). In Ohio, the same year, two McDonald's employees claimed that they were fired for trying to organize a union at their restaurant. Even at the McDonald's Squamish, British Columbia, which was successfully unionized in 1998, the management initially tried to combat the certification process by hiring fifty anti-union workers to keep the union from gaining a majority of employees at the restaurant (Hamstra).

The fast-food industry has been more difficult to unionize than other types of labor industries for several reasons. The industry is characterized by a high turnover rate, and it is difficult to cultivate enough support for a union when the majority of the workers are relatively new (Schlosser 184). Fast-food companies have generally hired the more disadvantaged members of society-- teenagers, the elderly, recent immigrants, and the disabled. They are hired because they are a cheap source of labor and less likely to rebel or complain, and often it is difficult for these members of society to find any higher paying jobs with better working conditions; therefore, most of these workers do not want to jeopardize their jobs by expressing their discontent (Schlosser 70).

This repeats what you wrote a few pages back, but I see your point.

Although low wages *are?* ~~is~~ the most notable complaint among fast-food workers, it is not simply higher wages and benefits workers hope to gain by unionizing. Workers trying to unionize, more than anything, want to be treated with more respect and to have a voice in the workplace. Accomplishing this can benefit the company as well as the workers. Studies have shown that the level of service a customer receives is the most important factor in whether they will be a returning customer. According to Jill Cashen, a representative for the United Food and Commercial Workers Union, "When workers are happier, when they have better wages and feel like they have a voice at work, their service is going to be better, and customers are going to come back and that's what helps build a good company." Therefore, keeping labor costs down may not be the best way to maximize profits if customers are unhappy with the service they are getting. Cashen also notes that past experience with large corporations has shown that increased wages for unionized workers has not translated into significantly higher prices for customers. She cites Kroger grocery store as an example; Kroger's workforce is entirely unionized, yet it is still the largest grocery store chain in the country.

Despite recent union successes, unionization is hardly gaining momentum. While not every fast-food

Gould 13

employee is pro-union, and not every employer is corrupt or greedy, there are plenty that are. Unionization may solve many of the wage and working condition issues, however, gaining respect for fast-food employees among the public is much more difficult.

Since unions are only part of your paper, do you want a conclusion that reflects your entire paper? Both my sisters work at Wendy's, so this paper is very interesting to me. Since you write mostly about the workers, should your title and thesis statement be more about workers? For another source, I'd suggest an interview with a student who works in fast food. This should be a good paper.

-Sean

Gould 14

Works Cited

Ayoub, Nina C. "Nota Bene." Rev. of <u>Youth at Work: The</u>
    <u>Unionized Fast-Food and Grocery Workplace</u>, by Stuart
    Tannock. <u>Chronicle of Higher Education</u> 25 May 2001:
    A20.

Broydo, Leora. "Worked Over." <u>Utne Reader</u>. Jan./Feb. 1999:
    20-21.

Cashen, Jill. Personal Interview. 10 Sept. 2002.

Gellar, Adam. "More Workers Challenge Bosses on OT
    Exemption." <u>Star News Online</u>. 5 Aug. 2002. 29 Sept.
    2002. <http://www.wilmingtonstar.com>.

"General Information on the Fair Labor Standards Act
    (FLSA)." U.S. Dept. of Labor Employment Standards
    Administration Wage and Hour Division. 29 Sept. 2002
    <http://www.dol.gov/esa/regs/compliance/whd/
    mwposter.htm>.

Hamstra, Mark. "Unions Seek Momentum from Canadian McD's
    Certification." <u>Nation's Restaurant News</u> 7 Sept.
    1998: 3. <u>MasterFILE Premier</u>. EBSCOhost. 15 Sept. 2002
    <http://web3.epnet.com/>.

Houten, Ben Van. "Moving on Up?" <u>Restaurant Business</u> 1
    July 2001: 15. <u>MasterFILE Premier</u>. EBSCOhost. 15
    Sept. 2002 <http://web3.epnet.com/>.

Royle, Tony. "Underneath the Arches." <u>People Management</u> 28
    Sept. 2000: 40.

Gould 15

Schlosser, Eric. Fast-Food Nation: The Dark Side of the

   All-American Meal. Boston: Houghton, 2001.

Wall Street Journal. "Canadian McDonald's First Outlet to

   Join Union." 21 Aug. 1998: B7.   *Shouldn't the title come first?*

Zipp, Yvonne. "Virtues of Work vs. Finishing Homework."

   Christian Science Monitor 15 Dec. 1998: 1. MasterFILE

   Premier. EBSCOhost. 15 Sept. 2002

   <http://web3.epnet.com/>.

Emily found Sean's comments valuable because they revealed another reader's response to her paper as well as useful ideas for improving it. Several of Sean's remarks highlight what worked well for him ("You give several good, specific examples"). Others inform Emily about a passage he found unclear ("I'm confused. This sentence doesn't seem to fit with the rest of the paragraph"). Remarks that specify his difficulty are particularly useful ("Do you mean they're afraid they'll be fired?"). In some of his comments Sean responds on a personal level to what Emily is saying ("That's an amazing statistic!"). Sean's longer commentary at the end of Emily's paper includes a personal response ("Both my sisters work at Wendy's, so this paper is very interesting to me"), but it also gives a response to the paper as a whole and makes several helpful suggestions.

Note that Sean's comments are framed in a positive and unintrusive way. When he offers suggestions, he usually does so in the form of questions, making it clear that the paper belongs to Emily and that final editing decisions rest with her ("Since unions are only part of your paper, do you want a conclusion that reflects your entire paper?"). Even when he notes a surface error, he asks rather than tells (Above the verb in Emily's "Although low wages is the most notable complaint . . ." Sean wrote "are?"), and it is clear that Sean's goal is to be as helpful to Emily as possible as she undertakes her revision. His comments are constructive, useful, and confidence-building.

In addition to responding to the valuable suggestions of her classmates and instructor, Emily discovered other ways to improve her paper over the next week. Each time she reread her draft, Emily noticed new possibilities for revising it. She spent many hours rephrasing, clarifying, and even rearranging sections of the paper, until she was ready to submit the polished draft that you read in Chapter 2, which is reprinted, with annotations on the following pages.

Gould 1

Emily Gould

English 12

Professor Katherine Humel

4 October 2002

Fast Food Comes at a High Price for Workers

The title is not underlined, italicized, or placed within quotation marks.

McDonald's, Burger King, KFC, Wendy's, and other popular chains have brought countless innovations to the restaurant industry, delivering food fast and at low cost year after year. Convenience and value have come at a price, however, and many believe that benefits to the public are outweighed by the costs that this giant industry imposes on its workers.

The writer introduces the reader to the paper's topic in her opening paragraph. For other opening strategies, see pages 187-90.

In his best-selling book Fast-Food Nation, Eric Schlosser shows just how much such popular chains revolutionized America's eating habits. In 1970, Americans spent $6 billion on fast food. By 2000, that figure had soared to $110 billion. Schlosser says Americans "spend more on fast food than on movies, books, magazines, newspapers, videos, and recorded music--combined" (3). Every day about a quarter of the U.S. adult population eats fast food in some form. Few, however, give much thought to the workers who prepare and deliver their meals.

The writer uses statistics to provide background for her topic.

The quotation is from page 3 of Schlosser's book.

Hiring teenagers to serve us food in a fast-food setting has become "so natural, so normal, and so

Gould 2

inevitable that people often think little about it," says Stuart Tannock, a lecturer in social and cultural studies at the University of California at Berkeley (qtd. in Ayoub A20). Nevertheless, while fast-food workers have become an essential component in the service industry, a fast-food job is usually viewed as undesirable, dead-end work.

"Qtd. in" is used when the person quoted is not the author of the source.

One-third of all workers under the age of 35 have gotten their first jobs working for restaurants (Yum! Brands), and about one-eighth of all workers in the United States have, at some point, worked for McDonald's (Schlosser 4). Yvonne Zipp of the Christian Science Monitor observes that such jobs have become "a teen rite of passage as universal as driver's ed" (1). They are ideal for teens because they require no special skills, and many believe that such jobs provide the educational benefit of teaching responsibility and good time and money management. These benefits may be more than offset by costs, however. Zipp cites a study by the National Research Council and the Institute of Medicine in Washington that teens who work more than 20 hours a week are "less likely to get enough sleep and exercise, less likely to go on to higher education, and more likely to use alcohol or drugs." These findings are disturbing, since four-fifths of American teens work at least part-

The writer integrates part of a quotation into her own sentence.

Gould 3

time during the school year, and of these, half work more than 20 hours weekly (Zipp 1).

Child labor laws offer some protection, governing the number of hours teens can work and the kinds of work they can do. Those who are 14 or 15 years of age may work up to three hours on a school day and up to eight hours on other days, for a maximum of 18 hours during a school week and 40 hours during a non-school week. They may work only between the hours of 7 a.m. and 7 p.m., except in the summer, when the hours extend to 9 p.m. Once they reach 16, however, teens may work an unlimited number of hours ("General").

These boundaries were set by the Fair Labor Standards Act of 1938, and many believe they are no longer suitable to current realities. At the beginning of the twentieth century, most teens left school at 16, and restrictive laws for children up to 15 years of age were designed to introduce them to the workforce before becoming full-time workers at 16. Today, however, 90% of teens graduate from high school at 18, and most work primarily for extra spending money or luxuries such as new cars. Relatively few now work to help support their families (Zipp 1).

Since 2000, Congress has been debating the Young American Workers' Bill of Rights, a bill that would update the 1938 labor law. If it is enacted as law, 14- and 15-

Notes are used for paraphrased as well as quoted material from sources.

For a print source the note gives the author's name and the specific pages where the information was found.

Gould 4

year-olds could work no more than 15 hours weekly, and
teens 16 and 17 would be limited to a 20-hour work week
(Kiger). While this bill would only affect work hours,
some critics of teen employment, such as Janine Bempechat,
assistant professor in Harvard's Graduate School of
Education, want to keep teens away from fast-food counters
altogether, claiming that they can get a similar sense of
responsibility and self-esteem from jobs such as peer
tutoring or volunteer work. Others, however, noting that
some teens use their paychecks to save for college, worry
that limiting hours could keep them from earning enough to
pay for tuition (Zipp 1).

Teens are also restricted in the kinds of work they
can do. Workers at 14 or 15 are not allowed to cook and
are limited to jobs such as cashier, bagger, or member of
the cleanup crew. More options are available to 16- and
17-year-olds, who can cook but cannot use hazardous
machinery such as automatic slicers, grinders, choppers,
or machines that form hamburger patties ("Prohibited").
Even though such regulations are intended to ensure safety
in the workplace, many employers are either not obeying
the laws or not doing enough to protect young workers. A
teen gets injured on the job every 40 seconds, and one
dies from a work-related injury every five days. Responding
to these alarming statistics, the U.S. Department of Labor

Notes for an Internet source or other sources without pages do not give page numbers.

A note identifies an anonymous source by the first word or two from the title.

Gould 5

has tried to crack down on violations of child labor laws
with heavy fines (Kiger). Funding for these efforts has
increased, with money going toward inspection of workplaces,
investigations, and occasional sweeps of industries
suspected of serious violations. The Department can impose
fines of up to $10,000 on employers who willfully break
labor laws and can sentence individuals to six-month jail
terms for each employee working in violation of the law.
One of the largest fines was incurred by a fast-food
company in Ohio, when a 15-year-old cut her finger while
using a meat slicer, a piece of equipment that should have
been off-limits to her according to federal law. The
company was ordered to pay $333,450 after it was found to
have 32 other unauthorized employees using similar
equipment, including one under the age of 14 (Pass and
Spector).

Notes for sources with multiple authors list all the last names that appear in the Works Cited listing.

    In recent years, reported cases of employer
misconduct have declined, but the injury rate among teens
at work has not seen a similar drop. Although fines for
violators are steep, critics worry that the Labor Department
is not doing enough to reduce violations. Only a thousand
inspectors are responsible for the safety of all 100
million workers in the nation. As a result, most employers
are not fined until someone is injured. Under the proposed
Young American Workers' Bill of Rights, an employer who

Gould 6

willfully ignores child labor laws could be sentenced to
as long as five years in prison for each teen who is
seriously injured on the job and up to ten if a teen dies
as a result of the employer's neglect. Regardless,
however, of whether stricter child labor legislation is
passed, companies and young workers alike have a strong
economic incentive to break whatever laws are on the
books. U.S. businesses save an estimated $155 million each
year by employing teens, and the economic gains that
result from hiring them to do jobs meant for older, more
experienced workers often outweigh the consequences of
getting caught (Kiger). Furthermore, teens are unlikely to
refuse an illegal assignment and risk losing the only job
they are qualified to hold.

The absence
of a note
indicates that
the writer is
expressing
her own
observations.

Because most fast-food jobs require little skill,
they are among the worst paying in the United States. The
fast-food industry pays minimum wage to a higher proportion
of its workers than any other sector of employment. While
a minimum-wage job may be a good source of spending money
for a teenager living at home, it is nearly impossible
for an adult to live off such wages, much less support a
family. Between 1968 and 1990, the boom years for
fast-food restaurants, the purchasing power of the minimum
wage dropped 40 percent, and even now, despite increases
mandated by federal law, it still purchases about 27

Gould 7

percent less than it did in 1968. At the same time, the
earnings of restaurant executives have risen dramatically.
Nevertheless, the National Restaurant Association opposes
any further increase in the minimum wage, and some large
fast-food chains, such as Wendy's and Jack in the Box,
have backed legislation that would allow states to exempt
certain employers from federal minimum-wage regulations
(Schlosser 73).

Schlosser is the source for all the information in this paragraph.

Critics of a higher minimum wage fear the effects of
increased labor costs on the restaurant industry. Scott
Vincent, director of government affairs for the National
Council of Chain Restaurants, says, "A lot of chains are
franchised, which means they're small businesses with thin
profit margins that can't handle more labor costs" (qtd.
in Van Houten). Higher wages, he maintains, would result
in reduced hiring, layoffs, or even closings. The only way
to compensate would be price increases, which would lessen
the appeal of fast food to customers with limited means
and therefore reduce business.

Acknowledgment phrases identify sources not familiar to the reader and establish their authority.

A spokesperson for the Coalition on Human Needs
expresses a contrary view, asserting that the effects of
previous increases in the minimum wage suggest that no
serious consequences to the restaurant business would
result, while low-income neighborhoods would derive
the greatest benefits from a minimum-wage increase

The writer presents opinions from both sides of a controversy.

Gould 8

(Van Houten). Author Eric Schlosser calculates that an increase of one dollar in wages would cause the price of a hamburger to increase only two cents (73). Furthermore, Jill Cashen, a representative of the United Food and Commercial Workers Union, argues that better wages and working conditions for workers would actually benefit the consumer:

> The service that customers get when going to shop is one of the main reasons why they'll come back and be repeat customers. . . . When workers are happier--when they have better wages and feel like they have a voice at work--their service is going to be better, and customers are going to come back, and that's what helps build a good company.

Without a minimum-wage increase, however, the pay that fast-food workers receive is unlikely to rise because they have so little bargaining power. The industry recruits part-time, unskilled workers, especially young people, because they are more willing to accept lower pay. Today, fast-food restaurants also hire disabled persons, elderly persons, and recent immigrants, for similar reasons (Schlosser 68, 70). When such employees grow dissatisfied, they are replaced quickly and easily, with little disruption of the restaurant's operations.

Since the writer identifies the interview source, no note is needed following the quotation.

Longer quotaions are indented one inch. No quotations marks are used.

The ellipsis signifies that the author has omitted some of the sources' words.

The note indicates that the information came from two discontinuous pages.

Gould 9

Fast-food restaurants see an annual turnover rate in employees of over 75% (White). To accommodate easy replacement of workers, companies are steadily reaching a goal of "zero training" for employees by developing more efficient methods and adopting the most advanced kitchen technology. The fast-food kitchen is like an assembly line. Food arrives at the restaurant frozen, and preparation, which involves little actual cooking, is regimented by a manual, which includes such details as how hamburger patties are to be arranged on the grill and the thickness of the fries (Schlosser 68-72). One college student who worked at Wendy's said, "You don't even think when doing work, and you never make any decisions. You're always told what to do. When you make hamburgers there are even diagrams about where the ketchup goes" (Williams). All these factors have contributed to the "de-skilled" nature of fast-food jobs, which corporations believe to be in their best interest because it increases output and reduces the cost of training and wages.

A note is needed when an interview source is not identified in the paper by name.

Others, however, claim that the high turnover in fast-food jobs costs employers more than they save through low wages. Fast-food restaurants lose at least $500 for each employee who has to be replaced. Managers are forced to spend time in recruiting, hiring, and training new employees, and additional staff is often needed to help

Gould 10

process applications. Current employees are also burdened with extra responsibilities when they pick up the tasks of replaced workers (White).

Other controversies involving wages have plagued the fast-food industry. In 1998, a Washington state jury found Taco Bell guilty of cheating as many as 13,000 workers out of overtime pay (Broydo 20), which, according to federal law, must be paid whenever an employee works more than 40 hours in a week and must be at least one and a half times the normal hourly wage ("General"). In the Taco Bell case, the jury found that managers had forced workers to wait until the restaurant got busy to punch in, had them work after punching out, and failed to record hours correctly. One worker claimed that she regularly worked 70 to 80 hours a week but was paid for only 40. While these are among the worst violations, there is evidence that many other companies deprive workers of earned overtime pay. The Employment Policy Foundation estimates that employees lose $19 billion in unpaid overtime wages every year (Broydo 20).

Fast-food restaurants adopt several other tactics as well to lower costs. Workers are employed "at will," meaning that they are employed only as needed, so if a restaurant is not busy, a manager can send them home early. Managers also avoid the cost of benefits for full-time

The writer uses transition words to provide continuity and coherence.

Gould 11

employees by hiring large crews and keeping all workers employed for less than 30 hours per week. Fast-food chains often reward managers who keep labor costs down, leading to such abuses as compensating workers with food instead of money and requiring them to clean the restaurant on their own time. When such abuses do occur, corporations try to distance themselves from responsibility. For example, the McDonald's corporation has no formal wage policies, so it accepts no blame for the abuses of its franchisees (Schlosser 74-75).

In various industries, dissatisfied workers have turned to labor unions to gain a voice in the workplace and to secure better wages and working conditions. At fast-food restaurants, however, union representation is rare. Organizers attribute their failed attempts to unionize McDonald's restaurants during the 1960s and 70s to the high turnover of workers and the corporation's opposition to unions. John Cook, U.S. labor-relations chief for McDonald's during the 1970s, said, "Unions are inimical to what we stand for and how we operate" (qtd. in Royle 40).

While the company no longer publicizes its anti-union stance, its efforts to forestall unions have continued. In 1998, two McDonald's employees in Ohio claimed that they were fired for trying to organize a union (Hamstra). In

Gould 12

1973, during a union drive at a McDonald's in San Francisco, a group of employees claimed that they had been threatened with dismissal if they did not agree to take polygraph tests and answer questions about their involvement in union activities. The company was found in violation of state law and was ordered to stop; nevertheless, the attempt to unionize was unsuccessful (Schlosser 76).

Ads for fast-food companies always show smiling, well-scrubbed, contented workers, and the corporations boast of their employee-friendly policies. Restaurants recruit workers with slogans such as "Everybody's Somebody at Wendy's" (Wendy's) and "A Subway restaurant is a really neat place to work" (Subway). On its website, McDonald's proclaims, "We're not just a hamburger company serving people; we're a people company serving hamburgers," and it claims that its goal is "to be the best employer in each community around the world" (McDonald's). While many thousands of teenagers who annually accept work serving fast food find the experience rewarding, many others regard the job as anything but friendly. As author Eric Schlosser concludes, "The real price [of fast food] never appears on the menu" (9).

Having established various problems at fast-food restaurants, the writer begins her conclusion by reminding readers of the public image they project.

The writer then concludes with a succinct statement of her theme.

Gould 13

Works Cited

Ayoub, Nina C. "Nota Bene." Rev. of <u>Youth at Work: The</u>
<u>Unionized Fast-Food and Grocery Workplace</u>, by Stuart
Tannock. <u>Chronicle of Higher Education</u> 25 May 2001:
A20.

Broydo, Leora. "Worked Over." <u>Utne Reader</u> Jan./Feb. 1999:
20-21.

Cashen, Jill. Personal Interview. 10 Sept. 2002.

"General Information on the Fair Labor Standards Act
(FLSA)." U.S. Dept. of Labor Employment Standards
Administration Wage and Hour Division. 29 Sept. 2002
<http://www.dol.gov/esa/regs/compliance/whd/
mwposter.htm>.

Hamstra, Mark. "Unions Seek Momentum from Canadian McD's
Certification." <u>Nation's Restaurant News</u> 7 Sept.
1998: 3. <u>MasterFILE Premier</u>. EBSCOhost. 15 Sept. 2002
<http://web3.epnet.com/>.

Kiger, Patrick. "Risky Business." <u>Good Housekeeping</u> Apr.
2002: 114. <u>MasterFILE Premier</u>. EBSCOhost. 15 Sept.
2002 <http://web3.epnet.com/>.

McDonald's USA. "Why McDonald's Has a People Promise and a
People Vision." 22 Sept. 2002.
<http://www.mcdonalds.com/corporate/promise/>.

Pass, Caryn G., and Jeffrey A. Spector. "Protecting
Teens." <u>HR Magazine</u> Feb. 2000: 139. <u>MasterFILE</u>

Sources are listed in alphabetical order.

Sources are not numbered.

Give the date when you consulted an electronic source.

For a source with multiple authors, only the first is listed with first and last names inverted.

Gould 14

Premier. EBSCOhost. 15 Sept. 2002 <http://
    web3.epnet.com/>.

"Prohibited Occupations for Non-Agricultural Employees."
    U.S. Dept. of Labor. Elaws--Fair Labor Standards Act
    Advisor. 29 Sept. 2002 <http://www.dol.gov/elaws/esa/
    flsa/docs/haznonag.asp>.

Royle, Tony. "Underneath the Arches." People Management 28
    Sept. 2000: 40.

Schlosser, Eric. Fast Food Nation: The Dark Side of the
    All-American Meal. Boston: Houghton, 2001.

Subway Restaurants. "Subway Job Opportunities." 22 Sept.
    2002 <http://www.subway.com/>.

Van Houten, Ben. "Moving on Up?" Restaurant Business 1
    July 2001: 15. MasterFILE Premier. EBSCOhost. 15
    Sept. 2002 <http://web3.epnet.com/>.

Wendy's International. "Welcome to Wendy's Career Center."
    22 Sept. 2002. <http://www.wendys.com/w-5-0.shtml>.

White, Gerald L. "Employee Turnover: The Hidden Drain on
    Profits." HR Focus Jan. 1995: 15. InfoTrac OneFile.
    21 Sept. 2002 <http://infotrac.galegroup.com/>.

Williams, Tamicah. Personal interview. 24 Sept. 2002.

Yum! Brands. "Great Jobs." 22 Sept. 2002. <http://
    www.yumjobs.com/>.

Zipp, Yvonne. "Virtues of Work vs. Finishing Homework."
    Christian Science Monitor 15 Dec. 1998: 1. MasterFILE

When a corporation's Web site is cited, list the corporation as "author."

Give the online location of electronic databases.

Gould 15

Premier. EBSCOhost. 15 Sept. 2002 <http://
web3.epnet.com/>.

11 *Producing and Proofreading Your Polished Draft*

TYPING AND PROOFREADING YOUR POLISHED DRAFT

Emily and Justin benefited from the comments and suggestions they received from classmates in their editing groups and from their instructors. They made further revisions in their papers and submitted them in polished form, in accordance with the assignment they had been given, which follows.

ASSIGNMENT   **Submitting Your Portfolio**

Submit the following items in your folder:

- Your typed polished draft
- All earlier drafts and outlines
- Your note cards in two packets:
    —those you used in your paper, in the order you used them
    —those you wrote but did not use
- Your research notebook

FORMAT FOR YOUR POLISHED DRAFT

The polished draft of your paper should be printed (using word processing software on a computer). A neatly handwritten paper may be allowed in rare cases, but only a printed paper presents a professional appearance. When you are communicating with others, appearance counts. Although the paper's appearance does not alter the content of your writing, it most certainly does affect the way your writing is received. Instructors try to be as objective as possible in judging student work, but they are still swayed, like all other humans, by appearances. Computer-printed papers give the impression of more serious, careful work, and they are certainly more inviting and easier to read. In the professional world, reports and correspondence are always computer-printed; anything less would be unthinkable. There is no reason to treat your college writing with any less respect.

Computer word processing offers the greatest benefits for composing, revising, copyediting, and printing your paper. With a word processor, you can make additions, deletions, corrections, and rearrangements of passages easily and at any time. The spell-check feature can identify errors in spelling and typing that you might otherwise miss. And, of course, the finished product has a polished, professional appearance.

When you compose your paper, follow the format exemplified by one of the sample papers shown in Chapter 2. In particular, pay attention to the following conventions.

Format for Computer-Printed Papers

The following are standard format guidelines for research papers. Individual instructors may wish to modify some of them according to their preferences. Check with your instructor if you have questions about the required format.

Paper

For computer printing, use plain white, heavyweight, 8½ × 11-inch paper. Print on one side of the paper only.

Ink

Use only black ink. Replace the cartridge in your printer if it no longer produces a dark copy.

Type Font

A high-quality printer, such as a laser or inkjet printer, produces the most readable, professional-looking papers. If your software allows a choice of fonts, choose Times Roman, a proportional-space font, or a monospaced font such as Letter Gothic or Courier. You can also use a sans-serif font such as Arial if your instructor approves. Never use a fancy font such as script. Use italics for book titles (*Moby Dick*) and foreign words, although underlining is also acceptable (Moby Dick). Do not use boldface (**bold**) for titles or section headings or for emphasis.

Spacing

Double-space (leave every other line blank) throughout the paper. This includes indented quotations and the list of works cited, which are also double-spaced. Do not skip additional lines between paragraphs, although it is acceptable to skip extra lines before a new section with a heading. Notice how Justin Stafford skipped extra lines before the "What I Found" section of his paper on page 31. Either one or two spaces is permitted after final periods or question marks, as long as you are consistent throughout.

Margins and Alignment

Set your margins at one inch at the top, bottom, right, and left of your paper. Choose "left" alignment for your text, not "full" alignment. Research papers differ from books such as this one, where the text is aligned with the right margin. Do not have the computer divide words with hyphens to achieve a straighter right margin.

Your computer may allow you to avoid a **widow line** or an **orphan line**—the typesetting terms for stranded lines. An orphan is the first line of a new paragraph printed as the last line of a page. A widow is the final line of a paragraph printed as the first line of a page. Notice how Emily Gould avoided a widow at the top of page 13.

Indenting

Indent each new paragraph one-half inch from the left margin. Indent long quotations one inch from the left margin only; do not indent from the right margin. (For additional directions, see pages 141–42.) Figure 11.1 shows an excerpt from a research paper demonstrating how margins and indentations should be handled.

The First Page

The format of your first page should resemble that of Emily's paper in Figure 11.2.

- **Page identification.** Your last name and the page number go at the top of the first page and each subsequent page. If you are using a standard word-processing program with a "header" feature, you can have it automatically

One-inch margin

moderately better by 14 months and substantially better at

age two (White, Kaban, and Attanucci 130).◄——————— Period follows parenthetical note in the text.

Indent paragraph one-half inch.

Second, Zajonc believes that older children enjoy a

significant advantage by having to assume the role of

"teacher." He explains the advantage as follows:

Approximately one-inch margin

Indent one inch for a long quotation.

One who has to explain something will see from

the other's reactions whether the explanation

Do not indent quotations from the right margin.

was well understood, and be prompted to improve

the explanation, with the consequence that his

Double-space throughout.

or her own understanding of the matter is

improved. (231)

Period precedes parenthetical note for an indented quotation.

In fact, the only firstborns who do not achieve

substantially better in these areas are those who have

done little teaching of their siblings (Smith 352).

Section headings are optional.

Skip 3 lines (double-space twice) before a section heading.

Middle Children

Psychologist Kevin Leman, a frequent talk-show

guest, describes a popular view of middle children in

The Birth Order Book: "They were born too late to get

the privileges and special treatment the first born

Figure 11.1 Format for the spacing and margins in a research paper.

put this header at the upper right of each page. Number the first page of the paper as page 1, even if you use a cover page. Do not precede the page number with *p.* or *page.*

• **Author information.** Type your full name, course information, and the date in the upper-left corner of the first page, about one inch from the top of the page. If you use an automatic header for the page identification, the author information goes on the first line of the paper itself, immediately below the header. A separate title page is needed only for lengthy reports (see page 237).

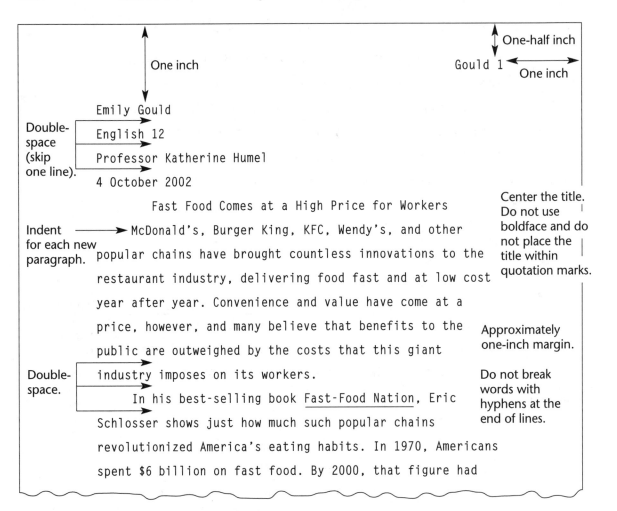

Figure 11.2 Format for the first page.

- **Title.** The title follows immediately under the author information. Writers have the option of whether or not to skip additional lines before and after the title. Only the first letter of each important word in the title should be capitalized; do not capitalize a word such as *the* (article), *and* (conjunction), or *of* (preposition) unless it is the first word of the title or the first word following a colon. Do not use underlining, italics, or bold for the title and do not enclose it in quotation marks. Of course, you should use standard punctuating conventions for titles of works that you include within your own title. For example:

The Depiction of Old Age in <u>King Lear</u>

and in "The Love Song of J. Alfred Prufrock"

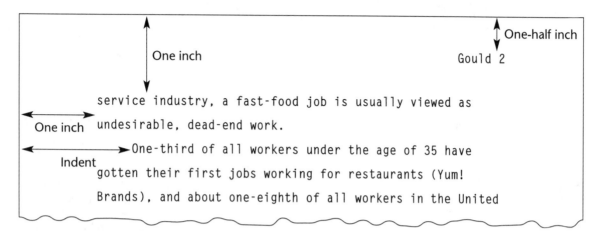

Figure 11.3 Format for subsequent pages.

- **Body.** Indent the first line of each new paragraph and double-space throughout. Do not skip additional lines between paragraphs.

Subsequent Pages

The format of subsequent pages is shown in Figure 11.3. If you use an automatic header, have the computer automatically place your last name and page number at the top right of each page. If not, type this information at the top right, and then double-space twice (skip three lines); the first line of text should begin one inch from the top of the page.

Tables and Figures

You can include *tables*—the presentation of data in columns—and *figures*—drawings, graphs, photographs, or other inserts—in your paper. Tables and figures can be either of your own creation or copied from a source (and duly acknowledged). A sample page from a research paper that includes a table is illustrated in Figure 11.4. Figure 11.5 shows a figure that the writer photocopied from a source he acknowledged.

Observe the following guidelines when you include tables and figures:

1. All tables and figures should be referred to within the paper (e.g., "Table 1 shows the variation among . . .," ". . . as can be seen in Figure 6," etc.). Place the table or figure as close as possible following its mention in the paper.

2. Tables and figures should be numbered consecutively (Table 1, Table 2, Table 3, . . . ; Figure 1, Figure 2, . . .). Each table should be given a clear explanatory label on the following line, and each figure should have an explanatory caption typed on the same line and placed below the figure. Each line begins at the left margin; it is not centered.

Reagan 8

Other statistics show that although the number of medical students in their thirties and forties is increasing, one's chances of being admitted to medical school decrease with age, as Table 1 demonstrates:

The table is referred to within the paper.

Each table or figure is given a number and a label.

Quadruple-space before and after each table or figure.

Table 1

Percentages of Men and Women Accepted by Medical Schools (1989)[a]

Raised lower-case letters are used for footnotes within tables and figures.

Age	Men	Women
21-23	73	67
24-27	58	55
28-31	49	53
32-34	46	51
35-37	41	46
38 and over	27	34

Each line of a table begins at the left margin (it is not centered).

Double-space throughout the table.

Source: Plantz, Lorenzo, and Cole 115

[a] The chart is based on data gathered by the American Medical Association.

The table ends with the source and footnotes (if any).

I have learned that there are many criteria other than age that medical schools consider when reviewing applications.

The paper resumes following the table.

Figure 11.4 Sample page with table.

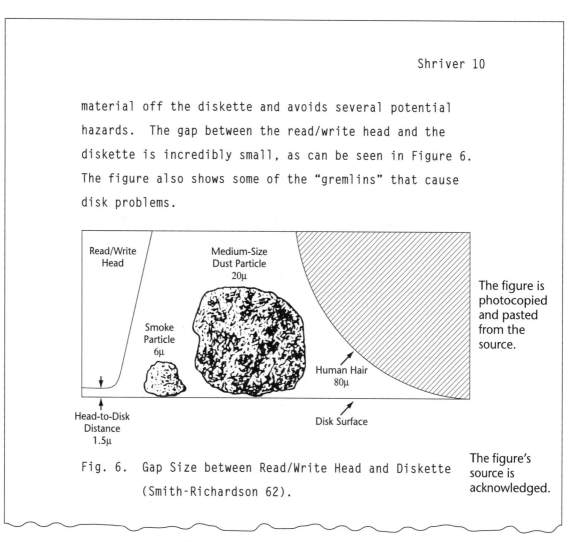

Shriver 10

material off the diskette and avoids several potential hazards. The gap between the read/write head and the diskette is incredibly small, as can be seen in Figure 6. The figure also shows some of the "gremlins" that cause disk problems.

Read/Write Head

Medium-Size Dust Particle 20μ

Smoke Particle 6μ

Human Hair 80μ

Head-to-Disk Distance 1.5μ

Disk Surface

The figure is photocopied and pasted from the source.

Fig. 6.   Gap Size between Read/Write Head and Diskette (Smith-Richardson 62).

The figure's source is acknowledged.

Figure 11.5 Sample page with a figure.

3. Double-space throughout, but skip three lines (double-space twice) both before and after a table or figure.

4. Lines may be drawn across the page (as in Figure 11.4, e.g.) to set a table or figure apart from the rest of the paper.

5. A table or figure may be photocopied from a source and pasted onto your page (see Figure 11.5). You may then wish to photocopy the entire page again.

6. If the table or figure is taken from a source, acknowledge the source on a line following the table or figure.

7. If you use footnotes (as in Figure 11.4), assign them raised lowercase letters (a, b, c, etc.) and place the notes below the table or figure (and source citation, if given).

List of Works Cited

Begin the list of works cited on a new page. (The exception is a very brief list, which you can begin after skipping three lines from the end of the text.)

- **Title.** Center the title *Works Cited* (or *Bibliography*) about one inch from the top of the page; that is, skip three lines following the page number.
- **Spacing.** Double-space between the title and the first entry and throughout the list. Do not skip additional lines between entries.
- **Entries.** Follow the guidelines in Chapter 6. Remember to "outdent" each entry; that is, begin each entry at the left margin and indent the second and subsequent lines one-half inch (five spaces). List items in alphabetical order. Do not number your entries. The list of works cited should include only works that you quoted or paraphrased in writing the paper, not works you consulted but did not use.

Refer to Figure 11.6 for a sample works-cited page.

Fastening the Paper

Fasten your paper with a paper clip in the upper left-hand corner. Do not staple or rivet pages together or place your paper in a cover unless you are requested to do so by your instructor.

Indent second subsequent lines of each entry one-half inch.

Three hyphens followed by a period indicate a second work by the same author.

```
                                                    Stafford 12


                              Works Cited
       American Association of Colleges of Pharmacy. "Career
                                                              Double-space
              Options." 16 Sept. 2002 <http://www.aacp.org/>.   throughout.

       ---. "Hospital and Institutional Practice." 16 Sept. 2002

              <http://www.aacp.org/>.

       Barefoot, Blake. Personal interview. 18 Sept. 2002.

       "The Career Interests Game." U of Missouri Career Center.

              14 Sept. 2002 <http://success.missour.edu/career/>.
```

Figure 11.6 Sample works cited page.

Title Page

A title page is standard only for a book-length report, a paper with multiple chapters, or a paper with preliminary material such as a formal outline or preface. If you use a title page, it should follow the format shown in Figure 11.7.

Title-page information is typed in the center of the page. Center each line, and leave equal space above and below the typed material. Most word-processing programs can automatically center material on a page from top to bottom.

Errors

Use the spell-check feature of your word-processing program and proofread to make your paper as error-free as possible before you print your final draft. For errors discovered during proofreading, neatly cross out a minor error with a single line, and write the correction above it. Never erase, and do not use correction fluid for making handwritten changes. Any page with a major error or numerous minor errors should be corrected on the computer and reprinted.

Format for Handwritten Papers

Most of the guidelines for computer-generated papers also apply to handwritten papers, with the following adjustments. Consult your instructor to determine if handwritten papers are acceptable.

Paper

Use lined, non-see-through 8½ × 11-inch loose-leaf paper. Never use sheets torn or cut from a spiral notebook. Paper should be college ruled (3½ lines per inch) and have a left margin line. Write on only one side of each sheet of paper.

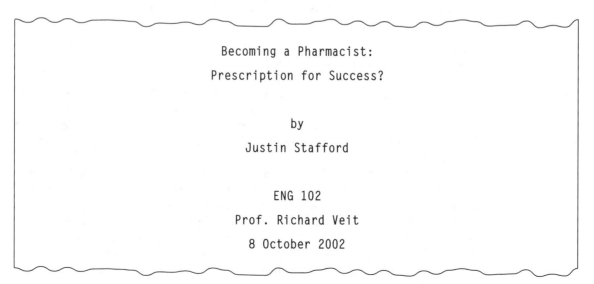

```
                  Becoming a Pharmacist:
                 Prescription for Success?



                            by
                     Justin Stafford



                        ENG 102
                   Prof. Richard Veit
                    8 October 2002
```

Figure 11.7 **Sample title page.**

Pen

Use a fine-point pen with dark blue or black ink. Never use a pen that smudges or that leaves small ink blotches when touched to the page.

Handwriting

Write in a neat, clear hand. Hard-to-read, distractingly fancy, or slovenly handwriting detracts from the effectiveness of your presentation. If you have difficulty with your handwriting, you would be wise to have your paper typed. Do not make your writing excessively large or leave excessive space between words. Handwritten papers with only a few words on each line are unpleasant to read because they demand constant eye movement.

Margins

Leave about a one-inch margin from the top and from the left of each page. That is, begin each page on the second line, and begin each line at the red margin line. Do not leave space for right and bottom margins, unless requested to do so by your instructor. The title and page numbers are placed as in typed papers.

Spacing

Single-space your paper unless you are requested by your instructor to double-space.

Errors

Handwritten papers should be error-free. Neatly cross out a minor error with a single line, and write the correction above it. Never erase or use correction fluid to make corrections. Any page with a major error or numerous minor errors should be recopied.

Excerpts from a handwritten paper are shown in Figures 11.8 and 11.9.

■ A FORMAL OUTLINE

The general, *informal outlines* that Emily Gould used in writing her early drafts (see pages 123 and 183) helped her organize her research materials. The length and complexity of a research paper require writers to have a plan for arranging it—one that is general and flexible enough so that they can develop and alter it as they discover new ideas.

Informal outlines are valuable, but most writers—both beginners and professionals alike—find it difficult and limiting to create a detailed, formal outline *before* they write. As you have now read many times in this book, writing is a learning process. Writers rarely know exactly how a paper will turn out before they write it. Even the best-prepared writers are usually surprised by the final form their writing takes. This occurs because our minds are actively at work when we write, and writing stimulates new thoughts that can take our writing in unforeseen directions.

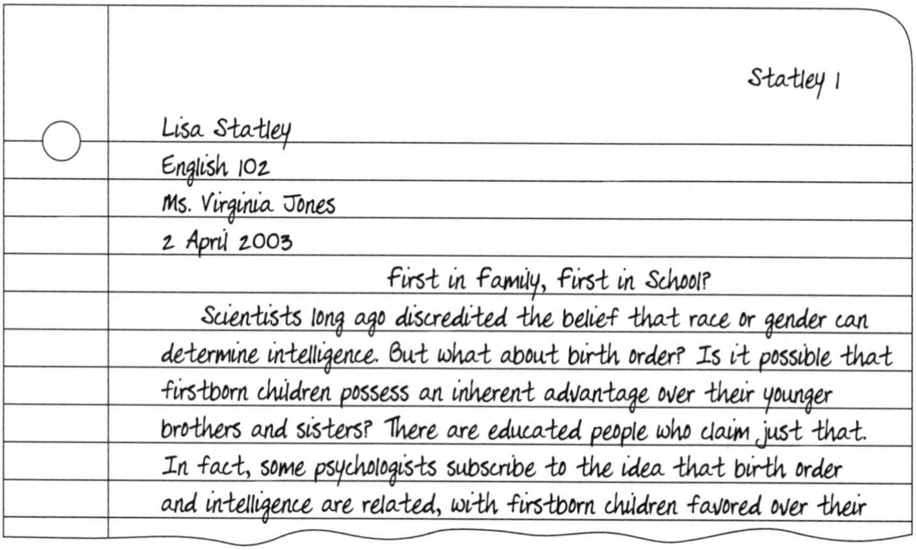

Statley 1

Lisa Statley

English 102

Ms. Virginia Jones

2 April 2003

First in Family, First in School?

Scientists long ago discredited the belief that race or gender can determine intelligence. But what about birth order? Is it possible that firstborn children possess an inherent advantage over their younger brothers and sisters? There are educated people who claim just that. In fact, some psychologists subscribe to the idea that birth order and intelligence are related, with firstborn children favored over their

Figure 11.8 Sample first page of a handwritten paper.

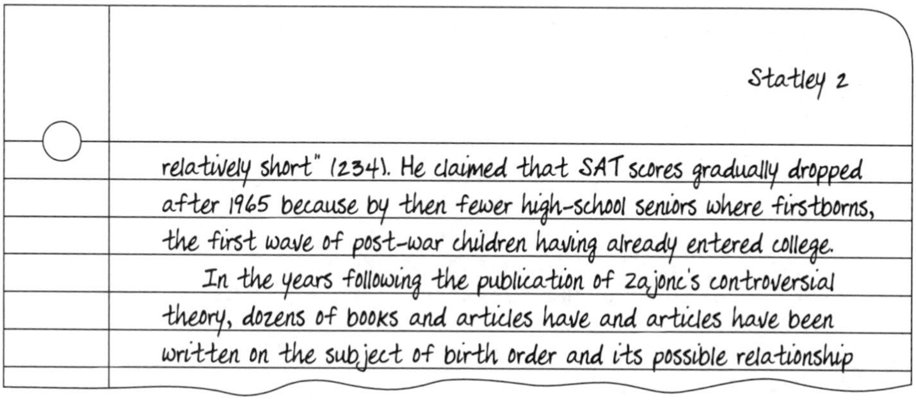

Statley 2

relatively short" (234). He claimed that SAT scores gradually dropped after 1965 because by then fewer high-school seniors where firstborns, the first wave of post-war children having already entered college.

In the years following the publication of Zajonc's controversial theory, dozens of books and articles have and articles have been written on the subject of birth order and its possible relationship

Figure 11.9 Subsequent page from a handwritten paper.

Although a *formal outline* is limited in usefulness when it is prepared before you begin writing, it *can* be useful as part of the revision process—when it is written *after* you have completed a preliminary draft. As a scaled-down map of your paper, the formal outline allows you to see its organization with clarity. It can point out the flaws of your arrangement and suggest new possibilities. Some instructors require that a printed, formal outline be included as a part of the research paper to make sure that their students have considered organization carefully. The detailed formal outline that Emily submitted with her paper is printed on the following page.

Fast Food Comes at a High Price for Workers

  I. Introduction
     A. Thesis: Benefits outweighed by cost to workers
     B. Background information about fast-food use
     C. Benefits and costs of teen employment

 II. Workplace issues
     A. Hours worked
        1. Current government regulations
        2. Proposals for new regulations
     B. Safety issues
        1. Restrictions on permissible jobs for young
           workers
           a. Teens endangered by lax enforcement
           b. Proposals for better enforcement
        2. Economic incentives for employers to violate
           laws
     C. Wages paid
        1. Minimum wage
           a. Decline in purchasing power
           b. Proposals for increase
              (1) Opposition from restaurants
              (2) Support from unions
        2. Lack of bargaining power by workers
           a. Unskilled work--duties highly mechanical
           b. High turnover
     D. Instances of unfair practice
        1. Overtime not paid
        2. Other abuses
     E. Unsuccessful efforts to unionize

III. Conclusion
     A. Benign public image created by restaurants
     B. Reality: high price paid by fast-food workers

An outline can be as detailed—or as general—as you wish. Emily's outline is reasonably complete, but she could have made it either shorter or longer if she wished. Compare it to this excerpt from a less detailed version of Emily's outline:

I. Introduction: Benefits of fast-food employment come at a price
II. Workplace issues
    A. Hours worked
    B. Safety issues
        1. Restrictions on permissible jobs for young workers
        2. Economic incentives for employers to violate laws
    C. Wages paid
        1. Minimum wage
        2. Lack of bargaining power by workers
    D. Unfair practices
    E. Unsuccessful efforts to unionize
III. Conclusion: high price paid by fast-food workers

On the other hand, Emily could also create a far more detailed outline of her paper. For example, she could expand Section II-C of her outline as follows:

C. Wages paid
    1. Minimum wage
        a. Decline in purchasing power
            (1) Adequate for many teens
            (2) Inadequate for supporting a family
        b. Proposals for increase
            (1) Opposition from restaurants
                (a) Support for exemptions from minimum wage
                (b) Arguments against wage increase
                    i) Loss of jobs
                    ii) Increased prices
            (2) Support from unions
                (a) Benefits to low-income neighborhoods
                (b) No harm to companies
                    i) Minimal increase in prices
                    ii) Happier workers
    2. Lack of bargaining power by workers . . .

When you are revising your paper, a detailed outline can help you see how each part fits into the whole. When you have difficulty in creating an outline, the cause is often a problem with the organization of your paper. Your attempts to create a logical outline can often suggest a workable rearrangement of material within your paper. For example, before Emily created her formal outline, she had placed a long quotation from a union representative about wages with her final section on unions. Only when she created her outline did she decide that it belonged more logically in her earlier section on the minimum wage.

On the other hand, a writer should not be a slave to a rigidly symmetrical outline. In the final analysis, the nature of your material and not form-for-form's sake should determine your outline.

Standard Numbering System

Formal outlines usually follow the format that Emily used. Notice that each major part of Emily's outline is divided into subparts. These subparts are indented and marked with numbers and letters, following this *standard system:*

Paper Title

    I. First major part of the paper
      A. First subpart of I
      B. Second subpart of I
        1. First subpart of B
        2. Second subpart of B
    II. Second major part
      A. First subpart of II
        1. First subpart of A
        2. Second subpart of A
      B. Second subpart of II
        1. First subpart of B
        2. Second subpart of B
    III. Third major part
      A. First subpart of III
        1. First subpart of A
        2. Second subpart of A
        3. Third subpart of A
      B. Second subpart of III
        1. First subpart of B
        2. Second subpart of B
          a. First subpart of 2
          b. Second subpart of 2
          c. Third subpart of 2
        3. Third subpart of B

Decimal System

The *decimal system* is also widely used for outlines, particularly for scientific papers.

    1. First major part
    2. Second major part
      2.1 First subpart of 2
      2.2 Second subpart of 2
        2.2.1 First subpart of 2.2
        2.2.2 Second subpart of 2.2
          2.2.2.1 . . .
          2.2.2.2 . . .
  3. . . .
    3.1 . . .
    3.2 . . .
    3.3 . . .

Some instructors who assign formal outlines require, in the interest of symmetry, that whenever a part is to have subparts, there must be at least two of them; that is, they prefer that there not be a part 1 without at least a part 2, and so on. For example, they would find level A1a in the following to be faulty because it is the only entry on its level (there is no A1b):

A. Hours worked
    1. Current government regulations
        a. Child labor laws
    2. Proposals for new regulations

It should be stressed that not everyone objects to lone subparts. For those who do, the preceding can be adjusted easily by incorporating the subpart into the part above it:

A. Hours worked
    1. Current government regulations: child labor laws
    2. Proposals for new regulations

Formal Outlines

1. Following are the parts of an outline for an argumentative paper. They appear in the proper order, but they have not been numbered or indented. Number them according to the *standard system* for outlining.

The Case against Saturday Morning Cartoons

Introduction
Background: description of current situation
Thesis: harm to children by Saturday morning cartoon shows
Counterarguments (those favoring these shows)
Positive-benefit arguments
Benefit to parents: babysitting
Benefits to children
Cartoon violence a harmless outlet for children's aggression
Children taught about life from cartoons
Free-market arguments
Programming determined by ratings, sponsors
Children's viewing up to parents, not networks
Censorship dangerous to our way of life
Refutation of counterarguments
Refutation of positive-benefit arguments
Damage to parents: deprived of interaction with their children
Damage to children
Shown only violent solutions to problems
Shown only the worst aspects of life
Refutation of free-market arguments
Morality, not only profits, a responsibility of networks

Parents unable to judge and screen all programming
Voluntary controls, not censorship, requested
Additional argument: danger to society of children's viewing
A nation of antisocial zombies
A nation of viewers, not doers
Conclusion: a call for reform

2. Renumber the preceding outline entries using the decimal system.

Topic and Sentence Outlines

The preceding formal outlines are examples of *topic outlines,* in which all the parts consist of phrases rather than complete sentences. In a *sentence outline,* the parts consist·of complete sentences. For example:

II. Various issues in the workplace affect employees.
   A. Limits on the hours teens can work are not always effective.
      1. Child-labor laws offer some but not complete protection.
      2. New laws have been proposed to update protections.
   B. Legislation is not always effective in keeping young workers safe.
      1. Laws seek to limit the kinds of jobs available to young workers.
         A. Teens are endangered by lax enforcement.
         B. Better enforcement has been proposed.
      2. Employers have economic incentives to violate safety laws. . . .

You can use either the topic or sentence outline method, but whichever you choose, be certain that you follow it consistently.

Like some of the other steps in research writing, the details of outline-writing may strike you as complicated—as undoubtedly they are—but they do serve a purpose. Use your informal and formal outlines to help you organize, write, and revise your paper. But remember that an outline is a tool to help you produce a better paper and not an end in itself. It is important at all times to remember the central goal of your research writing: to communicate what you have discovered in an effective way. Like all parts of the research process, the outline will work best and be of most help to you if you approach it with common sense.

EXERCISES | **Sentence Outlines**

1. Continue revising Emily Gould's outline on page 240 to make it a sentence outline.

2. Rewrite the outline in the preceding exercise beginning on the previous page to make it a sentence outline. Each line of the outline should be a complete sentence.

AND, FINALLY, PROOFREADING THE FINISHED PRODUCT

When you prepare your final draft, be sure that you observe formatting conventions described in Chapter 11, along with any others your instructor may specify. Before you submit your paper, read it through several times, slowly and carefully, looking for errors. Look for typing mistakes, misspellings, missing words, punctuation problems, and any other surface errors that may have escaped your notice in earlier readings. It is especially useful to have a friend proofread the paper as well, because by now you have become so familiar with what you have written that you may have difficulty noticing surface details.

Neatly cross out a minor error with a single line and write the correction above it. Never erase, and do not use correction fluid for making handwritten changes. Any page with a major error or numerous minor errors should be reprinted.

After proofreading their final drafts, Emily and Justin brought them to class, where their instructors gave them one final assignment:

Final Proofreading   ASSIGNMENT

Read the final drafts of the other students in your editing group. Do not mark on their papers, but if you find an error, point it out to the author so that it can be corrected.

At last, Emily and Justin submitted their final drafts. For both, the project had been difficult but rewarding work. Like their classmates, they had struggled with the previously unfamiliar process of research and research writing. They had uncovered and managed a large body of research materials. From these sources, they had created essays that had substance, form, and interest—essays they were proud of. They had also learned a great deal, not only about their particular topics, but also about research, about college scholarship, and even about the meaning of an education itself. It is likely that after the hard work of your own research project is completed, you too, like Emily, Justin, and many thousands of other students before you, will feel a well-deserved sense of satisfaction with what you have accomplished.

Other Citation Formats: APA Style and Numbered References

■ FORMATS OTHER THAN MLA

Although you will use the MLA parenthetical or footnote/endnote format to acknowledge sources in papers that you write for humanities courses (such as research papers in a composition class), other disciplines may require you to use different formats. Since many journals establish their own conventions for documenting sources, you are also likely to encounter various other formats when you conduct library research. A glance through scholarly journals in your college library will show you that dozens of different formats are in use—usually varying only in minor ways from MLA format or the formats described in this chapter.

Although it is not practical to describe all the different formats here, you should be familiar with the most commonly used formats for citing sources. It is probably unnecessary for you to memorize the details of any of them, but when you use a particular format, you should be prepared to model your own references carefully on sample entries, such as those in this chapter. Note the ways in which these formats differ from MLA format and pay close attention to the information that is presented in each entry, the order in which it is presented, and the punctuation used to denote and separate items.

Two principal formats, besides the MLA, are in wide use among scholars. The APA format gives special prominence to the source's publication date in all citations. In the numbered references format, each source is assigned a number in the list of works cited; each note in the paper refers to a source by its assigned number.

■ APA STYLE

Next to the MLA style, the most common format for documenting sources is that of the American Psychological Association—*APA style.* This format (or a variation of it) is widely used for course papers and journal articles in psychology but also in many other disciplines in both the social and natural sciences. Although APA format differs in many particulars from MLA format, the main difference is the prominence its citations give to the source's publication date. In fields where new theories and discoveries are constantly challenging past assumptions, readers must know if a writer's sources are up-to-date. Note how the date is featured in the following sample APA citations. Parenthetical notes in APA style always include the date, as in the following:

```
. . . tendency of creative people to be organized (Sternberg

& Lubart, 1995, p. 246).
```

Following is the listing for that same source, as it appears in the references page (list of works cited). Notice that the date is given in parentheses immediately following the author's name.

```
Sternberg, R. J., & Lubart, T. I. (1995). Defying the crowd:

    Cultivating creativity in a culture of conformity. New

    York: Free Press.
```

The particulars of APA reference style are explained in the following sections.

APA Bibliographic Citations (Reference List)

At the end of the paper, all sources are listed on a separate page, under the title *References* (not *Works Cited*). Like the MLA format, the APA also arranges works alphabetically, according to the first word in each item. See, for example, Figure A.4 on page 260.

In addition to the prominence given to publication dates, bibliographic citations in APA style differ from MLA listings in three principal ways:

1. In APA style, only the author's last name is given in full. Initials are used for first and middle names. Thus, an author who would be listed in MLA style as *Sternberg, Robert J.* is listed as *Sternberg, R. J.* in APA style.

2. Except for proper names, only the first word of the work's title (and, if there is a subtitle, the first word following the colon) is capitalized. Thus, a book title that would be listed in MLA style as *Defying the Crowd: Cultivating Creativity in a Culture of Conformity* is listed in APA style as *Defying the crowd: Cultivating creativity in a culture of conformity.*

3. Titles of periodical articles (and other works shorter than book-length) are not enclosed in quotation marks as they are in MLA style.

Other differences can be seen in the following sample entries.

Model Entries

Punctuation following italicized text is also italicized in APA style.

Books

Following are sample APA entries for books (accessed in print form). For online books, see Internet and Electronic Sources on page 254.

A Book with One Author

```
Macdonald, J. (2003). A free nation deep in debt: The financial

    roots of democracy. New York: Farrar, Straus and Giroux.

Wheelock, A. K., Jr. (1995). Vermeer and the art of painting.

    New Haven, CT: Yale University Press.
```

The complete names of publishers are given. Words like *University* and *Press* are not abbreviated.

A Book with Two to Six Authors

```
Reid, J. A., Forrestal, P., & Cook, J. (1990). Small group

    learning in the classroom. Portsmouth, NH: Heinemann.
```

All authors, not just the first, are listed last name first, followed by initials. An ampersand (&) is used before the name of the last author.

A Book with More Than Six Authors

```
Martin, S., Smith, L., Forehand, M. R., Mobbs, R., Lynch, T. F.,

    Renfrew, E. J., et al. (2003). Migratory waterfowl.

    Lincoln, NE: Wendell Press.
```

List only the first six authors, followed by *et al.*

Two or More Works by the Same Author, Different Years

```
Irwin, E. (2000). New . . .

Irwin, E. (2003). Lessons . . .
```

When two or more works have the same author(s), arrange the works chronologically, not alphabetically by title.

Two or More Works by the Same Author, Same Year

```
Bushman, D. E. (2003a). Development . . .

Bushman, D. E. (2003b). Lessons . . .
```

When the author(s) has two or more works in the same year, arrange the works alphabetically by title, and place lowercase letters (*a, b, c,* etc.) immediately after the year.

A Book with No Author Listed

Addison Wesley Longman author's guide. (1998). New York: Longman.

A Book with a Corporate or Group Author

Sotheby's. (1995). *Nineteenth century European paintings, drawings and watercolours.* London: Author.

A Book by a Government Agency

U.S. Department of Health and Human Services. Substance Abuse and Mental Health Services Administration. Center for Mental Health Services. (2002). *What you need to know about youth violence prevention.* Rockville, MD: Government Printing Office.

A Book with a Translator

Ramos, J. (1999). *Divergent modernities: Culture and politics in nineteenth-century Latin America* (J. D. Blanco, Trans.). Durham, NC: Duke University Press.

A Book with an Author and Editor

Shakespeare, W. (1591). *Henry V* (T. W. Craik, Ed.). New York: Routledge. (Edition published 1995)

A Book with an Editor

Stimpson, C. R., & Person, E. S. (Eds.). (1980). *Women: Sex and sexuality.* Chicago: University of Chicago Press.

A Book in a Later Edition

Skinner, E. (2003). *Women and the national experience* (2nd ed.). New York: Longman.

A Book in a Series

Matthee, R. P. (2000). *The Politics of trade in Safavid Iran: Silk for silver, 1600-1730.* Cambridge Studies in Islamic Civilization. New York: Cambridge University Press.

A Multivolume Book

Messenger, C. (1995). *For love of regiment: A history of British infantry, 1660-1993* (Vol. 1). Philadelphia: Trans-Atlantic Publications.

List all volumes of the work that you cite; for example, *(Vols. 2-3).*

A Paperback or Other Reprinted Book

Horwitz, T. (1999). *Confederates in the attic: Dispatches from the unfinished Civil War.* New York: Vintage. (Original work published 1998)

Selections from Books

A Selection from an Anthology

Baker, S. W. (1980). Biological influences on human sex and gender. In C. R. Stimpson & E. S. Person (Eds.), *Women: Sex and sexuality* (pp. 212-223). Chicago: University of Chicago Press.

Rushdie, S. (1992). A pen against the sword: In good faith. In Hirschberg, S. (Ed.), *One world, many cultures* (pp. 480-496). New York: Macmillan. (Reprinted from *Newsweek, 115,* February 12, 1990: 52-57)

An Article in an Encyclopedia or Other Reference

Harmon, M. (2002). Folk arts. In *The new encyclopaedia Britannica: Macropaedia* (15th ed., Vol. 19, pp. 306-338). Chicago: Britannica.

Morrison, T. (2003). In *Who's who in America* (57th ed.).

    Chicago: Marquis.

Hames, R. (1994). Yanomamö. In *South America. Encyclopedia of*

    world cultures (Vol. 7, pp. 374-377). Boston: G. K. Hall.

A Preface, Introduction, Foreword, or Afterword

Bradford, B. T. (2000). Foreword. In K. Winsor, *Forever amber*

    (pp. iii-xi). Chicago: Chicago Review.

Periodicals and Newspapers

Following are APA entries for periodicals and newspapers (when accessed in print form). For articles accessed online, see Internet and Electronic Sources on pages 254–55.

An Article in a Magazine

Block, T. G. (1995, September 11). Riding the waves. *Forbes,*

    156, 182, 184.

Jellinek, G. (2003, February). Record collecting: Hobby or

    obsession? *Opera News, 67*, 85.

Van Zile, S. (2003, January/February). Grammar that'll move you!

    Instructor, 32-34.

The date of a periodical is given (year first) immediately following the author's name. Months are not abbreviated. Neither quotation marks nor italics are used for article titles. All important words in a periodical's title are capitalized (*Opera News*). The volume number of a periodical is italicized and follows the name of the periodical (*Forbes, 156*). All page numbers are given immediately afterward. For magazine and journal articles (unlike newspaper articles), neither *p.* nor *pp.* is used. The Block article appeared on pages 182 and 184.

An Article in a Journal

A journal whose pages are numbered continuously throughout a volume:

Larter, R. (2003). Understanding complexity in biophysical

    chemistry. *Journal of Physical Chemistry, 107,*

    415-429.

A journal, every issue of which begins on page 1:

Mitchell, W. J. (2002). The surplus value of images. *Mosaic*
    35(3), 1-23.

The number *35*(3) tells you that the article appeared in volume 35, issue 3, of *Mosaic*. Only the volume number is italicized. Page numbers are not shortened, as they are in MLA style; pages in the Larter article are written 415–429 (not 415–29).

An Article in a Newspaper

Argetsinger, A. (2003, January 13). Lobbying gets old college
    try. *Washington Post*, p. B2.

Leonhardt, D. (2003, January 12). Defining the rich in the
    world's wealthiest nation. *New York Times*, national
    edition, section 4, pp. 1, 8.

An Editorial

Six sigma schools. (2003, January 15). [Editorial]. *Wall Street*
    Journal, p. A10.

A Letter to the Editor

Rothschild, M. (2003, January). [Letter to the editor].
    Kiplinger's, p. 14.

A Review

Flanagan, C. (2003, January 12). Get a job. [Review of the book
    What should I do with my life?]. *New York Times Book*
    Review, p. 4.

Glenn, K. (2000, January). [Review of the film *Man on the moon*].
    Premiere, 13, 20.

[Review of the book *Going to the territory*]. (1986, August).
    Atlantic, 120, 91.

Stearns, D. P. (1999, December). [Review of the CD *The well-*
    tempered clavier]. *Stereophile, 10,* 173, 175.

Other Sources

An Audio Recording

Dickinson, D. (Speaker). (1991). *Creating the future:*

    Perspectives on educational change [Audiocassette].

    Minneapolis, MN: Accelerated Learning Systems.

Mahler, G. (1999). Symphony No. 7 [CD]. United States: RCA Victor.

A Film, DVD, or Video Recording

Lee, S. (Director). (2003). *25th hour* [Film]. United States:

    Touchstone.

Mankiewicz, J. L. (Scriptwriter and director). (2003). *All about*

    Eve. [DVD]. Hollywood, CA: Studio Classics. (Film produced

    1950).

The classical Hollywood style [Videocassette]. (1995). Program 1

    of *The American cinema.* Washington, DC: Annenberg/CPB.

A Lecture

A source that cannot be retrieved by your readers, such as a classroom or public lecture which is not available in print or on recording, is not listed among your paper's references. However, it is cited in the paper in a parenthetical note: (*S. Granetta, classroom lecture, April 7, 2003*).

A Personal Interview

A personal interview that you conduct cannot be retrieved by your readers, so it is not listed among your paper's references. However, it is cited in the paper in a parenthetical note: (*B. Barefoot, personal communication, September 18, 2002*).

A Broadcast or Published Interview

Gross, T. (2003, January 21). [Interview with Kevin Spacey]. In

    Fresh air. National Public Radio. Wilmington, NC: WHQR.

Adiga, A. (2003, February). Trump speaks. [Interview with Donald

    Trump]. *Money, 32,* 28.

A Television or Radio Program

Harmon, R. (Director). (2000, January 1). The crossing

    [Television program]. Stamford, CT: History Channel.

Stone, S. (Reporter). (2003, January 9). [Report on Japanese comic books.] In *All things considered.* Washington, DC: National Public Radio.

An Unpublished Essay

Gould, E. (2002). Fast food comes at a high price for workers. Unpublished essay for Prof. Katherine Humel's English 12 class, University of North Carolina, Chapel Hill.

An Unpublished Letter or E-Mail

Unpublished correspondence cannot be retrieved by your readers, so it is not listed among your paper's references. However, it is cited in the paper in a parenthetical note: (*C. Cilano, personal communication, March 5, 2003*).

An Unpublished Questionnaire

Doe, J. (2003). [Survey of student attitudes on dating]. Unpublished raw data.

Internet and Electronic Sources

An Online Book

Irving, D. *Hitler's war.* (1977). New York: Viking. Retrieved January 19, 2003, from http://www.fpp.co.uk/books/Hitler/

A Print Periodical Accessed Online

Clinton, B. (2002, September 10). The path to peace. *Salon.com.* Retrieved January 20, 2003, from http://www.salon.com/news/feature/2002/09/10/clinton/

Falsani, C. (2003, January 10). Did respect for religion cloud 'clone' coverage? *Chicago Sun-Times.* Retrieved January 19, 2003, from http://www.suntimes.com/output/falsani/cst-nws-fals.html

Fineman, H., & Lipper, T. (2003, January 27). Spinning race. *Newsweek.* Retrieved January 19, 2003, from http://www.msnbc.com/news/861383.asp?

Young, A. J., Wilson, A. S., & Mundell, C. G. (2002). Chandra
     imaging of the x-ray core of the Virgo cluster.
     Astrophysical Journal 579(2), 560-570. Retrieved January
     19, 2003, from http://www.journals.uchicago.edu/ApJ/
     journal/issues/ApJ/v579n2/54935/54935.html

A Work Accessed in an Online Database

Use the following format when you access a work in an online database such as EBSCOhost, InfoTrac, LexisNexis, ProQuest, or WilsonWeb.

Jovanovic, R. (2002, August 5). Snowmobilers tied to rules of
     the road. *National Law Journal, 24,* B1. Retrieved January
     20, 2003, from InfoTrac OneFile database (Item A91884653).
Associated Press. (2003, January 9). Political inclination of
     the states. Retrieved January 20, 2003 from LexisNexis
     Academic Universe database.

Include an item number for the article, if available.

An Online Encyclopedia Article

Humpback whale. (2003). Encyclopaedia Britannica 2003.
     Retrieved January 28, 2003, from Encyclopaedia Britannica
     Online.

An Organization's or Individual's Web Site

The Coral Reef Alliance. (n.d.). Coral friendly guidelines.
     Retrieved January 21, 2003, from http://
     www.coralreefalliance.org/parks/guidelines.html
Hemming, S. (n.d.). [Home page]. Retrieved January 21, 2003,
     from http://www.sallyhemming.com/

Use (*n.d.*) for "no date."

Treatment of other sources, as well as detailed information about APA format, can be found by consulting the latest edition of the *Publication Manual of the American Psychological Association.* You can find the book in the reference section of most college libraries.

Notes in APA Style

Parenthetical notes in APA format are handled similarly to the MLA method, but with three notable differences:

1. The year of publication is included in the note.

2. All items are separated by commas.

3. Page numbers are preceded by the abbreviation *p.* or *pp.*

When a work is referred to as a whole, no page numbers are needed:

    In a study of reaction times (Sanders, 2003), . . .

Only the year is needed when the author's name appears in the sentence:

    Sanders (2003) studied reaction times . . .

Include pages when the source can be located more specifically:

    ". . . not necessary" (Galizio, 1999, p. 9).

Give the first word or two from the title when the author's name is unknown. Book titles are italicized; periodical titles in notes (unlike in the reference list) are enclosed in quotation marks; all important words are capitalized (also like reference-list citations):

    . . . the book (*Culture*, 2002).

    . . . the article ("US policy," 1999).

Only the year, not the complete date, is given in notes referring to periodical articles.

For a work with six or fewer authors, the note lists all authors' last names:

    (Andrulis, Beers, Bentley, & Gage, 2001)

However, only the first author's name is given for a work with more than six authors:

    (Sabella et al., 2003)

When the reference list cites two or more works written by the same author in the same year, use lowercase letters to differentiate them, as in reference-list citations:

    (Bushman, 2003a)

    (Bushman, 2003b)

These two notes cite different works by Bushman, both written in 2003.

When a note refers to more than one work, list the references alphabetically and separate them with a semicolon:

    (Earle & Reeves, 1999; Kowal, 2002)

Sample Pages in APA Style

Any paper written using MLA format can also be written in APA format. For example, Emily Gould could have used APA style for her paper on fast food.

A cover page is typically used for APA papers. The cover page is numbered as page 1, and a shortened version of the title precedes the page number on each page, as in Figure A.1.

The title is repeated on the opening page of the paper, numbered as page 2. Compare Figures A.2 and A.3 with pages from Emily's MLA-style paper that begins on page 11. Compare Figure A.4 with Emily's list of works cited on page 23.

```
                                              Fast Food 1


                        Running head: FAST FOOD


              Fast Food Comes at a High Price for Workers
                            Emily Gould
                University of North Carolina at Chapel Hill


                        Professor Katherine Humel
                            English 12
                            Section 16
                          October 4, 2002
```

Figure A.1 Sample APA cover page.

Fast Food 1

Fast Food Comes at a High Price for Workers

McDonald's, Burger King, KFC, Wendy's, and other
fast-food chains have brought countless innovations to the
food services industry, delivering our food faster and
cheaper over the years. Convenience and value have come at
a price, however, and many believe that benefits to the
public are outweighed by the costs that this giant
industry imposes on its workers.

In his book *Fast-Food Nation*, Eric Schlosser (2001)
shows just how much fast food has revolutionized America's
eating habits. In 1970, Americans spent $6 billion on fast

Figure A.2 Sample APA opening page.

Fast Food 2

Having teenagers prepare and serve us food in the
fast-food setting has become "so natural, so normal, and
so inevitable that people often think little about it,"
according to Stuart Tannock, a lecturer in social and
cultural studies at the University of California at
Berkeley (Ayoub, 2001). While fast-food workers have
become an essential component in the service industry, a
fast-food job is viewed as undesirable, dead-end work.

One-third of all workers under 35 got their first job
working for a restaurant (Yum! Brands, n.d.), and about
one-eighth of all workers in the United States have, at
some point, worked for McDonald's (Schlosser, 2001, p. 4).
Fast-food jobs have become such a common occupation for
teenagers that they become what Yvonne Zipp (1998) of the
Christian Science Monitor calls "a rite of passage" into
the American workforce. They are ideal for teens because

Citation of a source without author, date, or pages.

Citation of a source with a page reference.

APA parenthetical notes include the publication date. No page is given for a one-page source.

Citation of a source following author's name.

Figure A.3 Sample APA notes.

Fast Food 13

References

Ayoub, N. C. (May 25, 2001). Nota bene. [Review of the

Author's last
names and
first initials
are given.

     book *Youth at work: The unionized fast-food and*

     grocery workplace]. *Chronicle of Higher Education,*

     p. A20.

Article titles
are not
placed in
quotation
marks.

Broydo, L. (1999, January/February). Worked over. *Utne*

     Reader, 16, 20-21.

General information on the fair labor standards act

     (FLSA). (n.d.). U.S. Department of Labor Employment

Online sources
are cited in
this format.

     Standards Administration Wage and Hour Division.

     Retrieved September 29, 2002, from http://www.dol.gov/

     esa/regs/compliance/whd/mwposter.htm

Hamstra, M. (1998, September 7). Unions seek momentum from

     Canadian McD's certification. *Nation's Restaurant*

     News, 32: 3. Retrieved September 15, 2002, from

     MasterFILE Premier database (Item 1099749).

Titles are
capitalized
according to
the rules for
sentence
capitalization.

Figure A.4 Sample APA references page.

■ FORMAT FEATURING NUMBERED REFERENCES

Another common bibliographic format uses ***numbered references*** to identify sources. Variations on this format are used most widely in fields such as mathematics, computer science, finance, and other areas in the applied sciences.

Sources are assigned a number in the references page (list of works cited) and are referred to in the paper by that number rather than by the author's name. Items in the references list can be arranged either in alphabetical order or in the order in which references occur within the paper. Figure A.5 shows how the references list at the end of Emily Gould's paper might have looked if she had used this style. In this case, the references are numbered in the order in which they first appear in the paper.

```
                                              Gould 13

                        References
  1. Schlosser, Eric. Fast-Food Nation: The Dark Side of the
     All-American Meal. Boston: Houghton, 2001.
  2. Ayoub, Nina C. "Nota Bene." Rev. of Youth at Work: The
     Unionized Fast-Food and Grocery Workplace, by Stuart
     Tannock. Chronicle of Higher Education 25 May 2001: A20.
  3. Yum! Brands. "Great Jobs." 22 Sept. 2002.
     <http://www.yumjobs.com/>.
  4. Zipp, Yvonne. "Virtues of Work vs. Finishing Homework."
     Christian Science Monitor 15 Dec. 1998: 1. MasterFILE
     Premier. EBSCOhost. 15 Sept. 2002
     <http://web3.epnet.com/>.
```

Figure A.5 Sample list with numbered references.

Here is how the first three sentences with notes in Emily's paper would have appeared if she had used the numbered-references style:

Schlosser says Americans "spend more on fast food than on movies, books, magazines, newspapers, videos, and recorded music--combined" [1, p. 3].

> The paper's first note is numbered *1*.

Having teenagers prepare and serve us food in the fast-food setting has become "so natural, so normal, and so inevitable that people often think little about it," according to Stuart Tannock, a lecturer in social and cultural studies at the University of California at Berkeley [2, p. A20].

> The page reference follows the note number.

A later refer-
ence to a
source sited
earlier in the
paper.

One-third of all workers under 35 got their first job

working for a restaurant [3], and about one-eighth of all

workers in the United States have, at some point, worked

for McDonald's [1, p. 4]. Fast-food jobs have become such a

common occupation for teenagers that they become what Yvonne

Zipp of the <u>Christian Science Monitor</u> calls "a rite of

passage" into the American workforce [4, p. 1].

Note for
a source
without
pages

Apart from the use of reference numbers, there is no uniform style for citing bibliographic sources in this format. Individual items in the bibliography could follow the principles of MLA format, APA format, or yet some other format. If you are required to use numbered references for a course paper, be sure to check with your instructor for specific format details.

Another characteristic of papers using this format is that citation of page references is far less common than in either MLA or APA style. Usually, sources are referred to in the paper solely by their reference numbers, which are usually written within brackets:

Smith and Gurganus [6] showed that . . .

Often even the authors' names are omitted:

Other examples of this approach are [1, 4, 5]. In 1996, [3]

analyzed . . .

Instead of brackets, alternative formats that use numbered references place them either within parentheses:

Fort (7) disputes the findings of Byington (3) . . .

or as raised numbers:

It has been demonstrated[1] that artifacts that occur . . .

The raised number *1* in the preceding example refers not to a footnote or endnote but directly to the first source in the references list.

Appendix B

Footnotes and Endnotes

Scholars in the fields of art, dance, history, music, religion, and theater often use footnotes and endnotes, instead of parenthetical notes, to document sources. Although it should not be necessary for you to memorize the details of the format, you should know how to use this chapter as a reference guide whenever you need to write footnotes or endnotes. When you do, consult it carefully and be certain to follow the format exactly, paying special attention to the mechanics of arrangement and punctuation.

Figures B.1 and B.2 show how a portion of Emily Gould's research paper would have looked if she had used footnotes instead of parenthetical notes. (Compare them with her use of parenthetical notes on pages 18–19.) The excerpt in Figure B.3 shows what her "Notes" page would have looked like if she had used endnotes.

Footnotes and endnotes serve the same purpose as parenthetical notes—to identify and give credit to your sources for their specific contributions to your paper. In the same place in your paper where you would put a parenthetical note, put a raised number to refer your readers to the note. Number your notes consecutively throughout the paper, starting with number 1. For footnotes, type each note at the bottom of the same page where the reference occurs. For endnotes, type all notes, in numerical order, on a separate page following the paper but preceding the list of works cited.

SAMPLE FOOTNOTES AND ENDNOTES

The models in this chapter show the footnote/endnote format for works cited in Chapter 6. Note that complete information about a source is required only the first time it is cited in a note. Subsequent notes use an abbreviated format. (See sample footnote 21 in Figure B.1.)

Gould 8

Notes are numbered consecutively throughout the paper. The numbers are superscripts (raised slightly above the line).

for similar reasons.[19] When such employees grow dissatisfied, they are replaced quickly and easily, with little disruption of the restaurant's operations.

Fast-food restaurants see an annual turnover rate in employees of over 75%.[20] To accommodate easy replacement of workers, companies are steadily reaching a goal of "zero training" for employees by developing more efficient methods and adopting the most advanced kitchen technology. The fast-food kitchen is like an assembly line. Food arrives at the restaurant frozen, and preparation, which involves little actual cooking, is regimented by a manual, which includes such details as how hamburger patties are to be arranged on the grill and the thickness of the fries.[21] One college student who worked at Wendy's said, "You don't even think when doing work, and you never make

Double-space twice (skip 3 lines).

[19] Eric Schlosser, <u>Fast-Food Nation: The Dark Side of the All-American Meal</u> (Boston: Houghton, 2001) 68, 70.

After the first reference to a souce (see footnote 19), the abbreviated form is used (see footnote 21).

[20] Gerald L. White, "Employee Turnover: The Hidden Drain on Profits," <u>HR Focus</u> Jan. 1995: 15, <u>InfoTrac OneFile</u>, 21 Sept. 2002 <http://infotrac.galegroup.com/>.

[21] Schlosser 68-72.

Double-space within and between footnotes.

Figure B.1 A sample page from a paper that uses footnotes.

little disruption of the restaurant's operations.

Fast-food restaurants see an annual turnover rate in employees of over 75%.[20] To accommodate easy replacement of workers, companies are steadily reaching a goal of "zero

[18] Cashen, Jill. Personal Interview. 10 Sept. 2002.

[19] Eric Schlosser, <u>Fast-Food Nation: The Dark Side of the All-American Meal</u> (Boston: Houghton, 2001) 68, 70.

[20] Gerald L White, "Employee Turnover: The Hidden Drain on

Footnote 20 must be continued on the following page.

and training new employees, and additional staff is often needed to help process applications. Current employees are also burdened with extra responsibilities when they pick

Profits," <u>HR Focus</u> Jan. 1995: 15, <u>InfoTrac OneFile</u>, 21 Sept. 2002 <http://infotrac.galegroup.com/>.

[21] Schlosser 68-72.

[22] Tamicah Williams, personal interview, 24 Sept. 2002.

A line drawn on the page signals that the first footnote beneath it is continued from the previous page.

Figure B.2 Format for a footnote continued on the following page.

Gould 10

Notes

[1] Eric Schlosser, Fast-Food Nation: The Dark Side of the All-American Meal (Boston: Houghton, 2001) 3.

[2] Qtd. in Nina C. Ayoub, "Nota Bene," rev. of Youth at Work: The Unionized Fast-Food and Grocery Workplace, by Stuart Tannock, Chronicle of Higher Education 25 May 2001: A20.

[3] Yum! Brands, "Great Jobs," 22 Sept. 2002 <http://www.yumjobs.com/>.

[4] Schlosser 4.

[5] Yvonne Zipp, "Virtues of Work vs. Finishing Homework," Christian Science Monitor 15 Dec. 1998: 1, MasterFILE Premier, EBSCOhost, 15 Sept. 2002 <http://web3.epnet.com/> 1.

[6] "General Information on the Fair Labor Standards Act (FLSA)," U.S. Dept. of Labor Employment Standards Administration Wage and Hour Division, 29 Sept. 2002 <http://www.dol.gov/esa/regs/compliance/whd/mwposter.htm>.

[7] Zipp 1.

[8] Patrick Kiger, "Risky Business," Good Housekeeping Apr. 2002: 114, MasterFILE Premier, EBSCOhost, 15 Sept. 2002 <http://web3.epnet.com/>.

[9] Zipp 1.

[10] "Prohibited Occupations for Non-Agricultural Employees," U.S. Dept. of Labor, Elaws--Fair Labor Standards

Figure B.3 Sample notes page from a paper that uses endnotes.

Books

Following are sample entries for books (accessed in print form). For online books, see Internet and Electronic Sources on pages 273–74.

A Book with One Author

[1] James Macdonald, <u>A Free Nation Deep in Debt: The</u> <u>Financial Roots of Democracy</u> (New York: Farrar, 2003), 123-26.

Footnotes/endnotes differ from works cited entries in several particulars. The first line of each footnote/endnote is indented; the author's first (not last) name comes first; the publisher and date are enclosed in parentheses; and commas (not periods) separate major items. Also, unlike works cited entries (but like parenthetical notes), footnotes/endnotes give the specific page or pages from which the cited information is taken.

Second and Subsequent References—All Sources

After a work has been cited in one note, you do not need to repeat all the same information in subsequent notes that refer to that same source. For second and subsequent references to a source, footnotes/endnotes should contain the least amount of information needed to identify the source (usually the author and page number).

[2] Macdonald 45.

A Book with Two or Three Authors

[3] Robert L. Dingman and John D. Weaver, <u>Days in the Lives</u> <u>of Counselors</u> (Boston: Allyn, 2003) 88-103.

[4] Jo Anne Reid, Peter Forrestal, and Jonathan Cook, <u>Small</u> <u>Group Learning in the Classroom</u> (Portsmouth, NH: Heinemann, 1990) 110.

A Book with More Than Three Authors

[5] Stéphane Courtois, et al., <u>The Black Book of Communism:</u> <u>Crimes, Terror, Repression</u> (Cambridge, MA: Harvard UP, 1999) 248-49.

A Book with No Author Listed

[6] <u>Addison Wesley Longman Author's Guide</u> (New York: Longman, 1998) 11.

A Book with a Corporate or Group Author

[7] Sotheby's, Nineteenth Century European Paintings, Drawings and Watercolours (London: Sotheby's, 1995) 306.

[8] U of North Carolina at Wilmington, 2002-2003 Code of Student Life ([Wilmington, NC]: n.p., [2002]) 23-31.

A Book by a Government Agency

[9] United States, Dept. of Health and Human Services, Substance Abuse and Mental Health Services Admin., Center for Mental Health Services, What You Need to Know about Youth Violence Prevention (Rockville, MD: GPO, 2002) 3-4.

A Book with a Translator

[10] Julio Ramos, Divergent Modernities: Culture and Politics in Nineteenth-Century Latin America, trans. John D. Blanco (Durham: Duke UP, 1999) 97-99.

A Book with an Author and Editor

[11] William Shakespeare, Henry V, ed. T. W. Craik (New York: Routledge, 1995) 88.

A Book with an Editor

[12] Catherine R. Stimpson and Ethel Spector Person, eds., Women: Sex and Sexuality (Chicago: U of Chicago P, 1980), 11.

A Book in a Later Edition

[13] Ellen Skinner, Women and the National Experience, 2nd ed. (New York: Longman, 2003) 206-21.

A Book in a Series

[14] Rudolph P. Matthee, The Politics of Trade in Safavid Iran: Silk for Silver, 1600-1730, Cambridge Studies in Islamic Civilization (New York: Cambridge UP, 2000) 368.

A Multivolume Book
Volumes individually titled:

15 Crane Brinton, John B. Christopher, and Robert Lee Wolff, Prehistory to 1715, vol. 1 of A History of Civilization, 6th ed., 2 vols. (Englewood Cliffs, NJ: Prentice, 1984) 303.

Volumes not individually titled:

16 Charles Messenger, For Love of Regiment: A History of British Infantry, 1660-1993, vol. 1 (Philadelphia: Trans-Atlantic, 1995), 388.

A Book Published before 1900

17 Florence Nightingale, Notes on Nursing: What It Is, and What It Is Not (New York, 1860) 27.

A Paperback or Other Reprinted Book

18 Tony Horwitz, Confederates in the Attic: Dispatches from the Unfinished Civil War (1998; New York: Vintage, 1999) 177.

Selections from Books
A Selection from an Anthology

19 Myra Leifer, "Pregnancy," Women: Sex and Sexuality, ed. Catherine R. Stimpson and Ethel Spector Person (Chicago: U of Chicago P, 1980) 215.

20 George Lichtheim, "The Birth of a Philosopher," Collected Essays (New York: Viking, 1973) 109.

21 Salman Rushdie, "A Pen Against the Sword: In Good Faith," Newsweek 12 Feb. 1990: 52+, rpt. in One World, Many Cultures, ed. Stuart Hirschberg (New York: Macmillan, 1992) 487-88.

An Article in an Encyclopedia or Other Reference

22 Mamie Harmon, "Folk Arts," The New Encyclopaedia Britannica: Macropaedia, 15th ed., 2002.

23 "Morrison, Toni," Who's Who in America, 57th ed., 2003.

24 "Yodel," The Shorter Oxford English Dictionary, 1973.

25 Raymond Hames, "Yanomamö," South America, vol. 7 of Encyclopedia of World Cultures (Boston: Hall, 1994).

A Preface, Introduction, Foreword, or Afterword

26 Barbara Taylor Bradford, foreword, Forever Amber, by Kathleen Winsor, 1944 (Chicago: Chicago Review, 2000) iv-viii.

Sources in Periodicals and Newspapers

For articles accessed online, see Internet and Electronic Sources on pages 274–76.

An Article in a Magazine

27 Toddi Gutner Block, "Riding the Waves," Forbes 11 Sept. 1995: 182.

28 George Jellinek, "Record Collecting: Hobby or Obsession?" Opera News Feb. 2003: 85.

29 Susan Van Zile, "Grammar That'll Move You!" Instructor Jan./Feb. 2003: 33.

An Article in a Journal

Pages numbered continuously throughout a volume:

30 Raima Larter, "Understanding Complexity in Biophysical Chemistry," Journal of Physical Chemistry 107 (2003): 417-19.

Each issue begins on page 1:

31 W. J. T. Mitchell, "The Surplus Value of Images," Mosaic 35.3 (2002): 11.

An Article in a Newspaper

[32] Amy Argetsinger, "Lobbying Gets Old College Try," Washington Post 13 Jan. 2003: B2.

[33] David Leonhardt, "Defining the Rich in the World's Wealthiest Nation," New York Times 12 Jan. 2003, natl. ed.: sec. 4: 1.

[34] David Ranii, "New AIDS Drug Is Step Closer to Approval," News and Observer [Raleigh] 7 Nov. 1995: 1D.

An Editorial

[35] "Six Sigma Schools," editorial, Wall Street Journal 15 Jan. 2003: A10.

A Letter to the Editor

[36] Michelle Rothschild, letter, Kiplinger's Jan. 2003: 14.

A Review

[37] Caitlin Flanagan, "Get a Job," rev. of What Should I Do with My Life?, by Po Bronson, New York Times Book Review 12 Jan. 2003: 4.

[38] Kenny Glenn, rev. of Man on the Moon [film], Premiere Jan. 2000: 20.

[39] Rev. of Going to the Territory, by Ralph Ellison, Atlantic Aug. 1986: 91.

[40] David Patrick Stearns, rev. of The Well-Tempered Clavier, by J. S. Bach [CD], Angela Hewitt, piano, Stereophile Dec. 1999: 185.

Other Sources

An Audio Recording

[41] Dee Dickinson, Creating the Future: Perspectives on Educational Change, audiocassette (Minneapolis: Accelerated Learning Systems, 1991).

⁴² Gustav Mahler, Symphony No. 7, Michael Tilson Thomas, cond., London Symphony Orch., CD, RCA Victor, 1999.

⁴³ George N. Shuster, jacket notes, The Poetry of Gerard Manley Hopkins, LP, Caedmon, n.d.

A Film, DVD, or Video Recording

⁴⁴ 25th Hour, dir. Spike Lee, screenplay by David Benioff, Touchstone, 2003.

⁴⁵ All about Eve, dir. Joseph L. Mankiewicz, perf. Bette Davis, Anne Baxter, and George Sanders, Fox, 1950, DVD, Studio Classics, 2003.

⁴⁶ The Classical Hollywood Style, program 1 of The American Cinema, prod. New York Center for Visual History, videocassette, Annenberg/CPB, 1995.

A Government Document

See "A Book by a Government Agency" on page 268.

A Lecture

⁴⁷ Stephanie Granetta, class lecture, English 315, Richardson College, 7 Apr. 2003.

⁴⁸ Eleanor Kamenish, "A Tale of Two Countries: Mores in France and Scotland," public lecture, Friends of the Public Library, Louisville, 16 Apr. 2003.

A Pamphlet

⁴⁹ Golden Retriever Club of America, Prevention of Heartworm (n.p.: GRCA, 2004) 4.

⁵⁰ Who Are the Amish? (Aylmer, Ont,: Pathway, n.d).

An Interview

⁵¹ Blake Barefoot, personal interview, 18 Sept. 2002.

⁵² Kevin Spacey, Interview with Terry Gross, Fresh Air, Natl. Public Radio, WHQR, Wilmington, NC, 21 Jan. 2003.

[53] Donald Trump, "Trump Speaks," interview with Aravind Adiga, Money Feb. 2003: 28.

A Television or Radio Program

[54] The Crossing, dir. Robert Harmon, screenplay by Sherry Jones and Peter Jennings, History Channel, 1 Jan. 2000.

[55] Susan Stone, report on Japanese comic books, All Things Considered, National Public Radio, 9 Jan. 2003.

An Unpublished Essay

[56] Emily Gould, "Fast Food Comes at a High Price for Workers," essay written for Prof. Katherine Humel's English 12 class, Fall semester 2002.

An Unpublished Letter

[57] Cara Cilano, letter to author, 5 Mar. 2003.

An Unpublished Questionnaire

[58] Questionnaire conducted by Prof. Barbara Waxman's English 103 class, Feb. 2003.

Internet and Electronic Sources
An Online Book

[59] David Irving, Hitler's War, New York: Viking, 1977, 19 Jan. 2003 <http://www.fpp.co.uk/books/Hitler/> 177.

[60] Hank Richards, The Sacrifice, 1996, 3 Mar. 2003 <http://www.geocities.com/Area51/Vault/8101/>.

[61] Mary Wollstonecraft, Vindication of the Rights of Women, 1792, Bartleby.com, 1999, 13 Feb. 2003 <http://www.bartleby.com/144/4.html> ch. 4, para. 14.

Part of an Online Book

62 Edward R. Coyle, Spies and Their Work, <u>Ambulancing on the French Front</u>, 1918, 30 Apr. 2003 <http://www.ku.edu/carrie/specoll/medical/Coyle/Coyle04.htm#18>.

A Print Periodical (Newspaper, Magazine, or Journal) Accessed on the Publication's Web Site

63 Cathleen Falsani, "Did Respect for Religion Cloud 'Clone' Coverage?" <u>Chicago Sun-Times</u> 10 Jan. 2003, 19 Jan. 2003 <http://www.suntimes.com/output/falsani/cst-nws-fals10.html>.

64 Howard Fineman and Tamara Lipper, "Spinning Race," <u>Newsweek</u> 27 Jan. 2003, 19 Jan. 2003 <http://www.msnbc.com/news/861383.asp?>.

65 A. J. Young, A. S. Wilson, and C. G. Mundell, "Chandra Imaging of the X-Ray Core of the Virgo Cluster," <u>Astrophysical Journal</u> 579.2 (2002): 560-570, 19 Jan. 2003 <http://www.journals.uchicago.edu/ApJ/journal/issues/ApJ/v579n2/54935/54935.html>.

A Nonprint Periodical Accessed on the Publication's Web Site

66 Bill Clinton, "The Path to Peace," 10 Sept. 2002, <u>Salon.com</u> 20 Jan. 2003 <http://www.salon.com/news/feature/2002/09/10/clinton/>.

A Work Accessed in an Online Database

67 Rozalia Jovanovic, "Snowmobilers Tied to Rules of the Road," <u>National Law Journal</u> Aug. 5, 2002: B1, <u>InfoTrac OneFile</u>, 20 Jan. 2003 <http://infotrac.galegroup.com/>.

68 Noreen Parks, "Dolphins in Danger," <u>Science Now</u>, 17 Dec. 2002: 2-3, <u>Academic Search Elite</u>, EBSCOhost, 20 Jan. 2003 <http://web3.epnet.com/>.

[69] "Political Inclination of the States," Associated Press, 9 Jan. 2003, LexisNexis Academic Universe, 20 Jan. 2003 <http://web.lexis-nexis.com/universe>.

An Online Encyclopedia Article

[70] "Humpback Whale," Encyclopaedia Britannica 2003, Encyclopaedia Britannica Online, 28 Jan, 2003 <http://0-search.eb.com.uncclc.coast.uncwil.edu/eb/>.

An Online Review

[71] Roger Ebert, rev. of Identity, dir. James Mangold, Chicago Sun-Times Online 25 Apr. 2003, 29 May 2003. <http://www.suntimes.com/output/ebert1/wkp-news-identity25f .html>.

[72] Tony Eprile, "'Red Dust': Settling Scores in South Africa," rev. of. Red Dust by Gillian Slovo, New York Times Online 28 Apr. 2003, 29 May 2003 <http://www.nytimes.com/2002/04/28/books/review/28EPRILET.html?ex=1051761600&en=0f435a46a2f839eb&ei=5070>.

An Organization's Web Site

[73] The Coral Reef Alliance, "Coral Friendly Guidelines," 21 Jan. 2003 <http://www.coralreefalliance.org/parks/guidelines.html>.

A Personal Web Page

[74] Sally Hemming, home page, 21 Jan. 2003 <http://www.sallyhemming.com/>.

E-Mail

[75] Paul Wilkes, e-mail to author, 29 Dec. 2002.

Computer Software

[76] Atoms, Symbols and Equations, vers. 3.0, software, 2002 <http://ourworld.compuserve.com/homepages/RayLec/atoms.htm>.

[77] Twain's World, CD-ROM (Parsippany, NJ: Bureau Development, 1993).

Credits

Index

Parenthetical Notes (MLA Style): Quick Reference Guide

Detailed information on parenthetical notes can be found on pages 560–575.

PURPOSE

Use a note to identify the specific source location for a specific idea, piece of information, or quotation in your paper.

FORMAT

Give the specific page reference, preceded by the *least* amount of information needed to identify the source in your list of works cited.

PLACEMENT

Place the note following the passage.

MODEL ENTRIES

Standard Reference

Give the author and page(s):

>   A fear of thunder is common among dogs (Digby 237).

Author Identified in the Passage

Omit the author's name in the note:

>   Digby noted that dogs are often terrified of thunder (237).

An Anonymous Work (Unidentified Author)

Use the first word or two from the title:

>   ("An Infant's" 22)

A Work with Two or Three Authors

>   (Reid, Forrestal, and Cook 48-49)

A Work with More Than Three Authors

>   (Courtois et al. 112)

Two or More Works by the Same Author

Add the first word(s) from the title:

>   (Asimov, <u>Adding</u> 240-43)
>   (Asimov, "Happy" 68)

Two Authors with the Same Last Name

Include the authors' first names:

>   (George Eliot 459)
>   (T. S. Eliot 44)

A Multivolume Work

The volume number precedes the page number(s):

>   (Agus 2: 59)

Exception: Omit the volume number if only one volume is identified in your list of works cited:

>   (Agus 59)